THE
LICENSING BUSINESS
HANDBOOK

How to make money, protect
trademarks, extend product
lines, enhance merchandising,
control use of images, and
more, by licensing characters,
teams, celebrities, events,
trademarks, fashion, likenesses,
designs & logos!

By Karen Raugust

& THE EDITORS OF
THE LICENSING LETTER

EPM COMMUNICATIONS, INC.

Library of Congress Cataloging-in-Publication Data

Raugust, Karen, 1960-
The Licensing Business Handbook: How to make money, protect trademarks, extend product lines, enhance merchandising, control use of images, and more, by licensing characters, teams, celebrities, events, trademarks, fashion, likenesses, designs & logos
/ Karen Raugust
p. cm.
Includes bibliographical references and index.
ISBN 1-885747-43-8
1. Marketing. 2. Entertainment. 3. Sports. 4. Fashion. 5. Trademarks. I. Title.

THE LICENSING BUSINESS HANDBOOK
TABLE OF CONTENTS

THE LICENSING BUSINESS HANDBOOK
LIST OF FIGURES

INTRODUCTION

The licensing business has changed significantly since the first edition of this book in 1995. The market is crowded, as more properties of all types are licensed and an increasingly diverse group of manufacturers link their products to licensed properties. The rise in the number of licensed items is coupled with a decrease in retail shelf space devoted to licensing. Since the late 1990s, retailers have experienced a difficult business environment and have seen many properties that have not met expectations. Retail buyers tend to support a few licenses at a time and expect heavy promotional backing from licensees and licensors, as well as some sort of exclusive rights.

The business is now global; *The Licensing Letter* pegged retail sales of licensed products worldwide at $109 billion in 2001. Properties of all types cross borders and international markets account for a large share of licensors' and licensees' revenues. Meanwhile, developing technologies are allowing experimentation with e-commerce and opening up new product categories. Changes in technology over the next decade, whatever they may be, represent one of the most critical issues facing licensing executives today.

Licensing sectors that traditionally have accounted for a small portion of the market, such as art and music, have grown at a fast pace, while formerly robust sectors, such as entertainment/character and sports, have experienced difficult times. The corporate sector has progressed steadily to become the largest component of the licensing business. Overall, the maturation of the business has resulted in a leveling-off of retail sales of licensed merchandise in North America in the low $70 billion range. Total licensed product sales in the U.S. and Canada reached $70.3 billion in 2001, according to *The Licensing Letter*, down from a peak of $74.15 billion in 1999. Individual properties still succeed, of course; evergreens such as Peanuts and sudden hits such as Pokémon will always be with us.

Licensing covers a wide range of property types and product categories and can help meet a variety of company objectives. It should be noted that objectives vary depending on the type of property; an entertainment concern's goals differ from those of an artist, while the objectives of one corporate licensor differ from those of another. Licensing programs do not exist on their own; rather, they support the licensor's and/or licensee's overall corporate goals and strategies.

Notice that this book uses the term "licensing business" rather than "licensing industry." There is a reason for that. While people often refer to it as an industry, licensing is really a business tool that crosses over many separate industries, including apparel manufacturing, professional sports, museums, publishing, entertainment and so on. Executives from all of these recognize licensing as an effective marketing technique.

This book provides information on the basics of licensing for everyone involved, from the largest entertainment studios to sole proprietors selling one licensed product from a home office, from manufacturers to property owners, from one-person companies to large corporations, from beginners to experienced practitioners. It serves as an overview and introduction to the business and as a handy reference for those seeking answers to specific licensing-related questions.

It is impossible to offer an all-encompassing step-by-step method of launching a licensing program. Every effort differs in its objectives, target audience and property characteristics, a fact that has become more valid in today's crowded market. *The Licensing Business Handbook* provides a systematic approach that allows readers to develop their own licensing strategies. It illustrates the mechanics of entering into a licensing deal and outlines the issues to consider before introducing a licensing effort. Part I offers an overview of licensing; Part II illustrates potential strategies for licensors and licensees; Part III examines the details of licensing, including compensation, contracts, legal protection, tackling infringement, international licensing and promotions. Finally, the book includes a glossary of licensing terms and a list of answers to 45 frequently asked questions.

This all-new edition adds more than 60 pages of up-to-date information. It expands on a number of topics critical in today's business, including retail relationships, global licensing strategies, promotional techniques, and the impact of technology.

The Licensing Business Handbook is based on the knowledge of a network of licensing professionals, as gleaned in interviews, at conventions and seminars, through research and consulting and in informal conversations. Special thanks to the following executives, in alphabetical order, for reviewing this edition: Chris Johansen, Odyssey Marketing; David Koehser, Attorney-at-Law; Ken Markman, KKM Enterprises; Mary Morgan, The Morgan Network; Neil Newman, N² Marketing Communications; and Leigh Ann Schwarzkopf, General Mills. All the experts who have given EPM and its twice-monthly newsletter, *The Licensing Letter*, their insights over the years have created successful businesses by effectively using the licensing techniques you will learn in this book. *The Licensing Business Handbook* gives you the tools you need to make licensing work for you.

PART 1:
HOW THE BUSINESS WORKS

CHAPTER 1:
WHAT IS LICENSING?

Licensing is the process of leasing the rights to a legally protected (trade-marked or copyrighted) entity. The entity — known as the property — could be a name, a graphic, a logo, a likeness, a saying, a signature or a combination of these elements. The rights to a given property are granted for a specific purpose (usually for a product or products to be sold in retail stores), for a defined geographic area and for a limited time, in return for a negotiated payment.

TERMS AND DEFINITIONS

The owner of a property is known as the licensor, while the renter of the rights (usually a manufacturer) is called the licensee.

The basic component of payment is the royalty, generally a percentage of the manufacturer's selling price on every product sold. Contracts typically require a guaranteed minimum royalty payment, or a guarantee, a percentage of which licensees normally pay as an advance. (There are many variations in payment structures; see Chapter 7 for more on royalties and related issues).

In addition to merchandise, a property can be licensed for many nonproduct purposes. Examples include premiums, fast food or packaged goods promotions, television or print advertising, and services. Some licensors authorize their properties for entertainment vehicles, such as films, television series or live performances; Sesame Workshop licenses the right to create live shows featuring its characters to its stage show licensee, Vee Corporation.

The types of properties available for licensing vary and extend into a range of product categories. The Sunbeam logo appears on shower massagers and light bulbs; the Crayola name graces flowers and house paints; Polaris markets go-karts and snack machines; the 4-H organization has authorized fabrics; Jimmy Buffet has granted his Margaritaville label for margarita mix; Cartoon Network characters appear on cell phone accessories; and the NASCAR name identifies bowling balls.

A BRIEF HISTORY OF LICENSED PRODUCT MERCHANDISING

Merchandising began more than a century ago. In the late 1800s, banks featured the British puppets Punch and Judy, while blocks and games from Horsman took advantage of the fame of Palmer Cox's Brownies. Celebrities, including kings and queens, endorsed a variety of merchandise.

The first Peter Rabbit toy, based on the book character by Beatrix Potter, premiered in 1903. Many companies distributed banks and other products in the early 1900s that sported corporate trademarks such as Ford, Chevrolet, Pepsi, Dr. Pepper and Campbell's. Merchandised characters included the

Sunbonnet Babies, book characters introduced in 1902; the comic strip Buster Brown, with toys and games manufactured by Selchow & Righter and Steiff; and Amos and Andy, for which Marx manufactured toys.

Beginning in 1910, companies marketed dolls that looked like celebrities including Charlie Chaplin, while the first Kewpie doll (based on drawings published in *Ladies' Home Journal*) appeared in 1911. All sorts of merchandise during this period incorporated logos and brand names, such as Mr. Peanut, and fashion designers began to come into their own.

In the 1920s, some of the most popular licensed items featured film stars and animated and comic strip icons. Walt Disney granted his first license, for a Mickey Mouse school notebook, after that character debuted in *Steamboat Willie* in 1928. (Disney earned $300 on the deal.) Other companies sold products associated with The Green Hornet, film star Tom Mix, Little Orphan Annie and child movie star Baby Peggy.

Licensing really took off in the 1930s, with comic strips, comic books, film celebrities and radio stars especially popular. Top properties included Betty Boop, Popeye, Felix the Cat, Batman, The Lone Ranger, Mutt & Jeff, Dick Tracy, Charlie McCarthy and Jack Armstrong All-American Boy, as well as Babe Ruth, Shirley Temple, the Dionne Quintuplets, Jane Withers, Sonja Hennie, Gene Autry and Roy Rogers. Calendars, collectibles and banks continued to feature corporate trademarks during the 1930s.

Comics, films and radio shows remained strong in the 1940s, with Bugs Bunny, Casper the Friendly Ghost, Terrytoons, Tom & Jerry, Captain Marvel, Captain Midnight, Fibber McGee & Molly and Woody Woodpecker all appearing on licensed items. Pierre Balmain and Christian Dior were among the fashion designers who set up shop in the 1940s; meanwhile, consumers continued to desire products with corporate logos, such as Borden's Elsie the Cow.

Several fashion designers rose to prominence in the 1950s, including Pierre Cardin, Oleg Cassini, Givenchy and Valentino. Footwear designer Charles Jourdan was a licensor and a licensee, signing an agreement to manufacture Christian Dior shoes in 1959. Publishing properties ranging from Betsy McCall to the Bobbsey Twins appeared in the 1950s; baseball and hockey athletes authorized their likenesses for trading cards; and cosmetic company Revlon granted rights for a Miss Revlon doll. The first Peanuts book came out in 1952 and the first Snoopy licensed product, a plastic figurine, premiered in 1958. Entertainment-based properties included Shari Lewis, Rin Tin Tin, Emmett Kelly, Huckleberry Hound, John Wayne and Howdy Doody. The 1950s marked the debut of TV properties, which proved to be lucrative; Davy Crockett generated $300 million in retail sales of licensed merchandise, while Hopalong Cassidy rang up $70 million at retail.

The 1960s were characterized by several TV-based licensing programs, ranging from The Flintstones, Rocky & Bullwinkle and Yogi Bear to Dr. Kildare, Daniel Boone and As the World Turns. Sesame Street, soon to become a major force in licensing, premiered in 1969. Other entertainment and celebrity properties included Alvin and the Chipmunks, The Sound of Music, Twiggy and The Beatles. The NFL launched an organized licensing program in the early 1960s, the first sports league to do so on a systematic basis. A number of fashion designers introduced their first products, including Liz Claiborne, Laura Ashley, Adolfo, Geoffrey Beene, Oscar de la Renta, Anne Klein and Ralph Lauren.

In the 1970s, the Pink Panther maintained a roster of 250 licensees. Jay Ward opened a Rocky & Bullwinkle shop, one of the first such dedicated retailers, in Hollywood. The Muppet Show premiered in 1972, while Knickerbocker acquired rights to Holly Hobbie, for dolls, in 1974. Other entertainment properties during the decade included Planet of the Apes, The Six Million Dollar Man and Mork & Mindy. Many observers point to the licensing program surrounding the movie *Star Wars*, released in 1977, as the start of the "licensing business" as we know it today. That $2.5+ billion effort, driven by toy licensee Kenner, demonstrated the upside of licensing; people began to think of licensing as a career. Meanwhile, the first collegiate licensing agreements were put into place and more fashion designers launched their own operations, including Giorgio Armani, Bill Blass and Claude Montana.

The 1980s were characterized by the accelerated growth of the licensing business as it built upon the foundation created by the Star Wars phenomenon. The government allowed television shows based on toys for the first time and many of these, including He-Man, My Little Pony and G.I. Joe, went on to become significant licensed properties. The Smurfs, which began as a comic book in Belgium in 1957, debuted as a U.S. TV series in 1981 and generated $1 billion in retail merchandise sales. The Cabbage Patch Kids dominated in the mid-1980s with retail sales of $4 billion, including dolls. Among the other entertainment licenses of the '80s were Roger Rabbit, ALF, Thundercats, Dynasty, The Little Mermaid and Ghostbusters. Several properties springing from corporate advertising campaigns also made a splash during this decade, such as the California Raisins, Wendy's slogan "Where's the Beef?" and Budweiser's party animal, Spuds McKenzie. The late 1980s also witnessed the beginning of the rise of sports licensing, with the major leagues and colleges becoming more aggressive and customers — including those who had never been fans — demonstrating a seemingly insatiable demand.

The 1990s witnessed the maturation of the licensing business, including the first-ever annual declines in total sales of licensed merchandise, exacerbated by a recession in the decade's early years. Despite the challenges, several hit entertainment properties emerged, including The Lion King; singing groups The New Kids on the Block and the Spice Girls; The Simpsons; the Teenage Mutant Ninja Turtles; Mighty Morphin Power Rangers; PBS-aired properties including Thomas the Tank Engine, Barney and Teletubbies; Beverly Hills 90210; South Park; and Pokémon. More properties of all types became available for licensing, ranging from women's sports leagues (WNBA) and corporate brands (Duncan Yo-Yo) to artists (Todd Parr) and events (the millennium).

The first decade of the 2000s has seen a continued increase in corporate licensing, with a particular focus on brand extension. Music licensing has witnessed growth, especially in traditional retail channels (as opposed to concert venues), led by pop acts such as Britney Spears, 'N Sync and the Backstreet Boys. In the publishing area, numerous magazine titles have authorized branded products in related product categories. More artists have entered the licensing business, while others have extended into new categories; Thomas Kinkade authorized a licensed housing development and a series of novels. Non-profit groups, such as Boys & Girls Town, also entered licensing in greater numbers, albeit most with limited programs.

High-profile entertainment properties in the early 2000s have included Harry Potter, Monsters, Inc., Shrek and the Powerpuff Girls. In general, the entertainment sector of the business has been slow and television-based franchises have taken precedence over films as a foundation for retail licensing programs. Major sports licensors have winnowed down their licensee lists in an effort to regain control over their licensing strategies, while new properties, such as professional fishermen, began to extend their names into related products. Overall, the business has faced difficult economic times, resulting in consolidation among retailers, as well as among licensees and licensors in some sectors.

Figure 1 (page 7) shows total retail sales of licensed merchandise in the U.S. and Canada from 1982 through 2001, while *Figure 2 (page 8)* illustrates retail sales figures for properties of different types. The numbers in the latter are all associated with successful properties and should not be taken as the norm.

BENEFITS AND RISKS OF LICENSING

As a marketing tool that can be utilized across diverse industries, licensing benefits both licensees and licensors if done realistically and with common sense. At the same time, both parties should also be aware of the risks and challenges.

STRATEGIC CONSIDERATIONS

Licensing is not a strategy in and of itself, but rather is, like advertising, public relations and promotion, a tactic that supports a company's strategic objectives, both corporately and for the property. Objectives can include brand exposure (raising awareness for a property) or brand extension (including line extension into new markets and category expansion into new product classes). Licensing can also support financial goals, such as enhancing profit margins.

Corporate objectives governing a licensing program vary depending on the sector from which a given property comes. Trademark and brand licensors typically are more interested in extension or exposure than in supporting financial goals, since licensing revenues generally represent a fraction of

Figure 1

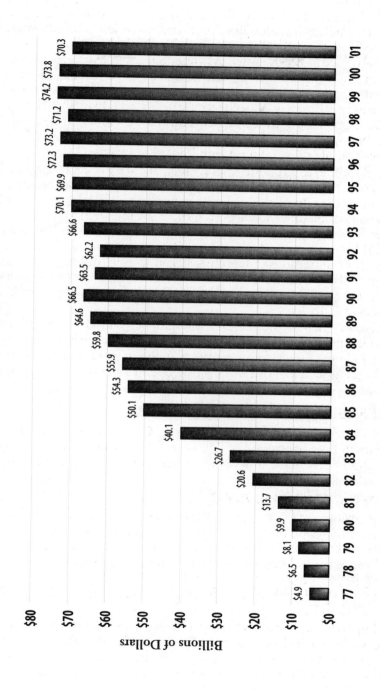

RETAIL SALES OF LICENSED MERCHANDISE
U.S. & Canada, 1977-2001

Billions of Dollars

'01	$70.3
'00	$73.8
99	$74.2
98	$71.2
97	$73.2
96	$72.3
95	$69.9
94	$70.1
93	$66.6
92	$62.2
91	$63.5
90	$66.5
89	$64.6
88	$59.8
87	$55.9
86	$54.3
85	$50.1
84	$40.1
83	$26.7
82	$20.6
81	$13.7
80	$9.9
79	$8.1
78	$6.5
77	$4.9

Source: The Licensing Letter. © Copyright 2002 EPM Communications, Inc.

Figure 2
SALES OF LICENSED MERCHANDISE FOR SELECTED PROPERTIES

PROPERTY	SALES	TIME PERIOD
Fashion/Corporate		
Aris (all brands)	$162 million	annually (2000)
Candie's	$96 million	annually (2000)
Caterpillar	$900 million	annually (2000)
Coca-Cola	$1 billion	annually (2001)
Everlast	$200 million	annually (2001)
General Motors (all brands)	$2 billion	annually (2001)
Non-Profit		
National Audubon	$38 million	annually (1999)
National Crime Prevention Assn.	$11 million	annually (1999)
Sierra Club	$473 million	annually (2000)
Entertainment/Character/Literary		
Barney the Dinosaur	$3.5 billion	lifetime (2001)
Caillou	$30 million	annually (2000)
Clifford	$100 million	six months (2002)
Digimon	$1 billion	lifetime (2000)
Marvel (all characters)	$400 million	annually (2000)
Mary-Kate & Ashley	$1.2 billion	lifetime (2000)
Mighty Morphin Power Rangers	$5.6 billion	lifetime (2001)
Paddington Bear	$160 million	annually (2001)
Sailor Moon	$2 billion	lifetime (2000)
South Park	$250 million	lifetime (2001)
Sports/Collegiate		
Kentucky Derby	$7 million	annually (2000)
National Hot Rod Association	$50 million	annually (2000)
NASCAR	$2 billion	annually (2001)
University of Tennessee	$100 million	annually (1999)
Art/Design		
Christian Riese Lassen	$100 million	annually (1999)
Marcoart	$5 million	lifetime (2001)
Precious Moments	$500 million	annually (2001)
StickWorld (Bill Attinger)	$30 million	two years (2000)
Suzy's Zoo	$40 million	annually (2002)
Thomas Kinkade	$200 million	annually (2001)

Notes:

• Retail sales figures include only licensed merchandise, not merchandise produced in-house or under contract. Figures are worldwide.

• These are randomly selected properties intended to illustrate a range of performance rather than a comprehensive picture; individual licenses within the same property sectors may vary drastically.

Sources: Company information and press releases, corporate annual reports and advertising, executive interviews, estimates by *The Licensing Letter*.

total revenues for the company (although brand extension income can be significant). Of course, some top management look to licensing to drive revenue more than as a means of achieving other objectives, but that outlook may not be realistic and may even be harmful to the brand.

An entertainment company, on the other hand, often views licensing royalties as one important part of the total potential profit picture for a franchise, along with fees from TV stations, syndication and home video profits, and global sales. If the total package is weak, the entertainment property will not go forward.

For a fashion licensor, licensing can support a brand-extension strategy by allowing the house to enter categories in which it does not have expertise (such as fragrances). It also may fit financial goals, if a company can create a product line at a higher margin through licensing than through in-house manufacturing or sub-contracting.

The same considerations hold true for licensees. Licensing is not an objective, but a tool to achieve corporate goals, whether they be to expand distribution, gain exposure, target new markets or enhance revenues through premium pricing. For licensees, as for licensors, licensing must work hand-in-hand with other tactics to support strategic objectives.

Licensing, especially in the initial stages, requires patience. While some licensors and licensees face pressure from top corporate management to achieve results quickly, it typically takes at least two years for revenues to start flowing consistently. Many properties, especially potential evergreens, need time to build; impatience can harm the program by hurrying the decision-making process and hampering common sense.

The next sections examine the benefits and risks of licensing for licensors and licensees, depending on their motives and strategic direction.

BENEFITS TO LICENSORS

For property owners, licensing can support corporate objectives in many ways. Many think first about the potential royalty income, often at the behest of top management. While property owners would not initiate licensing programs if they were not profitable—and many programs can generate significant revenues— it should be reiterated that, in many cases, revenue generation is not the primary or most logical reason for the effort. In some cases, property owners expect their licensing efforts to be self-liquidating but not necessarily profitable, since non-financial objectives take precedence.

That said, licensing certainly can bring financial benefits. While income may not be their primary reason for entering licensing, many property owners, even in the corporate sector, have turned licensing into a profit center. Harley-Davidson is one of these; close to 50 licensees sell products through specialty stores and Harley motorcycle dealerships to the brand's core customers and their families.

Several corporate, entertainment/character and other licensors have instituted a floor on minimum acceptable guarantees. These can range from

$5,000 to as much as several million per deal and ensure a certain financial benefit from any licensing foray, no matter what other benefits accrue to the property owner.

Fashion labels, such as Ecko and Mossimo, have turned to licensing as a less risky and less investment-heavy way to do business and, as a result, have experienced debt reduction, greater sales and improved margins. According to financial statements from designer Donna Karan in 2000, that house's gross margin improved from 29.4% to 32.4% in a year due to a greater focus on licensing.

A large percentage of licensing revenues, as compared to revenues from manufacturing, go directly to the bottom line. Martha Stewart Living Omnimedia reported in 2001, for example, that 99% of its revenues from merchandising went directly to EBITDA (earnings before taxes, depreciation and amortization).

Several owners of apparel labels have, at certain points in their lifespans, opted to become full-time licensors. They create cohesive, centralized brand marketing plans but accomplish all manufacturing and distribution through licensed manufacturers. In 2001, for example, Aris, owner of the XOXO, Fragile and Members Only fashion labels, opted for a 100% licensing strategy, signing a five-year exclusive deal with Mexico-based Grupo Xtra and several master licenses outside North America. Similarly, Stage II, owner of Cross Colours and other brands, transitioned from a manufacturing to a licensing strategy that same year. Brands such as Mossimo and Cherokee have moved to a direct-to-retail licensing strategy that has brought financial success to these formerly troubled properties.

In general, if a property owner's potential royalties from a licensed product line exceed its profit margins for the same items produced in-house (or out-sourced), licensing becomes an attractive alternative. Some licensors have made the move as a key means of surviving a bankruptcy filing; Converse, for instance, licensed its core footwear line to Global Brand Marketing and closed its manufacturing plants as it strove to emerge from Chapter 11.

Some fashion licensors move in the other direction, either to increase control over their brand activities or because they feel they can generate more profit by controlling manufacturing than through royalties. In 2001, Tommy Hilfiger acquired its European licensee, T.H. International, while Polo Ralph Lauren purchased its Italian licensee, PRL Fashion of Europe. The latter move, one of a series of purchases of licensed manufacturers, completed Polo's strategy of directly controlling all of its European activities. Such a move may affect single categories as well; Nautica brought its childrenswear business in-house in early 2001.

Entertainment licensors, particularly the major movie studios, have traditionally accounted for their licensing activities on a cash basis; that is, advances and guarantees are recorded on the books when they come in, rather than on a sales basis as actual royalties accrue (see Chapter 7 for more information). Thus high guarantees are often preferable from a financial point of view than high potential sales levels (although, as of 2001, changes in accounting rules may put the emphasis back on royalties). These licensors often face pressure from top management, which expects the consumer products division to deliver immediate and significant results, regardless of the property's realistic sales potential, and do not realize that it takes 18 to 24 months for actual royalties to accrue, even in the case of a successful program.

A non-financial benefit of licensing is its ability to create consumer awareness. Fans who see New York Yankees caps and jerseys on retail shelves (or on a passerby) think of the team and of Major League Baseball; this exposure to the property may spur them to buy merchandise or tickets. Similarly, displays of Clifford toys, apparel and gifts may prompt preschoolers and their parents to tune into the character's show on PBS or buy books featuring Clifford. The Nature Conservancy's licensed products raise exposure for the nonprofit organization's mission, in addition to generating income. Licensors such as Anheuser-Busch view licensing as one component of the marketing mix, along with advertising and point of sale materials, used to create positive associations among core consumers of Budweiser and the company's other beers.

For licensors of corporate trademarks and fashion labels, licensing is a method of extending their product lines into areas where they do not have manufacturing or marketing expertise or existing distribution channels. Cosmetics marketer Revlon's expertise lies in cosmetics, fragrances and other personal care products, but it has extended its reach into hair brushes, hair dryers, cosmetic kits and hair accessories through licensing. Revlon lacks experience in manufacturing and/or distributing these products, but its brand makes sense in these categories. Food brand owners often look to licensing as a means of adding new flavors (and strong co-brands) acquired from other food- or beverage-related licensors. Preschool toymaker Little Tikes launched a licensing effort in 1999 to target areas, such as footwear, bike helmets and computer accessories, where it lacked expertise and distribution.

Corporate licensors sometimes use licensing and co-branding to add positive attributes to their products and brands. AT&T, for example, has said that it looks to its potential licensees to bring attributes such as "speed," "fun" and "energy" to its products, complementing AT&T's existing image of "quality," "reliability" and "technological innovation."

New product categories, achieved through licensing, can expand a property's customer base. Many shoppers cannot afford couture or high-end designer clothing, but can purchase a bottle of fragrance tied to the same designer. The earth-moving vehicle brand Caterpillar licenses objects such as apparel, children's videos and books, and footwear, which exposes the brand to additional consumers in new venues.

Licensing may also provide an effective and relatively risk-free means for a corporate marketer to test a new product category. If the category proves successful during the test period, the licensor can either continue to license or set up an in-house operation to market the product line. The large investment required to set up a new division is more palatable once there are assurances the line will sell.

Similarly, a company can test or expand its brand internationally through licensing. Authorizing a licensee on the ground in Singapore to manufacture and distribute a product throughout Southeast Asia is often preferable to exporting, given cultural, economic and business differences. Licensing can be more cost-effective for the property owner as well, particularly if the product line must be altered for international consumption (perhaps even requiring a slightly different design for each region around the world).

Another important reason to set up a licensing program, particularly for owners of corporate brands, is to strengthen trademarks. Trademark rights arise from the use or intent to use a mark — the latter signaled by registering with the Patent and Trademark Office — in various classifications of goods and in various countries. Licensing strengthens a trademark by expanding its use to products outside the licensor's core categories.

In a hypothetical example, Harley-Davidson, the motorcycle company, would not want a manufacturer to distribute unauthorized Harley-Davidson lollipops, even if it has no intention of entering the candy business itself. The unauthorized item would imply an endorsement from the licensor, potentially harming its hard-earned brand image. Even if Harley-Davidson's trademarks are not registered in the food classification, its other trademark registrations and its exploitation and policing of its marks in various categories (some through licensing) demonstrate to the courts that the company is serious about protecting its trademarks and that an unauthorized company making lollipops was infringing on its rights. (See Chapter 8 for more on trademark registration.)

A note on the use of the words "trademark" and "brand" throughout this book: "Corporate Trademarks" is one of the property types used by *The Licensing Letter* to categorize and measure the size of the licensing business. It comprises corporate logos and brands that are available for licensing (see Chapter 2 for details). That usage — which is employed to distinguish corporate trademark owners from licensors of other property types — is different from the legal meaning of the word "trademark," discussed above. Licensors of all types of properties own legally protected trademarks in the latter sense.

The term "brand" is increasingly used to refer to a property — no matter what its source — if it is perceived as a brand by consumers and/or positioned as such by its licensor (a concept that will be discussed later in this chapter). Again, a brand in this sense does not necessarily originate in the Corporate Trademark sector. These differences should be clear given the context in which they are used.

Another benefit of licensing, especially for corporate trademark owners, is its effectiveness in helping to relaunch or reposition a brand or property. If a property targeted primarily toward teenagers is being repositioned as a younger children's property, or *vice versa*, the availability of licensed products appropriate for that age group is one way to achieve this. If an unexpected group of consumers embraces a property, a licensing effort can be repositioned to reflect that. Nickelodeon originally conceived SpongeBob SquarePants as a property for young children, but when it detected interest from college-aged males, it repositioned the property by authorizing older-skewing products such as soap-on-a-rope, which was true to the attributes of the property but appealed to the new fan base.

Samsonite is using licensing to help transform its brand positioning from that of a luggage brand to an upscale, fashion-driven travel brand. While licensing is not the only or even the primary tool for repositioning a property, it can be an important component of the overall marketing plan.

In some cases, licensing indirectly benefits licensors by creating an additional outlet for its core products or by-products. This is true for some food and beverage licensors that extend their brands into other categories. Nabisco supplies Oreos to Pillsbury for its licensed line of Oreo-flavored cake frostings and snack bars; Jim Beam-licensed charcoal briquets used by-products from the whiskey-distilling process as an ingredient.

A marketing-related advantage of licensing is that the availability of diverse licensed items enables cross-merchandising, which creates a bigger splash at retail. This is important for home furnishings designers and brands, for example, where cross-merchandising can help boost a property or line into bestsellerdom. It also holds true for other licensors, including fashion labels and artists. In fact, cross-merchandising and cross-marketing (e.g., techniques such as cross-couponing) provides value for virtually all property types. In a tough retail environment, buyers from Target, Wal-Mart and other store chains look favorably on properties whose licensors offer cross-merchandised in-store boutiques, supplemented by eye-catching point-of-purchase materials.

Licensing (in contrast with selling a property outright) allows owners to maintain control over their brand names and images. This is a particularly important concern for artists, who historically have sold manufacturers all rights to their designs. Selling an image outright may lead to uses that the artist does not support but has no control over. In addition, relinquishing ownership prevents artists from implementing an integrated cross-merchandising campaign.

Licensing, on the other hand, allows designers and artists to maintain full ownership and control of their creations. They have final approval over all uses of their designs and can terminate agreements that do not meet expectations. They can choose which products to license and whom they will authorize to sell them. In addition, they earn royalties tied to sales rather than a one-time upfront fee that, for a successful product line, is generally less than the royalty potential.

BENEFITS TO LICENSEES

For a manufacturer, a major benefit of licensing is the consumer awareness the licensed property brings to its product lines. A company lacking its own well-recognized brand name can immediately associate with a high-profile brand or property through licensing. The licensee benefits from the property's consumer awareness and avoids the time and expense of building an in-house brand from scratch.

Even if the manufacturer must pay a high minimum guaranteed royalty to the licensor, the cost is likely to be significantly less than the amount needed to create a proprietary brand. A toy company spends more to develop an original toy (often up to 10% of the net sales price) than a toy that trades on the borrowed equity of a license (less than 5%). A fragrance company often spends $15 million to $20 million in marketing funds to launch a brand-new fragrance, but can invest far less if the new line is based on an established designer name.

It is the inherent consumer awareness of the property that brings this financial benefit. A children's wear manufacturer gains instant recognition by linking with an established children's television series. A sheet and towel marketer benefits from the awareness gained through a relationship with a recognized apparel designer. A sports equipment maker attracts sports fans to its products through a major league association.

Licensing brings a manufacturer a built-in audience. A collectibles marketer that acquires rights to Elvis Presley automatically gains a large potential market of Elvis Presley fans. A bath products manufacturer associated with artist Glynda Turley attracts consumers that like her images. Lego was able to attract older consumers to its building blocks by linking with the Star Wars franchise.

In addition to pure recognition, a property can enhance licensees' products with positive attributes. These could include: quality (Ralph Lauren), fun (Looney Tunes), educational benefits (Sesame Street), an upscale image (Fabergé), spirituality (Thomas Kinkade) or value at a reasonable price (Route 66).

A manufacturer that wins rights to a license receives additional marketing clout. All of the licensed products attached to a single property help sell each other, while the core property and its promotional activity support all of them. The advertising for the Liz Claiborne apparel line creates demand for Bausch & Lomb's Liz Claiborne eyewear. Clifford books sold through Scholastic's trade and in-school channels increase children's desire for Clifford plush from licensee Toy Island. NASCAR die-cast vehicles help market NASCAR apparel, whether the two products are cross-merchandised, creating a memorable impact, or displayed separately, causing the consumer to spot the same brand twice within the store.

This marketing impact means licensees of certain properties, especially the highest-profile entertainment and character licenses, have little or no need to additionally advertise their products (with the exception of key categories such as toys). This is not true for *all* properties; licensees of many corporate trademark, fashion and sports properties, and a growing number from the entertainment sector, are *required* to contribute to advertising, often by forwarding a percentage of sales (on top of the royalty) to a central marketing fund or by being responsible for a certain level of expenditure per year to advertise the brand.

An operational advantage of licensing, in some cases, is that it allows manufacturers that rely heavily on art and designs — such as bedding, wallcovering, giftware and tabletop marketers — to limit the size of their full-time in-house art staff. They minimize the costs of art preparation, since the responsibility for developing the designs rests with the artist or other property owner.

On the other hand, while a well-chosen property can help round out a licensee's selection without significant internal development costs, most licensing relationships are more successful if the licensor works with the licensee's in-house creative staff. Combining the licensor's knowledge of the property and the licensee's of the product leads to the best outcome.

Acquiring a license can open up distribution channels for a manufacturer, although this situation is rare. Usually, licensors weigh a candidate's existing distribution network carefully when making a licensee selection. Sometimes, however, other factors (e.g., the quality of the licensee's products or its willingness to pay a high advance) may be more important to the licensor. The Ralph Lauren license opened the door for licensee Jones Apparel Group to expand its distribution internationally; Japanese toy company Tomy introduced its Tomica toy train brand to North America through a license with Amtrak; and mass market toy maker Mega Bloks was able to enter the specialty market by acquiring licenses such as Sesame Street and dealerships through a license with Harley-Davidson.

Some publically held manufacturers rely on announcements of license acquisitions to boost their stock price (or to generate enthusiasm for an initial public offering of stock). For example, having the Pokémon license during its peak benefited Hasbro's financial book value, although many analysts believe the company did not profit as much overall from the license in real terms as gross sales would indicate.

Of course, the hoped-for end result of associating with a license for most manufacturers is increased sales. WMS Gaming, a casino game maker, reported in 2000 that its revenues increased 72% and its net income rose four-fold in a year due to a license with Hasbro's Monopoly brand. Art-focused licensing agents have reported that licensees' sales have increased 20% when they moved from internally creating designs to licensing recognized art properties. Forward Industries generated $500,000 in one quarter from a new license with Motorola for cellular phone and electronic product carrying cases, representing a growing share of total sales.

All of these benefits of licensing, it should be noted, do not come solely from so-called blockbuster properties. Individual licensees of properties such as Mikhail Baryshnikov, Dr. Scholl's and Brut have been known to generate between $10 million and $100 million in retail sales annually from the licensed line. These are properties that maintained steady brand recognition among fans and/or regular customers without significant hype; that translates to strong day-in-and-day-out sales for appropriate licensees.

RISKS TO LICENSORS

Licensors bear relatively little of the financial risk of licensing. A portion of their royalty revenue comes in the form of a minimum guaranteed royalty, which licensees must pay regardless of how the products sell. While the amount of the guarantee varies, it is unlikely that a licensor would lose much money from a licensing deal, even with the investment in promotional, marketing and retail support that is critical to a property's success today. If the property owner is unable to secure a significant number of deals, on the other hand, its initial costs will not be recovered.

Of course, licensors must first develop the property, whether it be a collection of designs, a feature film, or a brand built over time. Theses costs can be significant, and licensing represents one revenue stream that helps property owners recoup them. For an artist, licensing may be the main method of earning back his or her investment; for other property types it may be one of many options. Yet the initial costs of developing a property of any kind are high, regardless of the costs attributable to the licensing effort itself. This is an especially important consideration for artists and entrepreneurs, who do not have big budgets and for whom this investment represents a high percentage of their revenues or assets.

Another financial risk is tied to the financial fortunes of a licensor's licensees. Not only has consolidation among licensees become common, but many long-time, trusted licensees have entered bankruptcy and several have ended up out of business. Licensors usually stand among the top creditors of these companies, due to significant royalty payments owed. When apparel manufacturer Logo Athletic filed for bankruptcy in 2000, two of the largest unsecured creditors listed in the accompanying paperwork were Players, Inc., the licensor of NFL athletes, and NFL Properties. Logo owed both more than $1.7 million.

One of the most significant risks of licensing, for the property owner, is the threat of losing control of a property. When a trademark owner produces all its branded products in-house or by subcontract, it maintains control over every detail, from design specifications and product quality to sales, distribution and marketing. With licensing, in contrast, the property owner transfers some of these functions to the manufacturer, creating an arm's-length relationship and the potential to lose control of the property, *if* it is not vigilant.

Property owners have the ability to select appropriate licensees and distribution channels, to approve all products and monitor quality, to dictate the terms of the licensing contract, to terminate agreements where the manufacturer does not meet expectations and to create integrated brand marketing programs. The more seriously a licensor takes these responsibilities, particularly licensee selection and product approvals, the less the danger of losing control over the program.

Still, it is worth remembering that this risk is inherent in the process of licensing. Designer Calvin Klein and his long-time underwear licensee Warnaco entered into a dispute, complete with lawsuits and countersuits, in 2000 over this point. Klein claimed Warnaco sold its licensed products, some of them unauthorized, in discount channels such as club stores, decreasing the value of his brand. (The suit was subsequently settled out of court.)

In another scenario, the licensors of Babar, Clifford Ross Co. and Nelvana, terminated a license with French publisher Editions Mango in 1997, claiming it had breached its contract by shipping outside its territory and not providing regular royalty reports. After termination, it allegedly continued to sell books and did not send back proprietary artwork, leading the licensors to file suit.

Why is the potential loss of control such a significant hazard? Licensors are in the business of owning properties. The value of those properties forms the basis of a licensor's operations and, therefore, maintaining their image is paramount. Relinquishing authority over a licensing effort decreases the value of a property or properties. Shoddy manufacturing hurts a property known for its "quality" (or any property, for that matter). Frivolous merchandise subtracts from an educational children's property. A fatty food item damages a property that promotes good health (such as the American Heart Association or a health magazine).

In other words, the licensor risks diluting its brand image and value unless it maintains control over its licensees and its licensing strategy. It is risky to license a property to a manufacturer and then let that company take it from there. It is also dangerous to license a property to an inappropriate manufacturer; a potential licensee that is known for making low-priced, low-quality items will not become a maker of quality, upscale items just because a licensor authorizes it.

The licensor's name appears on the products marketed by its licensees, so when a manufacturer sells a low-quality licensed product it makes a direct impact on the licensor's brand or property. In 2001, a man bought an IBM cordless phone from a licensee and accused both the property owner and licensor of consumer fraud (because the phone did not work properly and he alleged he was misled into thinking it was manufactured by IBM), which generated bad publicity for IBM when one of the New York City daily newspapers recounted the incident in a full-page feature.

Another potential danger to licensors is the possibility that a property's life will shorten if too many products are available. The market becomes oversaturated once consumer demand is satisfied, sometimes leading to a consumer backlash. At minimum, consumers will quickly move on to the next "hot" thing. This life-shortening phenomenon is most noticable in the entertainment area, but properties of any type are susceptible if the market is flooded with merchandise.

Product overproliferation is of most concern to licensors of evergreen properties, from art images to classic entertainment licenses. Avoiding oversaturation is critical for owners of corporate and fashion brands, for whom the brand comprises their core business. Licensing represents an ancillary revenue stream; its primary purposes are to support the core brand image, protect the company's trademarks, extend the brand into new product categories and increase awareness. The availability of too many licensed products not only shortens the life of the licensing effort but mars the integrity of the core brand.

The risk of oversaturation also affects licensors of short-term properties or fads, desite the fact that a property such as a stand-alone film (one that is not part of an ongoing or future franchise) has a naturally brief sales window for licensed merchandise. A strategy of offering as many products as possible during that time makes sense financially and from a marketing viewpoint. At the same time, when the number of products available exceeds demand, retailers will pull out of the property quickly, harming current and future sales potential. For both short- and long-term licenses, the goal is for supply to equal demand.

With a fad, where consumer awareness is immense but short-lived, licensors and licensees struggle to keep up with demand. Soon, shoppers become bored and move on to the "next big thing," creating an oversupply of products. Research reports such as *The EPM Fad Study* have shown, however, that many fads are able to recover from this oversaturation and ultimately become evergreen properties, as long as they possess inherent attributes that consumers continue to desire.

It should be noted that the perception of "failure" is often the result of too-great expectations for a property. Star Wars: Episode I drove $2 billion worldwide in product sales at retail, and many licensees were happy with their results. Yet too-high expectations — accompanied by high guarantees — resulted in a perception that the property failed and for some licensees, it did.

The steep rises and declines associated with some sectors of licensing, such as entertainment and music, require attention to staffing, with ramp-ups often followed by layoffs. Companies that keep staffs too big for too long run into financial problems; this was the reason behind some licensor failures in the early 2000s.

A final risk associated with licensing, for the property owner, is — as with most of the risks cited so far — a preventable one. When licensors do not live up to their end of the bargain during the course of a licensing agreement, they jeopardize their ability to license quality manufacturers in the future. Word gets around quickly in the close-knit and relationship-dependent licensing community. Licensors that are perceived as unethical or do not contribute their fair share to their alliances with licensees theoretically will have trouble finding quality manufacturers with which to work on the next property, or on the same property in the future. Of course, there will always be manufacturers lining up for a "hot" property or strong brand, no matter who the licensor is, but few properties are truly must-haves. Licensors without sterling reputations, developed over the long haul, will have trouble marketing their properties and may even jeopardize their livelihood.

RISKS TO LICENSEES

One of the major risks of licensing, for manufacturers, is a financial one. They are responsible not only for the required minimum guaranteed royalty payment to the licensor, but for other nonrecoupable investments as well, including research and development, retooling and marketing expenditures (e.g., advertising and point-of-sale materials) related to the licensed line. All of these outlays are sunk costs if the license fails. In addition, licensees may accrue extra variable costs associated with manufacturing and shipping the licensed products.

The royalty itself — the main component of payment for a license — is directly tied to sales and is therefore as much of a burden as fixed costs that are payable regardless of the number of units sold. The royalty does cut into profit margins for the licensed line, however. Licensees considering whether to acquire a license must weigh the hardship of smaller per-unit margins against the potential for additional sales.

The minimum guarantee against royalties, on the other hand, is payable no matter how many licensed items the manufacturer sells. Licensees must pay a sometimes-significant sum to the licensor and will not recoup this investment unless sales levels are high enough that royalty payments exceed the guarantee amount. In a perfect world, licensors and licensees negotiate guarantees to be fair and not to exceed expected royalties, but the unpredictable nature of licensing makes the guarantee a financial risk.

Increasingly, licensees are asking that guarantees be forgiven if a property, particularly in the entertainment sector, fails through no fault of theirs (e.g., a television show achieves low ratings or a movie does not open well, both of which prevent consumer demand). At the same time, licensors, especially if their stock is publicly traded, often carry advances (or a portion thereof) on their current books and count on future guarantee payments in their revenue projections. Thus they are unwilling to forgive contractual guarantees. Licensors may, rarely, forgive a portion of the guarantee under specific conditions; typically the amount will not be returned unilaterally but could be rolled over toward a future property or result in a lower guarantee on a future property.

Another economic consideration is that the upfront portion of the guarantee, known as the advance, can be high, especially for some entertainment properties. The laws of supply and demand dictate that a hot film or TV property can command a high advance; in addition, some entertainment licensors look to incoming advance money to help recoup production costs and therefore try to negotiate high upfront amounts. Manufacturers may view a large advance, coupled with other upfront investments associated with the licensed product line, such as retooling and research and development, as a barrier to acquiring the license. If the line fails, these expenditures are irretrievable.

Some licensors waive or reduce required advances in lieu of more product development, larger guarantees and/or higher royalty rates. More commonly, they are willing to share risk by creating graduated royalty and guarantee scales that reduce the licensee's risk before the property is established. (See Chapter 7 for more on royalties and guarantees.)

Even if a license is successful in terms of gross sales, it may not be profitable for a licensee, depending on the particulars discussed above. Major licensees such as Mattel and Hasbro have stated that they would like to reduce their dependence on licensing, this despite being associated with top entertainment properties. Their desire springs from the fact that royalties, investment costs, and/or other factors diminished the financial benefit of some of their recent licensed lines, even with robust sales, and that the ups and downs of licensing can be hard to bear.

One tactic that helps licensees accurately assess the financial risks of licensing is to understand the expectations of the retailers who will purchase the licensed line. Licensees must also manage their portfolio of licenses properly, risking only what they can afford to lose.

Another major risk of licensing, from the point of view of the licensee, is the difficulty of inventory control. Sales of merchandise tied to a popular property— especially a faddish one — can rise to higher-than-expected levels very quickly. Then, with virtually no warning, the desire for products falls off. It is a challenge for licensees, first, to meet demand while it is growing toward its peak; an inability to do so can cause bad feelings about the licensee's company on the part of both retailers and consumers. Then, and more importantly, manufacturers must try to ensure that no excess inventory is left when the peak ends. Selling off products at close-out prices often wipes out profits earned at the property's peak.

These quick declines also wreak havoc on year-to-year sales figures and, for public companies, with stock prices. Hasbro annouced in early 2001 that its worldwide sales of Pokémon merchandise dropped $240 million in one quarter, accounting for 75% of the company's total revenue decline for that period. The year before, it announced that its cumulative revenues from two key licenses, Star Wars and Pokémon, were down $500 million from the year before. Sales of wrestling toys and videogames industry-wide dropped 35%-45% in a two-month time period after the trend peaked, affecting all licensees and retailers involved.

Licensing is a gamble for manufacturers. They are betting that the property — and, more to the point, their own licensed line — will succeed. But the property as a whole could flop. In the entertainment area, if theaters showing a particular film are empty or a network cancels a television series after two episodes, the chances of selling truckloads of products are slim. If a newly launched apparel brand fails, licensed accessories are almost certain to fail, too. The XFL, a professional "extreme" football league, failed after its first season, leaving 20 licensees in the lurch. Italian scooter manufacturer Aprilia successfully sued the Spice Girls, saying its licensed product line failed after one of the Girls, Geri Halliwell, left the group.

More significant is the fact that, even if the property itself succeeds, some or all of the licensed products may not. People may like a film or television show but not want to purchase merchandise based on it; Universal's *Dr. Seuss's How The Grinch Stole Christmas* generated more than $200 million at the domestic box office, but consumers did not embrace much of the merchandise. A few products may just sit on store shelves, while shoppers scoop up other items based on the same property. Even billion-dollar properties do not drive success for every licensee.

The same is true for established fashion labels, corporate brands and other evergreen properties, despite their having a built-in market and a past record of solid licensed merchandise sales. Cadillac, the National Basketball Association, the Sierra Club and James Dean have all generated strong-selling licensed product lines, but each has been associated with at least some items that fizzled.

In some cases, there is a discernible reason for the failure of the product line: The target markets for the property and product did not adequately match, the price point of the product was too high or too low or the product category did not fit with the property's image. In other cases, there is no identifiable reason: The product fails, even though it seems to meet all criteria for success.

It should be noted, of course, that the opposite can be true as well. Sometimes the licensing and retail communities consider a property a failure or a nonstarter overall, but individual product lines make cash registers ring. Ray-Ban successfully promoted its sunglasses line in conjunction with the film *Men in Black*, even in the context of a minimal licensing effort for the property overall.

Complicating the issue is that retailers often stop purchasing product at the first sign of a decline or simply don't reorder once initial shipments have sold. Their goal is to avoid excess inventory, but the result is that they can prematurely end the life of a license that is still vibrant, albeit at a lower level than at its peak. The lack of retail support leaves licensees with inventory that can cause problems with subcontractors and harm retail relationships.

A final challenge for licensees is that their association with a property could lead to bad press or a consumer backlash if the property itself becomes the center of controversy. It may be deemed too violent, for example. Licensees who associate with living celebrities, including athletes or entertainers, are particularly vulnerable. Drugs, imprisonment, unproven accusations of crimes or any behavior unbecoming to a product spokesperson makes an attractive property unattractive in an instant.

Some merchandise is relatively controversy-proof, such as t-shirts marketed to a college audience. Other items, especially family-oriented ones, are prone to damage when controversies swirl around them. Each of the following properties, all of which have or had several licensees or endorsement deals, became controversial at some point in their lifespan: Beavis & Butt-head (thought to encourage children to light fires); Jurassic Park, Godzilla and Batman Returns (considered more appropriate for adults, yet products appealed to younger children); Mortal Kombat (accused by some of being too graphically violent); Barney the Dinosaur (deemed more commercial than is appropriate for a PBS pre-school television series); and O.J. Simpson (murder trial).

Most (but not all) of these properties drove a lot of merchandise sales, despite the controversy. Still, licensees face the risk that a property could unexpectedly become the target of criticism among a manufacturer's core market, the press or a vocal segment of the general populace, thus hurting its sales and image. The more popular the property, the more likely it is that controversies will arise.

Certain risks are inherent in licensing for both licensor and licensee. Designer brand Guess? parted with its 15-year infant products licensee Pour le Bébé due to a disagreement over royalty payments that eventually went to court. Whole product categories can experience licensing oversaturation (e.g., the licensed t-shirt market in 2000), adversely affecting licensors as well as manufacturers. Factors outside the control of the partners (e.g. constantly changing film release schedules or threats of writers', actors' or directors' strikes) can wreak havoc on a licensing effort. Both parties must consider these and other risks when embarking on a licensing program.

ROLES AND RESPONSIBILITIES OF THE PLAYERS

Each participant in a licensing relationship must fulfill certain responsibilities. Since every agreement is unique in its specifics, the roles of each partner vary depending on the deal; it is possible, however, to offer some guidelines as to how the duties are normally divided.

Licensors are responsible for creating the property (if new) and for preserving its overall integrity and longevity and setting a strategy that maintains its attributes. This role is sometimes termed "brand management," although the use of the word "brand," as discussed elsewhere, is often overused within the context of licensing.

One of the licensor's primary obligations is to legally protect its properties through trademark and copyright registration. Trademarks safeguard brand names and logos distinguishing the products of one company from those of others; copyrights protect creative elements of a property. Protecting rights in all categories is difficult and costly (see Chapter 8), but licensors must maximize protection within their means. Licensees desire a property because its uniqueness allows them to differentiate their merchandise from their competitors'. If licensors do not adequately protect a property, the likelihood of infringement rises and transgressions are less apt to be remedied, making that property unattractive to manufacturers. Therefore, proper legal protection is a prerequisite of licensing. The licensor — with some exceptions discussed later — bears the costs.

The licensor is responsible for creating the graphic look of a property and monitoring that licensees implement it consistently. Licensors maintain the image of their properties by putting together a style guide and other art reference materials to direct licensees on the proper use of the trademarks and copyrights. The style guide sets forth the allowable logos, likenesses, signatures, design variations and hangtags, as well as outlining any prohibitions. It offers a range of suggested artwork and includes specifications such as the proper use of colors. It often illustrates a variety of potential applications of the property on goods in selected product categories. Many licensors create "interim" style guides, smaller versions that provide for seasonal or other changes in the property. (Some licensors attempt to charge licensees for the style guide, which is expensive to produce, but this is not a widely accepted practice.)

Licensors are responsible for keeping the property fresh over time, by providing new designs, implementing consumer and trade promotions and, if appropriate, creating entertainment vehicles to support the brand. Licensees also play a role in rejuvenating and refreshing a property, mainly through the creation of fashion-forward and innovative designs and products.

Licensors also monitor the image of their properties by selecting licensees that will be able to preserve that image. As mentioned earlier, a licensee's track record speaks volumes about its ability to appropriately market and create products based on the licensor's property. The style guide and other tools are useless unless the licensee is capable of doing the job.

The licensor's next responsibility, once it has selected appropriate licensees, is to set up an effective product approval process and follow it diligently. Quality control is a major factor in maintaining a property's integrity. Licensors approve merchandise at several points during the manufacturing schedule, usually viewing conceptual drawings or models, preproduction samples and production samples. Licensees then have a period of time during which to make changes. Some licensors take this responsibility very seriously and are notorious for their strict and lengthy approval procedures. This diligence often pays dividends, though; these same licensors are generally those with the most sought-after brands (although licensees will always clamor for the most popular licenses, regardless of the quality-control process in place).

A careful approval process helps licensees, too: The better the overall brand image, the better the property will drive sales of their products. Licensors who are lax about approvals open themselves up to potential problems later when a faulty or inappropriate product devalues the property, making it unattractive to potential licensees and decreasing sales to consumers.

Overseeing anti-counterfeiting and anti-infringement efforts is the licensor's task (with a few exceptions). Infringement (the unauthorized use of a property) and counterfeiting (the manufacture of illegitimate merchandise) are big problems in the licensing business. Poor-quality knock-offs find their way into the marketplace, hurt the image of the infringed property and cut into sales of official products. Large licensors and smaller owners of hot properties tend to oversee the most active anti-infringement efforts, since the more popular a property is, the likelier it is to spur counterfeiting. In addition, these property owners have deep enough pockets to wage an effective — and therefore costly — anti-counterfeiting program. Still, preventing infringement is an important concern for all licensors.

Licensees' major responsibilities within the context of a licensing agreement include the design and manufacture of the authorized products, subject to approval by the licensor. (Licensors often participate in the product development process as well, with sometime controlling it completely and others taking more of an advisory role.) Licensees also handle sales and distribution, typically offering the licensed items to the same retail accounts that purchase their nonlicensed products. (If a licensor has a manufacturing business and utilizes licensing as a means of brand extension, its sales force might handle the licensed as well the core items for certain channels. For example, toy stores might carry licensed apparel based on a toy brand and would probably be serviced by the licensor's sales force. Generally, however, sales and distribution fall under the licensee's jurisdiction.) Licensees are also responsible for calculating manufacturing quantities, although licensors may maintain some control over this, especially for properties with a significant perceived threat of oversaturation (see Chapter 9).

Both licensors and licensees can assume responsibility for advertising and marketing, depending on the situation. Licensors sometimes strengthen their brands by advertising to consumers. They also advertise the property as a whole to the trade, so that retailers know where to purchase licensed products in relevant categories; a licensor might run an ad listing its kitchen-related licensees in the housewares section of *HFN*, a home furnishings trade magazine.

Licensees increasingly expect licensors, especially of entertainment properties, to play a role in selling the property to retailers, either jointly with licensees or in advance of licensees' sales calls. They also demand that licensors provide additional marketing support for the property in the form of point-of-purchase materials, co-op marketing dollars, retail promotions or other techniques (although they typically help finance these initiatives through their contributions to a central marketing fund). Retailers, too, desire this licensor-driven marketing activity. The existence of a strong licensor-backed promotional effort is a key factor in retailers' decision to purchase products based on a given property and of licensees' decision to tie in with that property.

At the same time, manufacturers advertise their licensed lines. In some categories, a licensee's investment in advertising is critical to the success of the entire property. The master toy licensee of a children's entertainment property advertises during Saturday morning cartoon shows; licensors and other licensees depend on this expenditure to strengthen the property overall. Licensors of corporate trademarks, fashion labels and some sports and entertainment properties view licensees' contribution to advertising as crucial and often require or encourage them to advertise, through monetary incentives or contractual obligations (see Chapter 7).

As licensors and licensees increasingly view themselves as partners, the lines between the roles and responsibilities of each side become blurred. In the 1980s and 1990s, the boundary between each party's responsibilities was clear; in the 2000s, the partners more often join together to accomplish their objectives. As with all else in licensing, each situation is different, depending on the property and the objectives of both partners.

THE ROLE OF THE RETAILER

Retailers, in their role as gatekeepers (standing between licensors and licensees on one side and the ultimate consumer on the other), have always been key players in the licensing business. Their interest in a given property determines whether that property will end up on store shelves. In some cases, retailers dictate who a property's licensees will be, by requesting or demanding their preferred suppliers. They can also cause the death of a property by refusing to buy more at the first sign of a decline (or even of slowing growth).

Retailers are key promotional partners for licensed properties (licensors often sell a property to retailers *before* selling to licensees) and, increasingly, serve as licensees in their own right. They often demand some sort of exclusivity on properties they support, ranging from a single exclusive product to full exclusivity, from a promotional window of six months to a permanent private-label arrangement.

For their part, retailers look to licensed properties as a way to differentiate themselves from other chains and to increase store traffic. They want to carry desirable products that can command premium prices and give them high margins (and often turn over faster) rather than competing on price alone. Toys 'R' Us said in financial statements in 2001 that its 80 basis-point increase in gross margin was largely attributable to its exclusive partnerships with licensed brands and properties.

Therefore, while licensing is essentially an agreement between a licensee and licensor, in practical terms retailers are so vital to the relationship they are considered a third partner. The existence of a strong retail partner is often considered the primary predictor of success for a property. (See Chapter 4 for more on retail relationships.)

OTHER MAJOR PLAYERS IN LICENSING

The two main players in any licensing agreement — the licensor and the licensee — rely on the expertise of licensing agents, consultants, attorneys and/or other service providers and partners.

Many licensors retain LICENSING AGENTS to manage their merchandising programs. Agents bring experience and industry contacts to the table, which can be especially valuable to a new licensor. Agents can also handle the approval process, oversee bookkeeping (including royalty compliance) and help with contract negotiation, among other services. For their efforts, they receive a percentage of all royalty income as well as, in some cases, a monthly retainer or fee. (See Chapter 5 for more on licensing agents.) Some act as short- or long-term consultants for select clients, rather than as commission-based agents, or as agents for specific product categories only.

The role of the agent has changed over the years as the business has become more competitive and many licensors have opted to handle their licensing business in-house. Their role has evolved from sales to brand management. They are involved in supporting and promoting the property, forging and maintaining retail relationships, and all aspects of licensing. Some entertainment-specializing agents invest monetarily in a property, such as helping finance a television show.

International sub-agents' role have changed in parallel fashion. These are agents in international territories retained by the master licensing agent or directly by the licensor to secure licensees and/or manage the property in their territory, which may consist of one country or a group of countries. (See Chapter 11 for more on international licensing and international sub-agents.)

Manufacturers also have help in the form of licensing consultants or manufacturers' representatives. These companies work with licensees to identify and acquire appropriate licenses. Like agents, they have expertise and contacts and specialize in licensing on a full-time basis. Manufacturers must attend to other aspects of their business and often do not have time or adequate staff to fully concentrate on acquiring licenses or administering licensing relationships.

Attorneys assist both licensees and licensors with contractual issues, guide them through the intricacies of trademark and copyright law and counsel them in their anti-counterfeiting activities. Most licensing executives find it essential to hire an attorney and strongly recommend retaining one who is an expert in licensing.

Some licensors and licensees retain promotions agents. When working on behalf of licensors, these companies brainstorm and implement appropriate promotional strategies on behalf of the property, help secure promotional partners, which can be retailers, packaged goods marketers, licensees, media companies, quick-service restaurants or other firms, and create and source premiums. Promotions agents also work on behalf of potential tie-in partners, helping them evaluate available licensed properties with which to associate and helping negotiate deals.

The roles of various partners and associated companies within the scope of licensing are not always clear-cut. Retailers are often licensees, manufacturers can be both licensees and licensors, and licensing agents can act as licensors and, in a few cases, licensees.

CHAPTER 2:
SOURCES OF LICENSED PROPERTIES

Licensable properties come from a variety of sources. The largest sector, according to *The Licensing Letter,* is Corporate Trademarks and Brands, which drove $17.8 billion in retail sales of licensed merchandise in the U.S. and Canada in 2001 and represented 25% of total sales of licensed goods that year. This segment includes brands such as Coca-Cola, Adidas, Pillsbury, Land Rover, and the M&Ms candy mascots.

The second largest source of licensed properties is the Entertainment and Character sector, which includes films, television programs and comic book characters and accounted for $13.7 billion in sales of licensed merchandise (19% of the market) in 2001. Fashion, with $11.5 billion (16%), and Sports, with $10.5 billion (15%) follow. *Figure 3 (page 28)* shows the share of retail sales of licensed merchandise in the U.S. and Canada in 2001, by property type. (Globally, Entertainment/Character licensing represents 25% of all licensing with Fashion at second place at 22% and Trademark/Brand third at 20%.)

Categorizing property types is not a clear-cut enterprise. *The Licensing Letter* attempts to organize properties according to the form they take first, but in these days of multifaceted franchises it is sometimes difficult to say which medium most influences consumer purchasing. Harry Potter, initially a book character, is classified under Publishing even though its licensing program is, as of this writing, influenced more by the film franchise. Pokémon began as an electronic game and is categorized under Toys/Games, but the associated WB television series probably drove the bulk of sales at the property's peak in 2000. In certain cases, a property's origin is not even obvious. Jimmy Neutron: Boy Genius was a film/TV/Internet property right from the beginning in 2001.

Figure 4 (pages 28-32) lists some examples that fall into each property type. The table's purpose is to provide an overview of the sorts of licensed properties that spring from each source and of the multiplicity of possible licensing programs. It is not a comprehensive list. In terms of success, of course, the source of a licensed property really does not matter, as long as there is a market for products based on it.

Every licensing program is unique and requires its own strategy. Common trends and similarities exist within each property type, however, and this chapter outlines them.

CORPORATE TRADEMARK AND BRAND LICENSING

Corporate trademark owners launch licensing programs for many reasons: to create brand awareness or "share of mind," to protect the company's trademarks, to develop new revenue streams and, especially, to enter new product categories in a relatively risk-free and cost-effective way. (The last is known as "brand-extension licensing.") Some corporate trademark licensors

Figure 3
2001 SHARES OF LICENSED PRODUCT RETAIL SALES, U.S. AND CANADA, BY PROPERTY TYPE

Dollar Figures In Billions

PROPERTY TYPE	2001 RETAIL SALES	PCT. ALL SALES
Art	$6.00	9%
Celebrities/Estates	$3.10	4%
Entertainment/Character	$13.70	19%
Fashion	$11.50	16%
Music	$1.60	2%
Nonprofit	$0.90	1%
Publishing	$1.80	3%
Sports	$10.50	15%
Trademarks/Brands	$17.80	25%
Toys/Games	$3.30	5%
Other	$0.10	<1%
Total	**$70.30**	**100%**

Source: The Licensing Letter;
EPM Communications

Figure 4
SELECTED PROPERTIES BY PROPERTY TYPE

ART
American Greetings card art
Amy J. Wulfing
Boris Vallejo
Cat Clan
Cat Hall of Fame
Cheryl Ann Johnson
Christian Riese Lassen
Colonial Williamsburg
Cynthia Hart
Deborah Brumfield
Donald Zolan
Edith Jackson
Flat Cats
Frank Frazetta
Grant Wood
Gre Girardi
Greenwich Workshop
Greg Spiers
Gwen Connelly
Hallmark card designs
The Hautmans
Helen Lea
Hillary Vermont
Hummel

Hunt Slonem
Ivory Cats
Jan Brett
Jared Lee
Joan Walsh Anglund
Jody Winger
John Grossman
Judith Ann Griffith
Judith Kruger
Judy Buswell
Leslie McGuirk
Lisa Frank
Mabel Lucie Atwell
Mary Engelbreit
Maxfield Parrish
Norman Rockwell
Olivia
Paul Brent
Picasso
Ruth J. and Bill D. Morehead
Precious Moments
Stephen Lawrence
Sue Dreamer
Suzy's Zoo

Continued Next Page

Figure 4 Continued

Thomas Hart Benton
Thomas Kinkade
Vicky Hart
Viv Eisner Hess
Winterthur Collection

CELEBRITIES/ESTATES
Abbott & Costello
Albert Einstein
Mikhail Baryshnikov
Bette Davis
Charlie Chaplin
Elizabeth Taylor
Elvis Presley
Emmett Kelly Jr.
Fabio
Humphrey Bogart
James Cagney
James Dean
Kathie Lee Gifford
Laurel & Hardy
Malcolm X
Marilyn Monroe
Martha Stewart
Martin Luther King
Roy Rogers
Wolfgang Puck

ENTERTAINMENT/CHARACTER
ABC Daytime
Alvin & the Chipmunks
Andy Griffith Show
Animaniacs
Archie & Friends
Austin Powers
Barney
Batman
Beavis & Butt-head
Beetle Bailey
Beverly Hills 90210
Blondie
Bob the Builder
Cabbage Patch Kids
Cartoon Network
Casablanca
Casper the Friendly Ghost
Coach
Dick Van Dyke Show
Felix the Cat
Fido Dido
Flintstones
Free Willy

Garfield
Godzilla
Gone with the Wind
Gumby
Hello Kitty
Home Improvement
Honeymooners
I Love Lucy
Indiana Jones
Inspector Gadget
It's A Wonderful Life
Jurassic Park
King Kong
King of the Hill
Lamb Chop
Lassie
Lion King
Looney Tunes
Marvel Comics (Spiderman, X-Men, etc.)
The Mask
Mickey Mouse
Mighty Morphin Power Rangers
Mr. Rogers Neighborhood
MTV
Mulan
Muppets
Nickelodeon
Nightmare Before Christmas
Nightmare on Elm Street
Peanuts
Popeye
Ren & Stimpy
Rocky & Bullwinkle
Sailor Moon
Sesame Street
Simpsons
Smurfs
South Park
Star Trek
Star Wars
Teenage Mutant Ninja Turtles
Teletubbies
Thomas the Tank Engine
Tom & Jerry
Wild Wild West
Wizard of Oz
Woody Woodpecker
Ziggy
Zorro

Continued Next Page

Figure 4 Continued

FASHION

Adrienne Vittadini
Alexander Julian
Anne Klein
Armani
Arnold Scaasi
Aspen
B.U.M. Equipment
Bebe Winkler
Bennetton
Beverly Hills Polo Club
Bill Blass
Bob Mackie
Body Glove
Bonjour
BOSS
Brittania
Bugle Boy
Burberry
Calvin Klein
Capezio
Carolina Herrera
Carter's
Charlotte Moss
Cherokee
Chic
Christian Dior
Cotler
Cross Colours
Crunch Gear
Danskin
Debra Mallow
Diane Von Furstenburg
Donna Karan
Easy Spirit
Faded Glory
French Toast
Gear
Generra
Gitano
Givenchy
Gloria Vanderbilt
Guess?
h.i.s.
Halston
Hang Ten
Health-Tex
Hugo Boss
J.G. Hook
Joe Boxer

Jones New York
Jordache
Jou Jou
Lightning Bolt
Lillian August
MacGregor
Marimekko
Members Only
Misty Harbour
Mossimo
Natori
Nautica
Nicole Miller
Ocean Pacific
Oleg Cassini
Oscar de la Renta
OshKosh B'Gosh
Perry Ellis
Pierre Cardin
Polo Ralph Lauren
Sasson
Todd Oldham
Tommy Hilfiger
Vera Wang
Wrangler

MUSIC

Backstreet Boys
Beatles
Brandy
Britney Spears
Country Music Association
Garth Brooks
Grand Ole Opry
Grateful Dead
Janet Jackson
John Lennon
K.I.S.S.
Madonna
'N Sync
New Kids On The Block
Prince
Rolling Stones
Spice Girls

NONPROFIT

American Heart Association
American Red Cross
ASPCA
Boys and Girls Clubs

Continued Next Page

Figure 4 Continued

CARE
4-H
Greenpeace
National Audubon Society
National Park Foundation
National Parks & Conservation
  Association
Nature Conservancy
National Wildlife Federation
Save the Children
Sierra Club
UNICEF
Wilderness Society
World Wildlife Fund

PUBLISHING
Arthur
Babar
Beatrix Potter
Berenstain Bears
Better Homes & Gardens
Chicken Soup for the Soul
Clifford the Big Red Dog
Cosmopolitan
Curious George
Eric Hill's Spot
Esquire
Essence
Field & Stream
Good Housekeeping
Harry Potter
I Spy
Kipper
MAD Magazine
Magic School Bus
Maisy
Old Farmer's Almanac
Paddington Bear
Pat the Bunny
Penthouse
Playboy
Popular Science
Rainbow Fish
Rand McNally
Reader's Digest
Richard Scarry
Sports Illustrated for Kids
Stuart Little
Sweet Potato Queens
Where's Waldo?
YM

SPORTS
Arnold Palmer
Babe Ruth
B.A.S.S.
Big Ten
Canadian Football League
Championship Auto Racing
  Teams (C.A.R.T.)
Colleges
Goodwill Games
Indianapolis 500
International Hockey League
Ironman Triathlon
Jack Nicklaus
Joe Montana
Major Indoor LaCrosse League
Major League Baseball
Major League Baseball Alumni
  Association
Major League Baseball Players
  Association
Major League Soccer
Michael Jordan
Minor League Baseball
NASCAR
National Basketball Association
National Football League
National Football League Players
  Association
National Hockey League
National Hockey League Players
  Association
Negro Leagues Baseball Museum
Negro Leagues Baseball Players
  Association
New York City Marathon
Pele
PGA of America
PGA Tour
PONY League
Professional Rodeo Association
U.S. Hot Rod Association
U.S. Olympic Team
U.S. Soccer
Wayne Gretzky
Wimbledon
WNBA
World Cup
World Wrestling Federation

Continued Next Page

Figure 4 Continued

TRADEMARKS/BRANDS

American Tourister
AMF
Anheuser-Busch, Budweiser
Arm & Hammer
Betty Crocker
Big Boy
Borden
Brut
Buick
Burger King
Caboodles
Cadillac
Campbell Soup
Celestial Seasonings
Chevrolet
Chiquita
Coca-Cola
Coleman
Colt
Converse
Coors
Coppertone
Croscill
Crown Crafts
Dr. Scholl's
Dunlop
Everlast
Fabergé
Farberware
Fieldcrest
Ford
Formica
Gateway
Good Humor
Harley-Davidson
Hawaiian Punch
Hawaiian Tropic
Hershey
Huffy
IBM
Jack Daniels
Jeep
Kawasaki
Keds
Kodak
Labatt's
Louisville Slugger
Mack Trucks
McDonald's

Miller
Molson
Mr. Clean
Pepsi
PEZ
Pillsbury
Rawlings
ReaLemon
Reebok
Remington
Revlon
Riddell
Rollerblade
Samsonite
Sharper Image
Snap-On Tools
Spalding
Stanley
Sunkist
Voit
Volkswagen
Winchester

TOYS/GAMES

Barbie
Betty Spaghetty
Crayola
Fisher-Price
Hot Wheels
LEGO
Matchbox
Monopoly
Mortal Kombat
Mr. Potato Head
Nintendo/Super Mario
Pac-Man
Play-Doh
Playskool
Pokémon
Polly Pocket
Sonic the Hedgehog
Street Fighter
Super Soaker

Note: This list of current and past properties is not exhaustive, but should give a sense of the sorts of licenses found in each sector.
Source: The EPM Licensing Letter Sourcebook; EPM Communications

also authorize licensed premiums for promotions or dealer incentives. (As noted in Chapter 1, "trademarks" and "brands" refer here to the properties a corporation has available for licensing; it does not signify trademarks in the legal sense or brand-positioned properties of other types.)

Corporate licensors' main concern is to avoid harming their core image, which is their reason for being. Revenues from corporate trademark licensing are usually minuscule when compared to sales of the company's major products. Inappropriate distribution, low quality and incompatible price points are among the potential dangers inherent in a corporate licensing program, if not well monitored.

A large and growing number of trademark owners are initiating licensing efforts. Their strategies vary—some are primarily promotional, some "lifestyle" and some extension—depending, in part, on the industry where the core brand originates. Some of the most common sectors include automotive (e.g. Volkswagen); food and beverage (Jack Daniel's, Sun-Maid); sporting goods (Everlast); electronics/communications (AT&T); restaurant/retail/hotel (Ritz Paris); housewares/home furnishings (Farberware); cosmetics/fragrance (Cover Girl); and footwear (Hush Puppies). The proprietors of properties in each of these sectors — which barely scratch the surface of potential branded licensing opportunities — all launched their licensing programs for different reasons and have embarked on unique licensing strategies.

One area of corporate licensing that has expanded significantly in the early 2000s is the brand-extension sector. In a best-case scenario, the corporation's in-house licensing department, external licensing agents, and licensees work directly with the company's brand managers to integrate the licensing effort with the brand strategy. A sample of brand-extension licensing includes:

- Baking soda brand Arm & Hammer into air filters and carpet cleaning systems
- Fitness club Bally Total Fitness into home exercise equipment
- Cereal brand Kellogg's into fruit and popcorn snacks and muffin mix
- Cleaning solution brand Mr. Clean into gloves and cleaning accessories
- Gun maker Smith & Wesson into alarms and other security products
- Lollypop and candy brand Chupa Chups into fragrances and cosmetics for teens

A great deal of corporate brand-extension licensing is invisible to consumers. When shoppers purchase a Revlon hair dryer or a Betty Crocker kitchen utensil, they often believe the product is made by Revlon or General Mills. This perception is a good reason for vigilant licensee selection and careful quality control.

ENTERTAINMENT AND CHARACTER LICENSING

The Entertainment and Character sector contains two groups of properties with very different traits: "hot" or short-term properties and "classic" or long-term ones. Short-term properties traditionally have been expected, no matter how successful, to have a lifespan of about three to five years. Sales reach their apex — sometimes spiking dramatically — in the first year or two of this cycle but by the end, merchandise sales are very limited. When licensors determine that their property possesses an inherently short life, they usually opt to maximize sales during the brief window of opportunity. (Sometimes the market gives them no choice.) Of course, there is always the risk that a property will fail altogether, resulting in a lifespan of zero years, with some properties' lives cut off prematurely by skittish retailers.

"Hot" properties' lifespans are getting even shorter than in the past. Films, whose lifespans have declined to as little as six weeks, are often viewed primarily as promotional opportunities. Other short-term properties (such as those from television or the Internet) can be over in as little as six months to a year.

Long-term properties have a potential lifespan of decades. Mickey Mouse, created in 1928, is certainly among them, as are Peanuts (1950) and Sesame Street (1969). When a licensor handles its property as a classic (or as if it will become a classic), its strategy is quite different from that for a short-term property. Too much merchandise in the early years could cause the property to fizzle out prematurely, making it more difficult to re-establish. In addition, licensors continuously must refresh the property through new product designs, promotional activity, advertising and new media and entertainment vehicles to ensure its longevity. Unlike with a short-term property, there is an emphasis on long-term "brand management."

Annual sales of classic-based entertainment licensing programs are likely to be less in any one year than that season's crop of "hot" properties, but will remain relatively stable throughout the years, rising and falling in cycles but hovering around a constant — and sometimes very significant — level.

Entertainment and character licensors increasingly position most of their properties, even brand-new ones, as classic franchises, in an effort to convince manufacturers and retailers of their longevity. Plans for media vehicles — films, TV, videogames, home videos and publishing — as well as retail and consumer goods promotions and other marketing activities, help sell potential licensees and retail buyers on these hoped-for classics-in-the-making. Some licensors even grant rights for all the individual properties in the franchise simultaneously to a single licensee. Of course, not all of these properties will succeed in becoming classics.

Properties that become fads and burn out after a short time can survive, post-peak, as evergeens, with ongoing sales at a level less than during the fad period but still viable. The Simpsons and Star Wars are examples. A change in the strategic direction of the licensing program paves the way for the transition from craze to classic. (See Chapter 5 for specific strategies applicable to long- and short-term properties.) No matter what strategy a licensor takes, of course, it is the consumer that dictates whether a property will become a classic or disappear. Just saying a property is a "classic" or a "brand" does not make it so.

Children's entertainment properties make up the bulk of this segment of the business — as much as 65% to 70%, according to estimates by *The Licensing Letter* — but licensed entertainment properties for teens and adults are viable as well. They may not generate the record-breaking retail sales of a blockbuster kids' property, but they can certainly represent a solid business for licensors and licensees; those involved with the cable TV property South Park in the U.S. in 1998-1999 found it lucrative to the tune of over $250 million at retail. Some properties, such as Star Wars, appeal to consumers of all ages.

While the bulk of entertainment/character properties come from the realm of television and film, there has been a rise in properties from other areas such as the Internet and home video. While these have tended to be niche properties to date, they have the potential to be successful for licensees that tie in. Core fans of Internet properties, such as Joe Cartoon, NeoPets.com, Bikini.com or the Mexican poperty The Net Gang, or of direct-to-video productions, such as the Baby Einstein series or Mattel's Barbie in the Nutcracker, often are receptive to relevant products.

Niche opportunities are becoming more common in general as the entertainment/character sector has become crowded. Properties such as the classic films Caddyshack, Yellow Submarine and Reservoir Dogs, for example, or the nostalgic Sid and Marty Krofft TV shows HR Puf 'n Stuf and The Bugaloos, have been the focus of limited licensing efforts. Other properties have extended to only one or a few products that make sense or are sought by consumers, as was the case for the film Cast Away and its hand-printed volleyball, "Wilson."

SPORTS LICENSING

Sports licensing was the fastest-growing segment of the business from the mid-1980s through the early 1990s, with average annual gains of 27% from 1985 to 1993, according to *TLL* data. In the mid- and late-1990s, the business started to mature, as well as suffering the consequences of labor unrest, anti-pro sports sentiment among some fans and, especially, the passing of sports-licensed apparel as a fashion statement. The declines have continued into the 2000s due to decreasing shelf space (both from the drop in the number of stores specializing in sports apparel and because retailers in general devoted less space to licensed sports merchandise) and due to increasing competition from brands such as Nike.

Sports licensing is primarily a fan-driven, seasonal phenomenon, with sales of products based on individual teams largely of regional interest. Event-related products sell best in the area surrounding the venues; Utah accounted for much of the Salt Lake City Olympic merchandise sold before and during the winter games in 2002. St. Louis Cardinals merchandise moves best in Missouri and Denver Broncos items in Colorado. Hockey products sell in the winter; baseball in the summer.

The four major leagues — Major League Baseball, National Football League, National Basketball Association and National Hockey League — are focusing on honing their licensee and product lists to focus on the most profitable programs, and on increasing their marketing efforts to their core fans (and young potential future fans).

Colleges and universities are also included in the sports licensing sector, since much of their sales of licensed merchandise is attributable to their sports teams. The University of Tennessee sold $100 million of licensed merchandise at retail in 1998, almost double the year before, due to a win in the Fiesta Bowl. About a quarter of sales were championship-related. Most sales of collegiate merchandise occurs regionally, although there are a few teams with a national following. Hundreds of colleges and universities have extensive licensing efforts, many handled by a handful of licensing agents specializing in this market.

NASCAR licensing intensified during the 1990s and 2000s, with retail sales surpassing $1 billion annually starting in 1998 and reaching $2 billion in the 2000s, putting it in the range of league licensing programs. Several other auto racing bodies also have merchandising efforts, with some focused on retail and others mainly on trackside sales.

One growing area in sports licensing in the early 2000s has been in out-doors-related properties such as World Championship Fishing, Team ProFish and B.A.S.S. (Bass Anglers Sportsman Society). Other sports properties range from minor professional leagues and amateur sports associations (e.g., the PONY softball league) to women's sports leagues and events. Almost any sports entity or event, from bowling to snowboarding, is the focus of some licensing activity. Many sell mainly at events, in pro shops and through their own online and mail-order catalogs.

FASHION LICENSING

Fashion licensing consists of non-personality-driven apparel labels, such as Ocean Pacific, Burberry and Carter's, and designer names such as Ralph Lauren, Liz Claiborne and Tommy Hilfiger. Licensing serves as a method of brand extension to place the label into product categories where the licensor does not have expertise (in manufacturing, marketing, design or distribution) or where licensing is more profitable than maintaining an in-house operation. Some brands, such as Chanel, historically have licensed very few products, while others, such as Ocean Pacific and Perry Ellis, are fully licensed brands whose owners manufacture nothing in-house nor under subcontract.

Say a women's fashion company that manufactures its core products, including women's, juniors', missy and large-sized sportswear, wants to extend its brand. For each expansion category, it would examine whether it has the expertise to design, manufacture and market the new products and whether its profit margin would be greater than the royalty it could expect through licensing. It also has to analyze the upfront costs of setting up an in-house operation for the new product line, an investment that would not occur if the line was licensed. Control over the brand is also an important concern; some designers have purchased their licensees or taken licensed lines in-house when they felt they were losing control over marketing, merchandising, design or any other facet of the line.

Fashion houses often opt for licensing when expanding into apparel for new market segments (e.g., menswear or childrenswear for a womenswear designer); accessories (hosiery, headwear, handbags, footwear, belts, scarves and jewelry); fragrances; and home furnishings. They may also decide to license outside manufacturers for certain products targeted to their primary market (such as denim or outerwear) and as an alternative to exporting when entering international territories.

The fortunes of fashion licensing mirror those of the apparel industry, which experienced some tough years in the 1990s and early 2000s. Some labels shy away from licensing in response to financial difficulties (for themselves or the industry), preferring to concentrate on core products controlled in-house. Jones Apparel Group took its licenses for handbags and shoes in-house in 2000 after acquiring its own footwear and accessories firm, Nine West. Conversely, other labels discover it is more cost-efficient to increase their licensing activity during fiscal downturns, when licensing royalties can exceed profit margins on goods produced in-house. Brands such as B.U.M. and Cherokee have taken this path, becoming full-time licensors, while Donna Karan's licensing royalties increased from 1% of total revenues to 5% in three years ending in 2000, according to the company's financial reports.

Most consumers are not aware that much of the fashion merchandise they buy is licensed. To them, all Ralph Lauren merchandise comes from Ralph Lauren's Polo Corp. but, in fact, the designer licenses his label for apparel, accessories, fragrances and home furnishings. Therefore, fashion licensors must maintain control over their licensing programs to ensure that licensed products do not harm the brand's positive image.

A trend in fashion licensing in the 1990s and 2000s has involved private-label agreements between retailers and fashion brands, whereby the licensor grants the retailer (often a mass merchant) exclusive rights to the property as a store brand. Mossimo became a private-label program at Target, for example. The licensee and retailer work together to develop the appropriate merchandise mix, hangtags and in-store signage; manufacturing is done under contract, often by one of the retailer's preferred vendors. The deal gives the retailer a point of difference from its competitors and is lucrative for the designer or apparel label, reducing costs and increasing revenues.

TOY AND GAME LICENSING

Toy and game makers (including those producing electronic gaming for computers and videogame consoles) are often perceived mainly as licensees, but many also own proprietary properties, which they license out . Some of these efforts are character-based and thus similar to the properties outlined in the section on Entertainment and Character licensing. Current and past examples include trolls in the early 1990s, which were licensed by several companies; Manley Toy Quest's Tekno the Robotic Puppy; the Razor scooter; MGA's doll line, Bratz; electronic game characters such as Sega's Sonic the Hedgehog and Nintendo's Pokémon; and board and card game properties such as Wizards of the Coast's Magic: The Gathering. Sometimes these toy-based licensing programs focus on additional products within the toy industry; JoyRide Studios announced in 2002 that it would produce collectible figures and vehicles based on a range of videogame titles.

Toy marketers are also active brand-extension licensors, like the companies discussed in the section on Corporate Trademarks and Brands. They want to capitalize on the equity they have built over time by positioning their properties not just as toy brands but as children's product brands. Through licensing, they expand into juvenile apparel, accessories, footwear, home furnishings, software, publishing and home video. A few of the licensors that have utilized this strategy include Fisher-Price, Hasbro (Playskool) and LEGO.

Some licensors of toy brands take a hybrid approach, employing a combination of character licensing and brand-extension methods within the context of their licensing program. For example, some Barbie products, such as apparel, are not heavily character-dependent but are identified with the Barbie brand or a sub-brand, while other items, such as CD-ROMs, utilize Barbie as a character.

MUSIC LICENSING

Several types of licensing, in addition to merchandise licensing, occur in the music industry. Owners of music copyrights grant authorizations to perform music, to record music in conjuction with advertising or as background in a product or entertainment production (e.g., in a home video), and to play over the air (in a restaurant or on the radio).

Although these situations are essentially outside the scope of this book on trademark licensing, an increasing number of licensed products, ranging from CD-ROMs to toys with electronic sound chips, require such rights. They are discussed in more detail in Chapter 8.

Music-related product licensing traditionally has been unique within the merchandise licensing business. Most musical acts have been handled by a half-dozen music merchandisers, which acted as licensees for certain product categories, including most of the apparel, souvenirs and other products sold at concert venues (which take a 40% cut of sales). The merchandisers also served as agents and sublicensed other companies for product categories where they lacked expertise either in manufacturing or distribution.

While this is still the case for many acts in the early 2000s (although some music merchandisers have gone bankrupt), more performing artists are taking matters into their own hands, retaining licensing rights and hiring licensing agents from outside the music industry with more retail expertise. This trend is partly due to the increased potential for music-related merchandise in mass-market outlets and the artists' growing awareness of the revenue potential of licensing. Although few musical acts drive significant merchandise sales at retailers like Wal-Mart and Sears, those that do — think New Kids on the Block, Garth Brooks or Spice Girls in the 1990s — are among the top properties during their tenure.

In response to lower venue sales, merchandisers and musicians have tried to cross over into mainstream retail, some with significant success. They are targeting product categories outside the t-shirts, tour jackets and collectibles typical of music-based licensing efforts, emphasizing items that appeal to customers in traditional shopping environments. The toy industry has been particularly ripe for such opportunities, with products such as dolls—depicting Britney Spears, Destiny's Child, Vitamin C, Brandy and others— interactive electronics and home karaoke machines.

Most music groups have narrowly defined audiences, which means that their fame tends to be transitory. On the other hand, they can be an effective means for licensees to reach a targeted audience, often one (such as teens) that does not embrace other licenses. It is critical, however, to target the correct (and often narrow) audience for the property; the Backstreet Boys and 'N Sync appeal to slightly different demographics, for example, even though many people identify both as tween-targeted properties.

A few music licenses, including The Grateful Dead, the Beatles and Elvis Presley, are the focus of robust and long-term merchandising efforts, but this is the exception rather than the rule. The average music-related licensing effort is short-lived.

A trend in the early 2000s has been the movement of musical artists, many from the rap genre, into the apparel category, as designers. Sean Combs was among the first; others include Jennifer Lopez, Carlos Santana, MC Hammer, Steve Harwell of Smashmouth, Lisa "Left-Eye" Lopes and Snoop Dogg.

PUBLISHING PROPERTIES

Most properties with origins in the publishing business are book characters (mainly for children), specialized book imprints (e.g., Rand McNally or Berlitz) or magazine titles. (Comic book properties are classified under Entertainment and Characters.)

Starting in the late 1990s, competition in the fragmented children's entertainment and licensing markets caused television and film distributors and retailers to favor TV and film properties based on existing franchises. The most popular of these are children's books, which have a life beyond entertainment. As a result, properties from the world of juvenile publishing have been among the most visible licenses in the business in the late 1990s and early 2000s. Examples of children's book properties, both entertainment-supported and standalone, include Curious George, Richard Scarry, Stuart Little, Maisy, Franklin, Goosebumps, Arthur, Clifford the Big Red Dog, I Spy, Olivia and Harry Potter. The classic Tolkien trilogy, The Lord of the Rings, for an older audience, has boosted its licensing activity with its transition into films.

Licensing programs based on children's books are, in general, handled like classic character programs, although their activity often receives a boost when they inspire entertainment vehicles, particularly television series. As books alone, their licensing efforts typically focus on a few products such as home video and plush, but their entry into television generates licensed items in all categories.

Content and brand names from adult book series and imprints are also licensed, usually for merchandise closely related to books, such as desk and wall calendars, CD-ROMs, electronic reference devices and other items that make sense given the content of the book series. Bookstores carry these products, as do other channels more commonly associated with licensed merchandise. Berlitz has authorized its name for a number of CD-ROM applications and computer calendars; the For Dummies brand has expanded into a variety of activity kits as well as electronic how-to and reference products; and Chicken Soup for the Soul has authorized products that incorporate the franchise's inspirational attributes.

A growing trend in publishing is the number of authors of adult nonfiction that have launched licensing efforts. These include Faith Popcorn (author of Clicking!); Mollie Katzen (The Moosewood Cookbook); and Jill Conner Browne (The Sweet Potato Queens).

Magazine properties that have introduced their brand names into retail product categories through licensing include Teen People, Sports Illustrated for Kids, Playboy, Penthouse, Elle, Cosmopolitan, McCall's, Food & Wine, Car & Driver and many others. Their licensing efforts usually include CD-ROMs and other content-driven items, as well as products related to their subject matter (e.g., Cosmopolitan handbags, Penthouse condoms, Food & Wine mustard). The growth in magazine brands available for licensing has been a significant trend in the early 2000s.

Some magazines have also proven popular as private-label store brands at mass market retail chains. Because they are closely associated with a particular topic and maintain high brand awareness with consumers, they make sense as identifying logos for merchandise. Meredith licensed its Better Homes and Gardens brand to Wal-Mart for its gardening departments.

Magazine-based licensing programs can be limited by publishers' desire to keep their advertisers, which account for a significant portion of revenues, happy. A magazine licensor would not authorize any products that might anger an advertiser by putting the publication's brand in competition with the advertiser's at retail. In many cases, the two product lines can peacefully coexist, but licensors should be aware of the possibility of a perceived conflict of interest.

NONPROFIT LICENSING

Licensed merchandise can generate income for a nonprofit organization—some attribute over 40% of total revenues to licensing royalties, others less than 1%— and create awareness for the group and its cause, resulting in increased membership and charitable contributions. More nonprofit groups, and with a wider variety of missions, are entering the licensing business every day, but many remain niche efforts with just a few products and little retail presence. (Many licensed products are sold through fundraising catalogs sent to the group's members and others.)

While large-scale programs are rare, opportunities exist for the right match of product and property. Much of the licensing is in gifts, stationery, publishing, and accessories, but some property owners have granted rights for items such as clocks (National Audubon Society's Original Singing Bird Clock), fabrics (4-H) and plants (Audubon).

The most high-profile nonprofit licensing programs are those launched by environmental groups such as the World Wildlife Fund (among the first to proactively pursue licensing in the late 1980s), the National Audubon Society, the Sierra Club, The Nature Conservancy, the Jacques Cousteau Society, Greenpeace, the National Parks and Conservation Society and many others. This sector is the largest within the nonprofit licensing arena.

Nonprofit organizations outside the environmental movement also have became active licensors, to various degrees. Some are relief agencies, such as CARE and Save the Children, while others are crusaders for good health, such as the American Heart Association. The American Red Cross, the National Crime Prevention Council, the National Fire Prevention Association, D.A.R.E. and the Humane Society of the U.S. are just a few examples of nonprofits with existing licensing efforts, illustrating the diversity of this sector.

Several challenges face nonprofit licensors. First, it is essential that none of their licensees' products detract from or contradict the mission of the group or are perceived to do so. Secondly, to generate significant revenues, licensing programs generally must appeal to children. While nonprofit groups view the youth market as an important target, experience shows that it is difficult for nonprofit-related licensed merchandise to succeed there. Although children tend to support causes, the fact that part of a product's purchase price goes toward a particular group's mission is not as significant an inducement to purchase as it is for adults. In addition, licensors find it tough to sell children's product manufacturers on a nonprofit license; manufacturers do not perceive it as a competitive advantage in the children's market, where they are fighting character merchandise for shelf space. Nonprofit groups must also have enough desirable artwork available each season to translate to successful products, which often requires a significant investment. The difficulty of meeting all these criteria has meant that, while more nonprofit groups are active in licensing, cumulative sales of their licensed products have remained flat in the late 1990s and early 2000s.

CELEBRITY LICENSING

Licensing of celebrities — both living and deceased — usually focuses more on promotional deals that involve the use of a famous person's name and likeness on packaging or premiums or in advertising than on licensed merchandise, although the latter is possible for many famous names. A celebrity with a high ratio of retail products to promotional deals on a worldwide basis, such as James Dean, still generates about 50% of licensing revenues from tie-ins. Others attribute closer to 80%-90% of licensing income to advertising and promotions, according to agents who specialize in this area. Merchandise rights are sometimes granted as part of a broader promotional deal; for example, a company for which a celebrity serves as a spokesperson may also sell memorabilia. (The figures for sales of celebrity-related licensed merchandise cited earlier in the chapter include retail merchandise only and exclude promotional income.)

Celebrities associated with products ranging from silk ties to plastic figurines include Marilyn Monroe, James Dean and Elvis Presley, who rank at the top in terms of worldwide personality-based merchandise sales; athletes such as Babe Ruth, Lou Gehrig and Wayne Gretzky; nostalgic and current entertainers such as Laurel & Hardy, Jane Seymour, Charlie Chaplin and Bette Davis; models such as Kathy Ireland, who has a home furnishings program, among other deals; politicians such as George W. Bush (products with a "W" logo) and Jesse Ventura (action figures), whose licensing royalties generally go toward charity and the official licensing program's primary objective is to maintain control over the celebrity's image; and celebrities from other walks of life, such as Anne McKevitt (a U.K. celebrity along the lines of Martha Stewart), Albert Einstein, Ernest Hemingway and Oscar Wilde.

One area of increase in the early 2000s has been in famous chefs, who are recognized from television shows, cookbooks or restaurant chains. They use licensing as a tool to enter retail product categories such as cookware and appliances, cooking ingredients (such as spices and sauces), frozen and packaged meals, kitchen utensils and soft goods. Examples include Wolfgang Puck, Emeril Lagasse and Graham Kerr.

The 1990s saw a rise in alliances between living celebrities and retail chains for exclusive brands. Ireland, Martha Stewart, Jaclyn Smith and Kathie Lee Gifford all partnered with major mass marketers for home furnishings and/or apparel programs. These private-label retail brands remain strong in the 2000s.

Many celebrity licensing programs are popular in international markets. Dean, Presley and Monroe succeed in many territories around the globe; Oscar Wilde, Sophia Loren and Greta Garbo are in demand in Europe; and Steve McQueen and Audrey Hepburn appeal to Japanese consumers.

Licensing of living celebrities can be risky for licensees in some cases; there is no way to guarantee how they behave or whether they stay popular. Estate licensing (licensing the names and likenesses of deceased celebrities whose estates are controlled by their heirs) is more predictable since consumers' perception of these personalities is not likely to change significantly — deceased celebrities will not be arrested or say anything controversial — although demand for their merchandise may rise and fall cyclically.

A small group of licensing agents represent most estate-based merchandising efforts on behalf of the celebrities' heirs. A few estates, notably Elvis Presley's, handle all product and promotional licensing in-house.

ART LICENSING

Art licensing includes museum-based licensing efforts, living and deceased fine artists, and designers who create images with products in mind. It has been among the fastest-growing licensing sectors in the late 1990s and early 2000s, both in terms of cumulative sales and, especially, in the number of participants.

Some museums are active licensors. Many, such as the Brooklyn Museum of Art, oversee small, upscale programs with merchandise distributed in their own and other museum shops. Others maintain reproduction licensing programs, where items from their collections are duplicated on retail products such as decorative accessories and home furnishings; Colonial Williamsburg's effort incorporates textiles, wall and floor coverings, furniture, pewter and brass objects, ceramics, house paint and moldings, while Mount Vernon sells products such as miniature reproductions of shoes worn by George and Martha Washington. Still others treat the name of their institution as a brand for certain product lines, such as Metropolitan Museum of Art silk scarves or Smithsonian science activity kits; these are often "inspired" by pieces in the museums collection rather than being replicas. Some institutions shy away from licensing altogether, preferring to maintain control of their products through in-house manufacturing or subcontracting.

The bulk of art licensing is attributable to individual artists (and photographers), both current and deceased. Artists (or their estates) with licensing activity include Pablo Picasso, M.C. Escher, Piet Mondrian, Thomas Kinkade, Jody Winger, Judy Buswell, Anne Geddes, Charles Wysocki, Warren Kimble, the Hautman Bros. and Mary Engelbreit, to name just a few. Their names, images, likenesses and/or signatures appear on licensed products from greeting cards to rugs.

From the point of view of licensing strategy, artists fall into one of two groups. Fine artists create art for art's sake, in which case licensing is a secondary concern; merchandising activity leans heavily toward publishing, gifts and stationery. The second group, which comprises the lion's share of the sector, involves designers who create art with merchandise in mind. Their licensing activity is wide-ranging, incorporating apparel, domestics, giftware, stationery, tabletop items, publishing, computer accessories and housewares, among other categories. They often specialize in a certain genre, such as sports, fantasy, whimsical children's, realistic, ethic-themed, illustrative, or nature art, as well as decorative patterns.

Artists and/or their agents often manage licensing efforts based on children's and illustrative art very much like a character program, and some of their work, such as Todd Parr's, make their way into entertainment vehicles such as a television series, which then multiplies mainstream licensing potential.

Consumers most often purchase art-licensed products simply because they like the way they look. They might not know or even care who the artist is; they just like the design of the product. They may choose a certain pattern as the basis for a whole room's decor but are not necessarily aware that the products are licensed and that a different manufacturer is responsible for each matching product. Of course, if the property is a recognized work of art (the Mona Lisa) or a famous artist (Keith Haring), name recognition also plays a role.

Some designers' names eventually become brands. Shoppers go out looking for Mary Engelbreit or Judy Buswell merchandise for their homes. When a designer achieves this level, he or she is more attractive to licensees and retailers. Not only can manufacturers and buyers choose from a group of designs that can be coordinated with other licensed products in-store but, more importantly, they benefit from consumers' awareness of the artist and can prominently display the artist's name as a selling point. This is the ultimate goal of most art licensing programs: To combine desirable artwork with a recognized name to maximize sales.

LIFESTYLE LICENSING

Some observers of the licensing business refer to "lifestyle" licensing as a separate property type. In fact, properties from any of the sectors discussed in this chapter can be positioned as "lifestyle" properties. The idea is that a property captures the essence of a lifestyle experienced or desired by its target audience. Martha Stewart, for example, appeals to consumers who would like to emulate the way of life she portrays in television and in books; while they may not actually live that life, they purchase products that connect them to it. The Mary-Kate and Ashley brand appeals to the same aspirational feelings in tween girls.

Art properties, fashion labels, home furnishings brands, extreme sports events and magazine titles are some of the many licenses that can be positioned as lifestyle properties, but they can come from anywhere. Mattel and MGM have marketed Barbie and the Pink Panther as lifestyle properties for girls and tween girls, respectively.

Some properties are what might be called "pure" lifestyle brands; Old Maui was created to reflect an upscale, nostalgic, weathered, vacationland lifestyle using the tagline "Distinguished Resort Goods." Products such as sunglasses, fruit and nuts, beverages and windchimes are among those that fit well with this true lifestyle brand. Meanwhile, the University of Hawaii created a beach brand called Kulanui; royalties go to the school (and to charity), but the brand conveys the essence of a sun-drenched lifestyle and is not identified with the institutional logo.

CHAPTER 3:
CHARACTERISTICS OF MAJOR PRODUCT CATEGORIES

Consumers can buy licensed merchandise in almost any product category. To illustrate, all of the following have been for sale: Hello Kitty cars, Joe Boxer toilet seats, Crayola plants and a Thomas Kinkade housing development.

Most licensed merchandise falls into one of 17 broad product segments, as shown in *Figure 5 (page 46-49)*. Some items are hard to categorize precisely; are lamps with bases made out of NFL helmets home furnishings or novelties? Since they are probably sold both in home furnishings departments and in specialty gift shops, they legitimately could be classified in either sector.

Some of the categories in Figure 5 are eclectic. The Accessories sector comprises everything from jewelry to backpacks, while items included in Gifts/Novelties range from signed memorabilia to novelty dog tags to animation cels. Licensors often break these categories down further, depending on the specifics of their businesses.

As *Figure 6 (page 49)* illustrates, Apparel is the largest product category overall in the U.S. and Canada, accounting for 13% of all retail sales of licensed merchandise in 2001, according to *The Licensing Letter*. Toys/Games (11%), Food/Beverage (10%), Accessories (9%) and Gifts/Novelties (8%) emerge as the second- through fifth-largest segments, respectively.

The relative importance of each category for a specific licensing program varies enormously depending on the type of property and the individual license. For an entertainment or character license with an audience primarily composed of children, toys and games can account for up to half or even two-thirds of total licensed product sales based on that property; for a teen entertainment license, videogames may account for a similarly high proportion. An adult-targeted license tends to be heavily gift- and novelty-oriented. Sports properties, on the other hand, tend to be weighted heavily toward apparel and accessories, with electronic games another significant category.

Corporate trademark licensing efforts, particularly those following a brand-extension strategy, differ from each other in terms of categories targeted, depending on where the core brand originates. A food brand may expand predominantly into food- and kitchen-related products; a sporting goods brand will target other sporting goods items as well as apparel, accessories and footwear. Fashion licensors tend to concentrate most of their activities in apparel, accessories (including eyewear and jewelry), footwear, beauty products (including fragrances), and home furnishings. Art properties typically are driven by gifts and stationery items, as well as books and products for the home.

Licensors are also increasingly looking at services, in addition to mer-

Figure 5

RETAIL PRODUCT CATEGORY BREAKDOWN FOR LICENSED GOODS

ACCESSORIES
backpacks
bandanas
belts
buckles
contact lenses
embroidered emblems and logos
eyeglass frames
hats and caps
jewelry
mittens and gloves
purses and handbags
scarves
shoelaces
small leather goods
socks and hosiery
sunglasses
ties
umbrellas
wallets
watches

APPAREL
boxer shorts
dresses
jackets
lingerie
nightshirts
pajamas
shorts
slacks
sportswear
sweaters
sweatshirts and sweatpants
t-shirts
underwear
uniforms

DOMESTICS
bath mats
bedspreads
blankets
cloth placemats
curtains
fabric
laundry bags
pillowcases
pot holders
sewing patterns
sheets
towels

ELECTRONICS
cassette/CD and video/DVD players
cell phone covers and accessories
clock-radios
clocks
foot massagers
hair dryers
karaoke machines and content
kitchen appliances
personal digital assistants (PDAs)
radios
telephones
vacuum cleaners
waffle makers
walkie-talkies

FOOD/BEVERAGE
candy
cereal
cakes and accessories
cookies
dairy products
edible baking decorations
fresh foods
frosting
frozen meals
gum
health bars
juice
meats
microwave meals
organic products
produce
snack foods
soda
sports drinks

FOOTWEAR
athletic shoes
beach footwear
designer shoes
hiking boots
shoelaces
slippers
socks and hosiery

FURNITURE/HOME FURNISHINGS
appliances
beanbag chairs
beds
bookcases

Continued Next Page

Figure 5 Continued

ceiling fans
chairs
chests
clocks
desktop accessories
housing plans and developments
lamps
paint
picture frames
tables
telephones
toilet seats and covers
wall coverings and wallpaper

GIFTS/NOVELTIES
air fresheners
animated alarm clocks
animation cels
bow-biters
ceramic gift items
ceramic mugs
chess sets
Christmas decorations and ornaments
cloisonne pins
collectibles
commemorative coins and plates
die-cast collectibles
gumball machines
key chains
lapel pins
lighters
magnets
milk caps
novelty watches
pencils
pencil toppers and erasers
pens
plush
pre-paid phone cards
PVC figurines
stickers
temporary tattoos and body art
t-shirts
wind socks

HEALTH/BEAUTY AIDS
adhesive bandages
bubble bath
condoms
combs and brushes
cosmetics
dental floss

disinfectants
fragrances
hair accessories
lotions and hand sanitizers
shampoo
soap
tissues
toothpaste and toothbrushes
vitamins

HOUSEWARES
acrylic and melamine tableware
baking and cooking supplies
cups, plates, bowls
glassware
insulated beverageware
juice box holders
laminated placemats
lunch kits
mugs
silverware
tableware

INFANT PRODUCTS
baby bags
bibs
bumper guards
cribs
diapers
diaper bags
high chairs
infant clothing
infant furniture
infant housewares
infant toys
mobiles
playpens
rockers
strollers

MUSIC/VIDEO
audiocassettes
book and cassette packages
CDs
LPs
spoken-word audiocassettes
videocassettes: theatrical, music,
    direct-to-video

PUBLISHING
activity books
address books
bath books

Continued Next Page

Figure 5 Continued

book and cassette packages
calendars
cloth books
coloring books
comic books
diaries
how-to books
magazines
music and talking storybooks
novelizations
novels
one-shot publications
post cards
posters
stickers
storybooks

SPORTING GOODS
backpacks
bicycles
bowling balls
camping equipment and tents
daypacks
fitness equipment
footballs, basketballs, baseballs
golf equipment and accessories
ice skates
inflatable water toys
ride-ons
rollerskates
skateboards
sleeping bags
slumber bags
sports equipment
sports jerseys
uniforms
vinyl pool and water slides
wagons
water bottles

STATIONERY/PAPER GOODS
birthday candles
bookmarks
checks
erasers
gift bags
gift wrap
greeting cards, packaged and single
invitations
memo boards
mylar and latex balloons
note cards

notepads
office supplies
paper party decorations
paper tableware
party goods
pens and pencils
postcards
rubber stamps and pads
school supplies
trading cards
Valentines

TOYS/GAMES
activity kits
board games
craft and model kits
die-cast vehicles and models
dolls
dominoes
electronic toys
finger toys
flying discs
Halloween costumes, makeup
and masks
kites
learning toys
marbles
milk caps
playing cards
plush, stuffed toys
puppets
puzzles
rack toys
radio-controlled toys
ride-ons
robotic toys
science kits
scooters
sound chip toys
trading cards
yo-yos

**VIDEOGAMES/SOFTWARE/INTERAC-
TIVE PRODUCTS**
arcade games
casino games
CD-ROM software
computer software,
digital greeting cards
e-mail messages
electronic games: handheld,
tabletop

Continued Next Page

Figure 6
2001 SHARES OF LICENSED PRODUCT RETAIL SALES
U.S. AND CANADA, BY PRODUCT CATEGORY

Dollar Figures In Billions

PRODUCT CATEGORY	2001 RETAIL SALES	PCT. ALL SALES
Accessories	$6.10	9%
Apparel	$9.20	13%
Domestics	$4.40	6%
Electronics	$1.00	1%
Food/Beverage	$7.30	10%
Footwear	$2.10	3%
Furniture/ Home Furnishings	$1.50	2%
Gifts/Novelties	$5.60	8%
Health/Beauty	$4.15	6%
Housewares	$2.60	4%
Infant Products	$3.10	4%
Music/Video	$1.55	2%
Publishing	$4.70	7%
Sporting Goods	$1.50	2%
Stationery/Paper	$3.40	5%
Toys/Games	$8.00	11%
Videogames/Software	$4.00	6%
Other	$0.10	<1%
Total	**$70.30**	**100%**

Source: The Licensing Letter; EPM Communications

Figure 5 Continued

Internet browsers and games
pinball games
simulation software
slot machines
videogames for all platforms
MISCELLANEOUS PRODUCTS
automotive accessories
gardening supplies including plants
hardware
luggage
vehicles: boats, trucks, all-terrain
    vehicles, trailers
SERVICES/NON-RETAIL
advertising
affinity credit cards
camps
educational and training materials
educational courses

live tours
lotteries
maid and other at-home services
marketing and promotional ties
premiums, ad specialties, incentives
restaurants
themed entertainment venues
travel services and tours

Note: Several products are listed in more than one category, since they are sold within more than one department or store type. Services/non-retail items are not included in the retail sales totals shown in Figure 6, above.

Source: The Licensing Letter; EPM Communications

chandise, to round out their licensing efforts. While these are not included in *Figure 6*, as they cannot be measured in terms of retail sales, their importance is growing for properties from sectors such as corporate trademarks, magazine titles and others.

Because every licensing program is unique, the overall product category breakdown of retail sales shown in *Figure 6* should not be taken as the norm for any individual property. With that caveat in mind, this chapter will briefly describe each of the major categories of licensed merchandise and outline the significant licensing-related trends in each sector.

ACCESSORIES

The Accessories segment includes wearable items outside of apparel. Examples include costume and fine jewelry, hair accessories, hosiery, belts, scarves, hats and caps, eyewear, handbags, backpacks and ties. Fashion properties, naturally, target this area heavily, but most other types of properties also do significant business in accessories. The category is eclectic; it includes everything from a Polo Ralph Lauren belt to NFL-licensed contact lenses featuring team logos.

The popularity of some licensed accessories is cyclical. So-called "conversational" accessories surged in the mid-1990s as ties and socks adorned with Tabasco bottles, Star Trek characters or Marilyn Monroe's likeness became popular gift items. In the late 1980s and early 1990s, sports-licensed caps became a hot fashion accessory, but sales declined as sports licensing weakened in the mid- to late 1990s and the headwear market became oversaturated. Character-licensed, shaped backpacks were among the novelty accessories that experienced an upturn in the late 1990s.

Conversely, a great number of accessories products exhibit strong staying power. Fashion-licensed belts, eyewear, fragrances, handbags and hosiery are lucrative categories for their licensors and, over the long term, become powerhouse brands within their respective industries. Calvin Klein-labeled eyeglass frames, which are licensed, are one of the top brand names in the eyewear business.

APPAREL

Apparel represents a major category for licensors of all types of properties. Products in this sector include inexpensive t-shirts screenprinted with a corporate trademark and distributed through mass market outlets or as premiums; leather jackets incorporating a sports logo and retailing for hundreds of dollars; designer-licensed furs with price points in the thousands; school uniforms tied to brands such as Carter's or Scholastic; and children's underwear and sleepwear featuring TV characters.

This naturally is the core category for fashion labels that choose to license rather than produce their lines in-house. Many designers and apparel brands utilize a mix of licensed and in-house merchandise as they target children, women and men; others license all categories. Apparel is also a core category for other property types, notably sports, and is important for many types of licensors.

As the market for licensed products becomes more competitive and success is increasingly difficult to achieve, the design of licensed apparel items is of the utmost importance. The appearance of a character or logo on a t-shirt, sweater or jacket is not enough to drive an impulse purchase. The item must be in tune with current fashion trends and integrate the licensed property in a uniquely eye-catching way. In addition, merchandise targeted to different retail tiers, or even different individual retailers, must be distinct for each in terms of design, materials, sewing techniques and other characteristics.

Some sectors of the licensed apparel business have struggled since the late 1990s. Several licensed t-shirt manufacturers have gone out of business or been acquired, as have key sports apparel licensees such as Apex, Starter and Pro Player.

DOMESTICS

The Domestics sector includes all soft goods for the home, including bedding (sheets, pillowcases, quilts and bedspreads); beach, bath and kitchen towels; placemats and tablecloths.

In children's domestics, character and entertainment licensing — and to a smaller extent sports — played a significant role during the mid-1990s, especially for products such as sheets and beach towels. In fact, in years where hot properties have been available (e.g., Barney in 1993), licensed merchandise has accounted for as much as 90% of the juvenile domestics business, according to practitioners. Yet the popularity of licensed domestics for children rises and falls cyclically.

Designers dominate the market for licensed adult-targeted domestics. Some are home furnishings specialists, such as Mario Buatta, while others are fashion designers, such as Ralph Lauren, who cross over into domestics with successful signature programs. The entry of high-profile apparel designers into the domestics industry was a key trend in the 1990s, although not all attempts were successful. Licensed designs also come into the domestics business from other home furnishings sectors; dinnerware patterns are licensed for tablecloths or curtain designs for bedding. Artists' images, such as those of Bob Timberlake and Warren Kimble, are also prevalent. While these are the key property types active in the domestics sector, properties of all stripes can be featured on domestics items.

Licensors, licensees and retailers agree that cross-merchandising of home-related products at retail drives sales, and all the types of licensing outlined in the preceding paragraph lend themselves to joint-display presentations. Licensing allows the creation of coordinated programs that involve products for every room, which can be merchandised together in retail concept shops highlighted by point-of-purchase materials.

ELECTRONICS

The electronics category incorporates products such as CD players, radios, alarm clocks and walkie-talkies. It includes novelty items such as telephones, as well as brand-extended and co-branded items for children and adults. The category has expanded as new electronic products are developed and as more manufacturers explore the potential of licensing.

In the 1990s, Mattel's Barbie was licensed for personal electronics, including telephones and radios, targeted to young girls; MGM-licensed televisions and stereos were aimed at adults for whom the MGM lion logo stands for entertainment; and Playskool electronics such as cassette players were intended to appeal to parents of preschoolers. In the 2000s, well-known consumer brands such as AT&T and Motorola have licensed their brands for products that make sense given their image and brand attributes, while Nickelodeon licensed its brand for a line of karaoke machines.

Licensing has been a factor in the personal-care appliance segment, which includes blow dryers, curling irons and the like. The cosmetic organizer brand Caboodles, the cosmetics brand Revlon and the hair-care brand Vidal Sassoon were among the properties licensed for hair dryers during the 1990s. Similarly, Dr. Scholl's, the foot-care brand, is licensed for electric foot-massage products. Kitchen appliances are another area of activity, with brands such as Betty Crocker featured on all types of kitchen electronics and characters such as Hello Kitty tied to items such as waffle irons, not to mention other appliances such as vacuum cleaners.

New licensed categories emerging in the 2000s include personal electronics such as cell phones and accessories and personal digital assistants (PDAs). For example, Cartoon Network licensed its characters to Fone Range for novelty cell phones and accessories; Pamela Anderson was licensed to Eruptor Entertainment for downloadable personal organizer content; Mattel licensed Hot Wheels for cell phone face plates; New Line licensed Austin Powers and Lord of the Rings for branded browsers; Disney has a deal with Hitchison Telecom for wireless content in Hong Kong; Michael Jordan is featured on a branded Palm Pilot sold through Tower Records. Some of these categories have seen great success in other countries, particularly Japan, but are in their infancy in North America as of 2002.

A growing number of licensed products in other categories have electronic components, such as toys, figurines and even t-shirts that contain sound chips. Since these are sold in the retail tiers where their non-electronic equivalents are available, they are categorized as such (e.g., sound-chip toys in the Toys and Games category).

FOOD & BEVERAGES

Traditionally a bigger category in countries, such as the U.K., France and Japan, than in the U.S. and Canada, licensing in food and beverages is rising in North America. The majority of food and beverage licensing centers on brand extension or co-branding, and these continue to comprise the main area of growth. Licensing is a preferred technique for expanding food brands' presence into new food- and beverage-related categories. Sunkist soft drinks, Dole frozen fruit bars and Seagram's mixers are just a few examples of substantial revenue-generating licensed line extensions within the food and beverage sector. Brand-extension within the consumables category often involves the use of ingredients; the licensor sells its products to the licensee as part of a co-branding agreement joining the licensees' and licensors' flavors and brands.

In general, other property types have had less presence in the food and beverage category in the U.S. Most property owners outside the food industry have little experience with grocery store distribution and little knowledge of how food brands are developed. At the same time, food manufacturers typically are not familiar with licensing and need to be sold on its value as a marketing tool. Yet this is changing, with character/entertainment, sports, non-food brands and other properties linking their names and images with food and beverage products. Food & Wine magazine, for example, targets its customers with upscale licensed products such as mustards, sauces and oils. Chefs such as Wolfgang Puck and Emeril Lagasse are also active licensors in this category.

Since it takes a great deal of time and money to launch a food brand, and because of the high industry failure rate for new products, food manufacturers are typically not interested in acquiring rights to what they perceive as short-term properties. They seek licenses that have the legs necessary to make their substantial upfront investment in the brand worthwhile. There have been exceptions to this rule, however, such as Ghostbusters licensed cereals in the 1980s and Teenage Mutant Ninja Turtles cupcakes around 1990.

All types of food products can benefit from licensing if the fit is right; a small worldwide sampling includes Rugrats canned pasta, Dilbert vegetarian burritos, Colt 45 malt liquor, Richard Scarry organic foods, Popeye frozen and canned spinach, Oreo ice cream, SpongeBob SquarePants Cheese Nips, Smithsonian chocolates, Simpsons frozen dinners, South Park packaged meats and Flintstones Fruity and Cocoa Pebbles breakfast cereals.

FOOTWEAR

Brand-extension licensing is a significant force in the footwear industry, primarily in conjunction with fashion labels and sporting goods brands. Most sporting goods companies (e.g., Spalding, Wilson) view athletic footwear as a natural extension of their sports equipment lines. Similarly, apparel brands and designer labels from Tommy Hilfiger to Chic consider footwear (dressy, casual or athletic, depending on the brand image) to be a key category. These labels often extend into footwear through licensing rather than through setting up in-house operations; the trademark owners do not usually possess the expertise to become footwear manufacturers.

Sports celebrities frequently license their names for signature lines of athletic footwear. The products are usually part of a larger endorsement deal between the athlete and the shoe maker, where the celebrity appears on behalf of the company in promotional events for the trade and consumers, as well as corporate advertising. Sports leagues and other sports entities also consider footwear an important category.

Character licensing plays a role in the children's footwear industry, in association with all types of shoes, as well as beach flip-flops, sandals and slippers, incorporating both short- and long-term properties. Most are sold at mass market retail outlets. In years with several strong children's licenses, observers estimate that as much as 90% of sales in the children's mass-market footwear category can be attributable to licensed lines.

FURNITURE AND HOME FURNISHINGS

This category includes, among other products: furniture, lamps, wallpaper and floor coverings. As with the domestics category discussed earlier, home furnishings and apparel designers (e.g., Alexander Julian), manufacturers that own brands and designs originating in other home-related categories (Waverly), and artists (Bob Timberlake) are among the licensors most active in this category. Artists in particular have identified home furnishings as a growth area; Timberlake furniture from licensee Lexington is among the top-selling brands in that industry.

Several museums maintain active licensed reproduction programs within the home furnishings market. The Hearst Castle and the Winterthur estate are among those that license wall and/or floor coverings, while other institutions grant licensees the right to replicate works of art, such as sculptures, as decorative accessories. Personalities associated with home decor, crafts and other domestic pursuits (such as Martha Stewart or B. Smith) are also active licensors of home furnishings products.

A few character and sports licensors have authorized the use of their properties on juvenile beds, wall borders and lamps. For the most part, however, home furnishings is a small category for these licensors. Most short-term properties are not appropriate since home furnishings represent a large investment for consumers, who expect their purchase to last a long time and do not want the product to outlive the license.

Some relatively new products within this category that have attracted the interest of licensors in the early 2000s include paint (licensed by Disney, Polo Ralph Lauren and Crayola, among others) and other building supplies, home plans (the Forbes Collection) and even housing developments (Thomas Kinkade).

GIFTS AND NOVELTIES

The Gifts and Novelties sector is one of the broadest in licensing, ranging from key chains and miniature plastic figurines retailing for a dollar or less to animated cels and crystal figurines that cost thousands of dollars. The category includes limited-edition products that are produced specifically as collectibles, upscale items intended for gift-giving and low-priced novelties that are purchased on impulse. Many products can be categorized here and in other sectors, depending on where they are sold and their purpose; for example, small die-cast automobiles could be considered toys but are often collected and therefore considered as part of this category.

Most types of properties are active licensors of gifts and novelties. Sports memorabilia, entertainment and character collectibles, novelties featuring the images of pop or classic musicians, gifts based on artists' designs and corporate-licensed merchandise based on nostalgic advertising art are all common. Fashion labels are not well represented in this segment, although some designer-licensed decorative items for the home can be categorized here.

Limited-edition collectibles have grown into a significant area of the gift market, ranging from NASCAR collectible die-cast fishing boats and cars, sculptures commemorating Mark McGwire's record-setting homerun, and Rocky & Bullwinkle animation cels signed by Jay Ward to lithographs featuring the artwork of wildlife artists the Hautman brothers. Limited editions are often numbered and come with verification of authenticity. The collectible portion of the market tends to go through ups and downs, with certain products increasing in popularity as others wane.

HEALTH AND BEAUTY

Fragrances are a particularly active segment of the licensed portion of this industry, representing a key category for fashion designers and celebrities in particular. Perry Ellis, Elizabeth Taylor and Mikhail Baryshnikov are just a few of the properties involved with lucrative, long-term licensing deals for fragrances. Signature scents associated with Calvin Klein or Ralph Lauren can generate in the tens and even hundreds of millions of dollars in wholesale volume annually. Many high-profile fashion designers count fragrances among their top-selling categories, licensed or otherwise. Fragrance marketers have to spend millions to launch new brands; a recognized license helps lower the investment and strengthen the potential for success.

Children's cosmetics, colognes and bubble baths are another active area; licensors have authorized properties from Godzilla to Scooby Doo for children's products. *The Licensing Letter* estimates that, in a year with several strong children's properties, nearly 20% of retail sales in the juvenile health and beauty market can be attributable to licensed products.

Personal care items for adults are associated with licensed properties from the art and fashion sectors, as well as brand-extension efforts on behalf of personal care lines. Examples have included Burberry, Jordache, Elite Model Agency, Vidal Sassoon, Dr. Scholl's, Revlon, Brut, Hallmark, Glynda Turley, Mary Engelbreit and Thomas Kinkade, among many others. Sports properties and sport-related trademarks, including Ironman Triathlon, Gold's Gym and NASCAR, have granted rights for sunblock, soaps and bandages.

Rock and heavy metal musical groups, magazine brands such as Playboy and edgy entertainment properties such as South Park have authorized condom makers to link with their properties; this category is not appropriate for every property, of course. Meanwhile, licenses such as Titan A.E. and Buffy the Vampire Slayer, targeted to tweens and teens, have extended into body art and temporary tattoos. Properties such as Coleman, which is associated with camping, have licensed items including hand sanitizers and personal disinfectants.

HOUSEWARES

Food brands are among the most visible licensors in the housewares industry. Properties including Pillsbury, Betty Crocker and Campbell's Soup build upon their equity by expanding into kitchen-related non-food products ranging from bakeware to dishes.

Various home-related brands also extend into housewares through licensing, including wallpaper, tablecloth and ceramics marketers, creating cross-promotional and co-display opportunities. Cookware maker Farberware has granted rights for food storage containers and cutlery under its brand name, for example. Home furnishings and apparel designers license their names, signatures and designs for dinnerware, glassware, cookie jars and mugs. Artists are increasingly active in this category, authorizing products that can be cross-merchandised with their licensed domestics and home furnishing items. Chefs also lend their endorsements to signature products in this category.

Primary product categories within the housewares segment for character, entertainment and sports licensing include thermal beverage containers and lunch kits, children's dinnerware and beverageware, ceramics ranging from salt and pepper shakers to cookie jars, and baking supplies, such as cake pans and cookie cutters.

INFANT PRODUCTS

This category contains a variety of items. Many could be categorized elsewhere (e.g., infant apparel under Apparel, layette under Domestics and infant toys under Toys/Games), but they are classified together here since they are often gathered in dedicated departments at retail. That means one buyer is responsible for purchasing all infant products.

Most property types are represented in this sector. Artists create designs that lend themselves to infant products due to appropriate themes or colors. Fashion labels sometimes extend their brands into the infant category, while the four major sports leagues and colleges have licensed companies for bibs, diaper bags and infants' and toddlers' apparel. Artists (including John Lennon, who created images for his children that are now licensed) also target the infant category if appropriate.

Character and entertainment properties, especially those that appeal to young children and their parents, are also active in infant products. In fact, several licensors of classic and not-so-classic characters have created subbrands in the 1990s and 2000s targeted specifically toward new parents. They are infant versions of classic characters, often utilizing pastel colors and cuddly graphics, but sometimes featuring the same characters on younger-skewing products. With classics, the purpose is to capitalize on the property's equity — parents have a nostalgic affinity toward the brand — and to build on this value by offering infant-themed merchandise that appeals to parents. With newer properties, the infant products allow younger siblings of the already-young fans to join in the fun; these properties are admired by parents, although they do not carry the same nostalgic weight as the classics. Examples of properties that have extended into the infant category include Looney Tunes, Barney, Blue's Clues and Teletubbies.

MUSIC AND VIDEO

Video distributors or record companies are often listed as licensees for home video or soundtracks, respectively, on entertainment-based licensee lists. Most of these agreements are essentially distribution contracts. They take existing intellectual property such as television episodes or theatrical films and distribute them in the new form of home video or recorded soundtracks. While this type of licensing is a legitimate, necessary and significant part of marketing a property, this book does not deal in-depth with these sorts of agreements. (Distribution licenses are also not included in the retail sales totals outlined in *Figure 6*). This section focuses on contracts that grant rights to an existing trademark (and associated copyrights) for the purpose of creating a wholly new product based on it.

Many property owners authorize home video or record companies to create original programming or music based on their properties; the resulting products are what the numbers in *Figure 6* represent. For example, the Simpsons during their peak were licensed to Geffen Records for a musical recording called "The Simpsons Sing The Blues," combining character voices and well-known musicians, while a music recording based on the TV series Bob the Builder ("Can We Fix It? Yes We Can!") was a bestseller in the U.K. in 2001. The sports leagues have experimented with original videos; the NBA licensed CBS/Fox Video for a series of videocassettes combining popular music with NBA game footage. Full-length direct-to-video feature films based on established entertainment franchises have been a growth area since the late 1990s, with Scooby Doo, The Lion King and other Disney properties, and The Land Before Time series among the success stories.

Publishing properties lend themselves to the creation of licensed audio and video. Licensors of several magazine properties, including Cosmopolitan, Car & Driver, Esquire, Reader's Digest and Sports Afield, have authorized the use of their names for special-interest videotapes, the content of which relates to the editorial focus of the respective publications. Periodicals such as Cosmopolitan have extended into music CDs, as have other properties, such as Martha Stewart and the Professional Bull Riders Association. Fashion designers and magazines have developed music CDs as promotional tools.

Children's book properties find their way into original video (or audio) programming that features original plots starring the characters in the book. The success of these products often serves as a prelude to a television series.

Video — whether original productions or existing entertainment distributed in this form — is a key element of children's entertainment licensing programs. When young children own videos, they play them repeatedly. Their frequent viewing strengthens their relationship with the characters and ultimately engenders demand for other licensed products. For this reason, and because video is often the product most closely related to the original entertainment vehicle, children's character licensors take this category seriously, especially when considering strategies for preschool properties. (Music recordings used to comprise an important category as well, but age-compression has rendered the children's music category insignificant for most properties. The success of Bob the Builder and a few others indicates that there are opportunities here, however.)

PUBLISHING

Publishing is another diverse product category. It includes books, comic books, magazines, trading cards, posters, limited- and open-edition prints and calendars. It represents a leading category for sci-fi fantasy properties such as Star Trek or Star Wars and for preschool entertainment properties; there are opportunities for virtually any property type.

Licensed books—from children's picture, bath and activity books to expensive coffee-table titles, from novelizations and original novels to "Making Of" books—can drive sales of other licensed merchandise, much as television series, films or home videos can. In 1990, Star Wars' first-ever original books became a best-selling series and are credited with single-handedly rejuvenating the property's licensing program between movie trilogies, transforming it into a classic franchise.

Licensing is a significant factor in children's books. In *Publishers Weekly*'s bestseller charts each year, licensed children's books make up a significant proportion of the top 50 titles, in strong years representing more than 80% of the top-selling titles (each with more than 300,000 unit sales in a single year). A Lion King storybook made the top 20 in *PW*'s list of the all-time bestselling children's books, published in 2002.

Comic books are a potential category for both children's and adult properties, although teen and preteen males form the core of comic book readership. Licensors have granted rights for many entertainment and even sports properties to comic book publishers, while several adult-targeted book properties from authors such as Stephen King, Anne Rice and Clive Barker have inspired graphic novels.

Comic books are sold primarily through comic book shops, which are known in the trade as the "direct market." (Young children's titles are distributed mainly through mass merchants.) Some comics retailers and manufacturers view licensing as a way to bring new readers into comic book stores, although industry observers debate the effectiveness of licensed comics in attracting — and keeping — additional customers. All told, licensed titles comprise a small percentage of the total market.

Trading cards have been a staple licensed category for sports properties, and are still important, although the industry has contracted severely since its peak in 1991. Some entertainment and other properties are also appropriate for trading cards; the electronic game/television property Pokémon was among several popular licensed trading card and trading card game lines since 1999.

The bestselling non-sports lines are usually targeted toward a definable fan base made up of consumers who desire any type of collectible product and will continue to purchase as fresh designs become available. Examples of non-sports cards in the 1990s and early 2000s have included those featuring corporate trademarks such as Harley-Davidson and Coca-Cola; contemporary and nostalgic artists, especially those specializing in fantasy art, such as Olivia; celebrity properties such as Abbott & Costello; and classic entertainment properties such as The Simpsons.

Prints and posters range from fine art reproductions (in limited or open editions) licensed by wildlife, floral and other artists, to mass-market one-sheets (posters) portraying musicians, celebrity heartthrobs and automobiles. Licensed calendars and desk calendars incorporate virtually every type of property geared toward an age group that is old enough to use these products. Licensed diaries and journals, many of which are sold through bookstores as well as stationery and gift shops, feature art, entertainment, character, sports and corporate trademark properties, among others.

In some countries, such as the U.K., magazines are an important licensed category for children's TV properties. They help maintain awareness for the property and allow children to increase their connection with it through contests, prizes, puzzles and added information. Kids also tend to spend more time on the magazine than on the show. In the U.S., magazines are usually limited to multicharacter, long-term franchises such as Nickelodeon, Sesame Street and Cartoon Network, although single characters/shows such as Barney have also been featured in their own publications. Some properties outside entertainment (e.g. fashion or corporate trademarks) may authorize magazines; these are largely promotional tools and are often created in-house or through a joint venture rather than being licensed.

SPORTING GOODS

Line-extension licensing is common in the sporting goods industry, with sports-equipment manufacturers authorizing other sporting goods companies to manufacture items for which they do not have distribution or manufacturing expertise but want to market under their brand umbrellas. Wilson licensed golf equipment or Spalding licensed backboards are examples.

Athlete-endorsed and league-licensed merchandise are also prevalent. Most player-based licensed programs involve a signature line of products, including soccer balls, golf clubs, baseball bats, hockey sticks or football helmets; aerobics champions and fitness experts authorize lines of exercise equipment and accessories. Many of these products, as in the footwear category, are part of a larger endorsement deal. An NBA or WNBA player might endorse a brand of basketballs and backboards, for example, including a signature line under his or her own name.

The NFL licenses footballs, helmets and protective equipment; Major League Baseball authorizes bats, balls and gloves; the NBA grants rights to basketballs and hoops; and the NHL signs companies for skates, helmets, protective equipment, hockey pucks and in-line roller skates. The Professional Bowling Association licenses bowling balls (as do properties such as Disney, NASCAR and Coca-Cola). Events organizers, such as the Salt Lake 2002 Olympic organizing committee, may license sporting goods.

A number of sports products for children are also licensed, including non-regulation balls, plastic bats and child-sized plastic hockey sticks. Toy companies that have set up or purchased sports divisions make many of these items. Licensors targeting juvenile sports equipment include the major sports leagues and colleges, owners of sporting goods brands, sports events and proprietors of character and entertainment properties.

In addition to the products mentioned above, other merchandise in the sporting goods category includes bicycles, scooters, sports toys, ride-ons, roller skates and skateboards, all of which feature licensed sports properties, corporate trademarks (Huffy, Kawasaki, Hot Wheels) and characters.

Some property types, such as fashion designers or artists, are rarely active in this category, but anything is possible. Licensed golf club covers feature the logo of the music group The Grateful Dead, for example.

STATIONERY AND PAPER GOODS

The Stationery and Paper Goods category incorporates products from greeting cards and writing paper to party goods, gift wrap, balloons, pens, pencils, erasers, pencil cases, folders, notebooks and school-related products.

Art and artists are important licensors in this category; in fact, the Stationery and Paper Goods sector is, along with Gifts and Novelties, one of the largest for contemporary artists and designers, fine artists and their estates, and museums. Their works are reproduced on greeting cards, gift wrap, gift boxes and virtually every other type of stationery item.

Licensors of almost all property types authorize stationery and paper items. Children's entertainment and character properties play a role, especially in paper partyware (paper plates, napkins, decorations and party favors), balloons, greeting cards and back-to-school products. *The Licensing Letter* estimates that 15%-25% of all paper school supplies sales are attributable to licensed merchandise in some years, while industry observers estimate that as much as 90% of all paper party goods are licensed, at least during periods where a variety of strong properties are offered.

Sports properties including the major leagues, trademarks including Nike, and fashion brands including Gitano have granted rights for stationery and paper goods, particularly school supplies. Properties such as Dilbert and a few corporate trademarks have extended into office supplies, still an emerging category, but one that makes sense for some properties.

TOYS AND GAMES

Between 40% and 50% of total retail sales of toys and games in the U.S. and Canada are attributable to licensed merchandise each year, according to *The Licensing Letter*. The figure is at the high end of that range in years where many of the best-selling toys are licensed — such as 1993, when Barney, Star Trek, Jurassic Park, Disney and other licensed toys were among the top 20 sellers — and at the lower end in years such as 1992, when the best-selling toys were mostly basics such as LEGO, Barbie, Hot Wheels and other non-licensed merchandise. Those cyclical ups and downs have continued throughout the 1990s and 2000s and will in the future, depending on the depth of children's properties available in a given year. In 2002, for example, properties such as Harry Potter and Monsters, Inc. drove significant toy sales.

Within the toy industry, action figures are one category where licensing drives a significant proportion of sales, especially for film and television properties whose audience is composed of males, such as Star Wars and Batman. Comic book and videogame characters, as well as sports celebrities, also inspire action figure lines. (Consumers purchase many action figures as collectibles rather than playthings.)

Other segments of the toy industry where licensing accounts for a large portion of revenues include:

- board games, licensed from comic book, book, sports and entertainment properties;
- dolls, especially fashion dolls based on celebrities or musicians, such as McFarlane Toys' K.I.S.S. line; character dolls, such as Cabbage Patch Kids; those with clothes designed by fashion designers, such as Bob Mackie-licensed Barbies; and sports dolls such as WNBA Barbie;
- plush, based on book characters such as Arthur, entertainment properties such as Teletubbies and classic characters such as Winnie the Pooh; this became an important sector as the number of preschool properties proliferated in the 1990s and 2000s.

Any toy that is popular at a given time will attract interest from licensors; scooters, finger toys, talking/sound-chip-enhanced toys, robotic animals, dueling tops and juvenile karaoke machines are among the categories that have become popular in the early 2000s; all have featured at least a few licensed lines.

VIDEOGAMES, SOFTWARE AND INTERACTIVE CONTENT

Console videogames and computer software comprise an important licensed category, especially for entertainment and sports properties but for other types as well. Like publishing, it is significant not only for its revenue potential but for its role in maintaining a property's consumer awareness and in creating new content.

The Licensing Letter estimates that more than 60% of the total videogame market in the U.S. and Canada can be attributed to licensed products in a given year, depending on what properties are available. Videogames drive some licensing programs, especially those for the often-elusive male teen market. For those consumers, videogames are one of the most important entertainment vehicles, with as much power as filmed entertainment to spur sales of other merchandise among that group. Sports properties, from the NFL and its players to extreme sports practitioners such as Tony Hawk, have also inspired successful videogame lines, primarily for boys and young men.

With the proliferation of interactive platforms, particularly in the videogame segment, where new introductions such as Microsoft's Xbox and Sony's PlayStation 2 join existing products such as the Gameboy, some licensors have carved up the category to maximize guarantees. Granting rights to several companies, each for one or a few platforms, brings in more revenue up front, but can compromise attempts at implementing cohesive marketing efforts in the category. Many licensors are looking at broader agreements, sometimes authorizing one licensee for all computer and console platforms worldwide.

Computer software is a significant licensed category, not just for entertainment properties but for sports, corporate trademarks, nonprofit groups and others. Any property that is associated with a defined topic (e.g., the Sierra Club with the environment) or is a source of content (any entertainment vehicle or magazine) is appropriate for computer software. Properties from Cosmopolitan to Arthur to Barbie have starred in CD-ROMs intended for reference, recreation or education, while The Simpsons and the Far Side are among the many licenses associated with computer utilities such as fonts, screensavers, sound effects, wallpaper and calendars. Some property owners have authorized licensed computer accessories such as specialized keyboards.

One interactive product category that has become active in licensing is slot machines and other casino games. Properties including Monopoly, The Pink Panther, Playboy, Wheel of Fortune, Harley-Davidson, Survivor, Elvis, Betty Boop, The Addams Family and Tabasco, among many others, have lent their names to slot or other casino machines, sometimes very profitably. Developments in this sector became a key trend in 2001-2002.

As new technologies develop, licensors will benefit from additional opportunities, although each new generation brings with it risks as property owners face the dilemma of how to get their feet wet at an early stage without knowing which new platforms, if any, will become the future standard. Many large entertainment licensors, in particular, want to be significant content providers in future interactive technologies (such as interactive television); the question is whether to invest in technologies through joint ventures or subsidiaries, or whether to license at first to minimize risk but then face the possibility of not being well-positioned in the future.

The late 1990s and early 2000s have given rise to several new interactive opportunities. The Internet has become an effective method of promoting properties of all sorts. Most licensors are experimenting with their own websites to expand awareness of their properties and sell merchandise, as well as to enhance the user's fondness for the property through interactive games, contests and entertainment vehicles (e.g., online serials or webisodics).

The Internet will play an increasingly important part in the licensing business for virtually all properties. So far the benefits have been largely promotional, but licensed categories such as animated e-mail messages and digital greeting cards are starting to emerge. FunMail offers animated e-mail and wireless messages in Asia featuring licensed characters such as Hello Kitty, Garfield, South Park and Mashimaro, a popular character in Korea. Disney content is available through wireless devices, also in Asia. Players Inc. has licensed its NFL players for content on The Loup, an interactive network for teens. Playing card brand Hoyle is licensed for online and handheld games.

Payment structures for interactive categories may differ from those for other segments, as will be discussed further in Chapter 7. Some interactive products are distributed free, for example, while others, such as slot machines, generate potentially royalty-earning income beyond the sale of the product itself.

OTHER PRODUCT LICENSING OPPORTUNITIES

Several products do not fit neatly into any of the categories listed above. They include automotive accessories, gardening supplies, hardware and luggage. Properties of all types have entered these categories.

Growing areas include plants and flowers—which have been licensed by Crayola, Ernest Hemingway and the Audubon Society—and vehicles, including cars, trucks, earth-moving equipment, all-terrain vehicles, snowmobiles, speedboats and trailers. Corvette, Tonka and Polaris are among the properties that have been linked with vehicles of various types.

SERVICES

More licensors are looking into licensing their properties for services or other non-retail programs as they seek new ways to exploit their assets profitably and enhance their property image. Some of the more active sectors here include:

- Restaurants and bars, associated with properties such as Harley-Davidson, Cheers, Cosmopolitan (in the U.K.) and Popeye
- Entertainment venues such as Star Trek video arcades, Seventeen dance clubs and ESPN skate parks
- Advertising, promotions and marketing materials featuring properties such as Dilbert
- Live tours and ice shows such as those starring Disney or Sesame

Street characters

- Theme park rides for Spider-Man and many others
- Travel services, tours and camps licensed by Discovery Channel, The History Channel and National Geographic
- Educational and training courses and materials such as Money magazine's financial planning courses or Hot Rod magazine's and NASCAR's automotive repair classes
- Affinity credit cards such as those for nonprofit groups
- Lotteries, linked with properties such as Elvis, Beetle Bailey, Harley-Davidson, Elvira and others
- Premiums, business incentives and advertising specialties such as those authorized by sports events such as the Olympics
- Maid, gardening and other at-home services associated with properties such as Whirlpool

Films and TV series can also be licensed, although it is more common for entertainment vehicles to occur through co-production arrangements or other deals outside of a straight licensing agreement.

It can be difficult to monitor service licensing deals, even more than with product licensing agreements, and a consumer's bad experience with a service tends to degrade the property's reputation more than a bad experience with a product. Many licensors use a secret shopper-type program to ensure that the service does not reflect badly on its brand or property. Despite the risks, however, these opportunities can be lucrative and awareness- and image-enhancing.

CHAPTER 4:
DISTRIBUTION OF LICENSED MERCHANDISE

The characteristics of a property and its target market dictate which stores should distribute the licensed merchandise associated with it. Products inspired by an upscale fashion brand sell in department and specialty stores, including a designer's own stores, while items featuring a teen-oriented entertainment property are appropriate for trend and/or music stores such as Sam Goody or Spencer, among other outlets.

Monitoring the distribution of merchandise is a crucial means of protecting a brand's image; an upscale licensor's core business can be hurt if discount stores carry its licensed products. For example, one Calvin Klein licensee sold Klein-branded underwear in warehouse/club stores, which the designer claimed harmed his image, ultimately taking the licensee to court.

Moving a property into inappropriate channels — that is, locations where target customers do not shop — is a waste of resources. Some observers noted that products linked to Star Wars: Episode I and distributed through upscale channels did not sell while many of those in mass channels did; the program for Episode II was adjusted accordingly.

Retailers are looking for ways to differentiate themselves from their competition and licensed merchandise can help. Chains seek exclusive licensed promotions and merchandise deals, which can increase traffic and sales and turn that retail outlet into a preferred shopping destination. Exclusive arrangements are becoming the norm, whether a full exclusive involving all products or a single exclusive line (e.g. Playmates' Simpsons Treehouse of Horror playset at Toys 'R' Us in fall 2000). Direct-to-retail licenses, where the retailer becomes the licensee, are also on the rise, especially for fashion, corporate and celebrity brands. This important trend will be discussed at greater length later in this chapter.

Distribution of licensed merchandise is primarily the licensee's responsibility, but licensors can — and are increasingly expected to — make the sales job easier by coordinating promotions and concept shops, preselling their properties to retailers and attending sales calls with their licensees. In fact, licensors often pitch their properties to retailers first, then use interest from one or more chains to attract licensees to the property. Retailers also have preferred vendors and often dictate which licensees they want licensors to select.

The retail landscape is constantly changing. Stores go out of business (e.g. Montgomery Ward), expand (Carrefour), merge (Best Buy and The Musicland Group), partner (K•B Toys and Sears) and reposition their strategies and images (Toys 'R' Us). Yet, regardless of these changes, retailers' power has increased to the point where they have become a third equal partner (or even the most powerful player) in the licensing relationship.

Figure 7
SELECTED RETAIL STORES BY DISTRIBUTION CHANNEL

UPSTAIRS *(Higher-Priced, Lower-Volume)*
Department Stores, Upscale
Bloomingdale's
Dillard's
Famous-Barr
Lord & Taylor
Marshall Field's
May
Nieman-Marcus
Nordstrom
Rich's
Saks Fifth Avenue
Woodward & Lothrup
Specialty Stores
Athlete's Foot
B. Dalton
Champs
Disney Store
FAO Schwarz
Gap
Musicland
Nicole Miller
Sam Goody
Sanrio Surprise
Spencer Gifts
Suncoast
MID-TIER
Department Stores
Fred Meyer
J.C. Penney
Kohl's
Mervyn's
Sears
SteinMart
DOWNSTAIRS *(Higher-Volume, Lower-Priced)*
Discount Stores,
National and Regional
Ames
Bradlees
Hills
Kmart
Meijer
Pamida
Rose's
ShopKo
Target
Venture
Wal-Mart
Zellers

Category Killers
Barnes & Noble Superstores
Bed, Bath & Beyond
Books-A-Million
Kids 'R' Us
Sports Authority
Staples
Toys 'R' Us
Grocery and Drug Stores
A&P
CVS
Food Lion
Kroger
Rite-Aid
SuperValu
Walgreens
Convenience and Variety Stores
Ben Franklin
Circle-K
Dollar General
Family Dollar
7-Eleven
Warehouse Clubs
Price Costco
Sam's Club
ON-SITE VENUES
Arcades/Amusement Parks
Concession Stands
Restaurants
Theme Parks
Trackside
DIRECT RESPONSE
Home Shopping
Internet
Mail-Order Catalogs, Property-Specific
and Third-Party

Note: This list is not exhaustive. It provides an overview of the types of stores in each channel, but represents a small sample of the chains in each. Also, in some instances a given company may define one or another chain in a different category.

Source: The Licensing Letter;
EPM Communications

DISTRIBUTION CHANNELS

Virtually all distribution channels carry licensed merchandise, including brick-and-mortar retailers, direct-response marketers and on-site venues. *Figure 7 (page 66)* illustrates a sampling of distribution tiers and some of the stores that fall within each.

The lines between channels are sometimes blurry. Licensors often sign one licensee for department and specialty stores and another for the mass merchant tier, but the difference can be hard to distinguish. A store such as Target is usually considered a discount department store but some licensors view it as more upscale than Kmart or Wal-Mart and more as a mid-tier outlet (the level between upscale department stores and discounters).

Licensees that sell to mass merchants and those that sell to department stores may both target mid-tier stores such as Mervyn's. Similarly, chains such as Bed, Bath and Beyond or Petsmart have qualities of both specialty stores and mass merchandisers. Licensors should keep this discrepancy in mind when granting licenses.

The number of distribution outlets available, as well as the potential overlap among them, leads many licensors to be precise when identifying licensees' distribution rights. One major entertainment licensor lists 80 separate distribution tiers in an appendix to its licensing contract; this reduces confusion over which specific distribution channels are allowed.

DEPARTMENT STORES

Department stores, along with specialty retailers, are viewed as "upstairs" distribution channels, meaning their prices are higher and volumes lower than mass merchants such as Wal-Mart or Target.

Fashion and designer labels often trace a large proportion of their sales to upscale department stores (along with specialty outlets). These retailers also carry other property types, such as entertainment, sports or corporate trademarks, but in general mass retailers (see below) rely more heavily on licensed merchandise than department stores do. Licensors often view upscale department stores as useful for establishing a property or creating high-profile promotions, but the bulk of sales for many properties are attributable to mid-tier and mass outlets.

Some upscale department stores have just one or a few units, others own many outlets in several states or within a given geographic region and still others have expanded nationally or internationally. Most are shopping center anchors. Examples include Saks Fifth Avenue, Bloomingdale's, Macy's, Marshall Field's, Hecht's, Dillard's and Famous-Barr.

MID-TIER DEPARTMENT STORES

Mid-tier national department store chains include J.C. Penney, Mervyn's and Sears; regional mid-tier chains include Fred Meyer, Kohl's and SteinMart. They have lower prices and less service than upscale department stores but higher prices and more service than discounters. These stores used to be considered in the same category with department stores, but over time they have become a distinct distribution tier.

Some so-called "upstairs" properties (e.g., higher-end fashion labels) target upscale department and specialty stores only, but many, especially in the character/entertainment and sports sectors, focus on "mid-tier and up." This strategy supports an upscale image but allows for greater volumes sold. Mid-tier chains are increasingly looking for exclusive deals, as are virtually all types of retailers, to distinguish themselves from their competitors.

MASS MERCHANDISERS

Mass merchandisers, or discounters, are characterized by low prices, low margins and limited customer service and drive much higher volumes than department stores. Some, such as Target, are discount department stores, while others, such as Toys 'R' Us, are discount specialty stores, usually of the warehouse or category killer type.

While mass merchants are the most significant channel for licensed merchandise in terms of total dollars, they may not be the best route—either initially or over an entire lifespan—for a given property, depending on its attributes. This despite the mass merchants' far greater revenue-generating potential compared to their more upscale rivals.

Like upscale and mid-tier department stores, mass merchandisers, both national and regional, are increasingly seeking exclusives from licensors, whether it be a single product or a full line of merchandise, or an exclusive promotional window.

Big 3 Discount Chains

The major national discount department store chains are Kmart (in bankruptcy as of 2002), Wal-Mart and Target. They sell a great deal of licensed merchandise across virtually all property types; any mass market property must earn shelf space here to succeed nationally.

The Big 3 use licensing extensively to differentiate themselves from their competition. They not only participate in exclusive licensed promotions, but also license properties for private label lines. Kmart has licensed Jaclyn Smith's name for apparel and Martha Stewart's for domestics. Wal-Mart has licensed Better Homes and Gardens from Meredith for its gardening departmants. Target has associated itself with fashion labels such as Cherokee and Mossimo, as well as characters such as Hello Kitty and art brands such as 2 Grrrls. The list of exclusives in this market is a long one; details will be discussed further later in this chapter.

The Big 3 chains are competitive with other store types in most product categories. For example, Wal-Mart is the top U.S. toy retailer, commanding nearly 20% of the market, followed by the toy specialist Toys 'R' Us.

Regional Discounters

Aside from the Big 3, other discount department stores operate on a regional basis. They include Venture, Pamida, ShopKo, Meijer, Rose's, Hill's and Fred Meyer. These chains have similar buying and merchandising structures to the Big 3 national discount chains and rely on licensed promotions to distinguish themselves from their regional competition.

Many regional discount chains, including Ames, the biggest discount retailer after the Big 3, have found themselves in difficult financial straits in the late 1990s and early 2000s, as they try to compete with the expanding operations of Wal-Mart and Target.

Category Killers

So-called "category killers" are big-box superstores specializing in one product category. Those with substantial licensed merchandise offerings have included Toys 'R' Us (toys), Kids 'R' Us and Babies 'R' Us (children's apparel), Home Depot (building and decorating supplies), SportMart (sporting goods and sports-licensed apparel), Bed, Bath & Beyond (domestics and other products for the home) and Barnes & Noble Superstores (books), to name just a few. Some category killers are regional while others are national.

The competitive advantage of these stores lies in their ability to charge lower prices and carry a wide selection of merchandise within one category; they can have ten times the square footage of an average mall-based specialty store. Shoppers give up customer service for the increased variety, convenience and low prices.

For category killers, licensed merchandise has historically served more to enhance the variety of their merchandise mix than to differentiate them from their competitors. This is beginning to change, however; chains such as Lowe's (building and decorating) and Border's (books) are among the many to tie in with licensed properties on a short- and/or long-term basis.

SPECIALTY CHAINS AND INDEPENDENTS

Like department stores, specialty stores are considered upstairs distribution channels. They offer a comparable level of merchandise in terms of quality, but specialize in one product category. They are usually small and compete not on price or variety but on a shopper-friendly atmosphere and on the desirability and uniqueness of the products they stock. Some are regional or national chains while others are single-store sole proprietorships.

Toy Stores and Chains

Specialty toy stores face competition from Toys 'R' Us, which they cannot beat in terms of price or selection. Some participate in promotions with licensed properties. FAO Schwarz (a division of The Right Start), an upscale national chain, utilizes a number of limited-time in-store concept shops and promotions with children's entertainment properties and has freestanding year-round Barbie boutiques.

Children's Book and Toy Stores

Stores selling children's books and educational toys became a force in distributing licensed products in the late 1990s. Stores such as Noodle Kidoodle, Zany Brainy and Imaginarium were key to the distribution strategy of educational entertainment properties for preschool and school-age children. These stores have undergone consolidation in the 2000s—Noodle Kidoodle and Zany Brainy merged under Zany Brainy, which then declared bankruptcy and was purchased by The Right Start; Toys 'R' Us bought Imaginarium; Learningsmith and Store of Knowledge went out of business — but are still considered an important outlet for certain types of children's properties. They are also attractive promotional partners for these licenses.

The problems within this distribution channel have affected product categories that rely heavily on these stores as customers; plush makers Eden (now defunct) and Applause attributed their financial difficulties in part to the decreased shelf space available at educational children's book/toy outlets.

Gift Shops

Gift shops run the gamut from independent one-shop operations to national mall-based chains (e.g., Spencer Gifts) to airport gift shops. Some concentrate on upscale gifts and sell items such as artist-licensed ceramics, tabletop items and stationery. Others, including Spencer, specialize in trendy novelties, often exclusive, associated with older-skewing entertainment properties and corporate trademarks like beer brands. Gift chains, particularly national ones, use licensed promotions to enhance their reputation as a unique shopping destination.

Specialty Apparel Stores

Specialty apparel stores range from independent shops and regional chains to large, national chains including The Gap. Their dependence on licensed merchandise varies: The Gap and The Limited, for example, stock private-label merchandise based on their own brand, whereas others carry licensed goods based on designer, character and sports properties and occasionally participate in licensed promotions.

Many specialty apparel stores are targeted toward one demographic segment. Hot Topic, for example, is a growing chain targeting tween and teen girls. It is a frequent participant in licensed promotions and has been a direct licensee for appropriate properties.

Sporting Goods Stores

Most sporting goods outlets carry sports and fitness equipment licensed from athletes or sports leagues. They also stock apparel from licensees of the professional leagues, NASCAR and colleges, as well as merchandise associated with events such as the Olympics on a short-term basis. Increasingly, they carry licensed apparel and other products based on sporting goods and footwear brands.

Some participate in promotions with leagues, colleges and other licensors, for example highlighting local team merchandise and offering free or discounted tickets to games. Some sporting goods chains have gone out of business or are suffering financially; most are reducing the shelf and floor space they devote to licensed sports products, especially tied to the major leagues and colleges.

Fan Shops

Fan shops are stores specializing in licensed sports apparel; Champs is one example. They became an important channel in the 1980s and helped drive the transformation in sports licensing during that time from a seasonal to a year-round business. The business since has returned to being seasonally driven, and these stores have done the same, concentrating on whichever sports are in play. Many have experienced financial difficulties; Champs, for example, has closed a significant number of stores. Fan shops are typically mall-based, regional chains and face competition from category killers, sporting goods stores and every other outlet that sells licensed sports merchandise. Like sporting goods chains, fan shops often utilize promotions with local teams and with the major leagues.

Footwear Stores

Mall-based footwear stores such as Kinney Shoes sell licensed footwear, primarily associated with fashion designers or brands. Some also sell accessories and hosiery, which may be licensed. Athletic footwear stores including Lady Foot Locker and FootAction USA sell athletes' signature footwear lines, shoes associated with sporting goods brands and, sometimes, licensed sports apparel.

Some chains, Payless ShoeSource among them, have been partners in licensed character promotions to support their children's shoe departments, as well as developing exclusive licensed footwear lines.

Bookstores

The majority of books are sold through national bookstore chains, such as Barnes & Noble and Borders (as well as Amazon.com and other web-based booksellers). Independent bookstores are also a factor, although they are experiencing tough times competing against the chains.

Many bookstores sell non-book merchandise, known in the trade as "sidelines." These include bookmarks, diaries, toys, videotapes, audiotapes, games and puzzles, calendars, CD-ROM software and plush figures. Most feature book-related properties or artists' designs, but others spotlight characters, trademarks, celebrities and other properties. Some publishers co-package books with plush, videotapes or other licensed products, bringing them into bookstores.

The major bookstore chains have been increasingly active in creating licensed promotions and sometimes act as direct licensees. Barnes & Noble, for example, has tied in with Curious George, Eloise and other literary property, and is the publishing licensee for the character Spookley the Square Pumpkin and the toy brand Huggy Buggy.

Entertainment "Fan Shops"

A number of specialty stores focusing on licensed entertainment and character merchandise appeared during the 1990s. These shops cater to baby boomers who seek products based on favorite TV shows and films. The offerings range from t-shirts and videotapes to collectibles and action figures and nearly all of it is licensed and entertainment-based. These stores compete on the basis of their uniqueness, rather than on other factors such as price. Most are independent outlets or small regional chains; examples have included TV Land and We're Entertainment.

Property-Specific Stores

At its peak, this segment included The Disney Store, which started in 1987, Sesame Street Retail Stores (1990) and Warner Bros. Studio Stores (1991); Coca-Cola is among the corporate trademark licensors that have entered the market. Not all succeed; Nickelodeon announced in the late 1990s that it was shuttering its dedicated shops, and Warner announced the same thing in 2001 after its parent company, Time-Warner, merged with AOL. Mary Engelbreit Studios closed its property-specific stores (except one) in 2002, while Disney has discontinued many stores, especially in the U.S. Eleven NASCAR Thunder stores shut down in 2001.

The surviving retailers market themselves not just as shopping destinations, but also as entertainment venues. Video walls, activities for children, costumed characters and galleries of animation art are among the draws, in addition to the merchandise itself.

While property owners still open dedicated stores, they are often limited to one flagship store (such as the Pokémon store in Manhattan), rather than a full chain. Fashion designers (Steve Madden) and artists (Thomas Kinkade) are among those that oversee successful property-specific one- or multi-store operations.

Museum Shops

Museum shops are high-end gift retailers, usually located in the museum for which they are named. They distribute merchandise featuring their institution's logo, collections and special shows, as well as items based on other museums' images and upscale fine art- and designer-licensed gifts. Some of the goods found in museum stores are sourced directly by the museum, rather than licensed.

The Museum Company is a national mall-based chain that carries museum-licensed merchandise and other licensed gift items. It, like many other chains in all sectors, has closed stores and entered bankruptcy in 2002.

Comic Book and Trading Card Stores

Some comic book stores — both chains and independents — sell comic book-related merchandise, especially in categories such as trading cards, action figures, role-playing games, toys and t-shirts. Most of these are licensed products based on comics, fantasy art, sports, Japanese anime and manga, teen- and adult-skewing films and sci-fi entertainment. Trading card stores have exhibited a similar propensity to expand their product offerings, blurring the line between the two types of store. Both experienced difficult times in the 1990s and beyond as the comic book and trading card markets declined.

Comic book and trading card stores carry a heavy percentage of secondary-market (used) merchandise in addition to new products.

Video Stores

Video stores represent a natural outlet for entertainment merchandise because of the fit between the core category and licensed entertainment goods. Some national chains attribute as much as 10% or more of their merchandise mix to licensed products. Historically, sell-through video stores such as Musicland have accounted for the bulk of licensed merchandise sales in this channel, rather than rental video stores, for which licensed merchandise had a high price point and was a difficult sell.

Still, some video rental stores sell videogames, figurines, candy and plush. One notable example is the Blockbuster chain, a subsidiary of Viacom, which has increased its floor space for licensed merchandise. (Blockbuster focuses on renting videos, but also has a sell-through business.) Independent video rental stores remain leery of licensed products.

Music Stores

Stores selling music CDs and cassettes are becoming increasingly important outlets for licensed merchandise tied both to music groups and to edgy entertainment properties that appeal primarily to male teens. Chains including The Musicland Group's Sam Goody (part of Best Buy) and Tower Records have devoted more shelf and floor space to products such as t-shirts and gifts. Some stores reserve small areas for licensed merchandise, while others create sections measuring in the thousands of square feet. Many of the products are full exclusives or are exclusive for a period of six weeks or so before going into wider distribution.

Computer, Videogame and Electronics Stores

Dedicated software retailers sell a limited amount of related licensed merchandise, primarily computer-related items (e.g., mousepads) and videogame accessories (joysticks or gloves), as well as licensed books with tips on game play. Of course, much of the software itself is tied to licensed sports or entertainment properties.

Electronics stores also carry some licensed merchandise. Radio Shack has done several exclusive licenses for holiday-themed radio-controlled vehicles, such as with Stuart Little.

FOOD AND DRUG CHAINS

Grocery stores are a significant outlet for licensed merchandise, in part because many food lines are licensed. Food-related brand-extension licensees record sales in grocery stores, as do marketers of character-based snacks. Packaged food companies often participate in short-term entertainment promotions that focus on the grocery store channel.

An increasing number of supermarkets and drug stores sell licensed nonfood items based on all types of properties, with examples ranging from kitchen gadgets to children's books, collectibles, school supplies, toys and greeting cards. Some are experimenting with endcaps featuring licensed t-shirts, party goods or other merchandise. Customers tend to want to get in and out of drug and grocery stores as quickly as possible, but they are open to impulse

Figure 8

SUMMARY OF MAJOR HOME SHOPPING CHANNELS THAT SELL LICENSED MERCHANDISE

NETWORK	DESCRIPTION
QVC	QVC is broadcast to 79 million homes in the U.S., as well as 27 million in Germany and 8 million in the U.K. In 1999, it took 111 million phone calls and shipped 76 million packages. Thirty-one percent of its programming is devoted to jewelry. It often sells licensed merchandise linked to designers such as Louis Dell'Olio, celebrities such as Joan Rivers, sports properties such as the Olympics and artists such as Thomas Kinkade and Warren Kimble, as well as entertainment licenses. An official American Bandstand Library boxed set of collectible CDs sold 40,000 units; an M&Ms candy dispenser sold out in an hour (representing 59,000 units and $59 million in sales) while an additional 31,000 units of M&Ms licensed merchandise sold in a two-hour period. Total QVC sales reached $2.8 billion in 1999.
HSN	HSN (the Home Shopping Network) took 75 million calls and shipped 41 million packages in 2000, when it had total sales of $1.8 billion. Licensed merchandise includes products based on ABC Daytime soap operas, celebrity-designed items such as those from actress Susan Lucci, segments featuring home designer Christopher Lowell, as well as television programming, sports properties and other types of licenses.
ShopNBC	The newest and smallest of the three networks, ShopNBC (formerly known as ValueVision), had sales of $462 million in 2001, with 13.4% of that attributable to e-commerce. The company bought FanBuzz.com, an e-commerce company specializing in online shops that sell licensed sports merchandise, in 2002. It sells team-licensed products on-air as well, along with celebrity programming such as that featuring Star Jones. NBC-themed merchandise is prominent, including an NBC Store and Olympic merchandise (such as the U.S. team's Roots beret) that gained popularity through NBC's Olympic's coverage in 2002.

Note: This table provides a snapshot of each company's activity but contains only a fraction of the licensing activity of each. All three networks are active in online sales as well as on air.

Source: EPM Communications

purchases of licensed goods.

While food and drug chains compete mainly on price, selection and quality of fresh foods, they are also becoming more frequent licensed promotional partners as they try to differentiate themselves from other stores in their area and make themselves a destination for shoppers. Grocery chain Ralph's and drug chain CVS are among those that have experimented with licensed properties, offering free movie tickets with purchases of a certain amount and carrying exclusive merchandise.

In-store bakeries also offer licensed products in the form of decorated cakes featuring characters or sports logoes.

DEALER NETWORKS

Dealer networks are retail or wholesale outlets that sell a brand's core products and sometimes distribute licensed merchandise. For example, hardware stores (and hardware co-ops like TruServ or Do-It-Best) might stock licensed Snap-On Tools caps, Corvette showrooms may display Corvette auto vacuum cleaners and Budweiser distributors might sell Bud can coolers to convenience stores along with the beer. John Deere dealerships, which number 4,000 in North America, sell John Deere licensed apparel and collectibles, while Polaris dealerships sell Polaris all-terrain vehicles and other brand-extension products. Corporate trademark licensors and/or licensees also offer licensed merchandise premiums, intended for consumers or the trade, through dealer networks. These may be sourced directly by the company or through an advertising specialty distributor.

VARIETY AND CONVENIENCE STORES

Variety stores sell stationery and back-to-school products, insulated beverageware, health and beauty items, lunch kits and paper partyware, among other licensed products, while convenience stores such as 7-Eleven carry licensed food products, beer-licensed novelties and other low-priced items. These types of outlets are not destinations for licensed merchandise, but impulse purchases can occur.

CONCESSION STANDS

On-site concession stands at concert and sports venues sell music-licensed products, arena and trackside concessions hawk sports merchandise and theme park concessions offer entertainment novelties. Merchandise is often theme park- or arena-specific so it does not compete with goods sold through traditional retailers; much of it is sourced directly rather than licensed.

Some sports properties attribute the bulk of their licensed merchandise sales to arenas or trackside locations, which are often supplied by a single on-site licensee. The National Hot Rod Association, for example, says that 75% of its $50 million in annual sales of licensed merchandise occurs at the venue, while 90% of the $2 million in annual sales for the Preakness and Belmont horse racing stakes occurs at those tracks. Conversely, 90% of Kentucky Derby licensed product sales take place at traditional retail locations.

RESTAURANTS AND ARCADES

Theme restaurants such as Cheers bars at airports, Popeye's Fried Chicken restaurants and the Harley-Davidson Café (all of which are licensed) sell property-specific merchandise in-store, while videogame and pinball arcades, including The Star Trek Experience in Las Vegas (a full entertainment venue) offer an opportunity to distribute licensed merchandise based on characters from the games. As with concession stands, this merchandise is usually exclusive to the arcade or restaurant and is often outsourced instead of licensed.

Themed restaurants are down from their peak in the 1990s, with some of the highest-profile examples, including Planet Hollywood, experiencing financial difficulties. Yet they still offer some opportunities for sales of appropriate merchandise.

MAIL ORDER

Mail order is an important distribution channel for licensed merchandise. Signals, Sharper Image, Wireless, Athletic Supply, Sound Exchange, The Mind's Eye and many other catalogs have sold licensed products ranging from mugs and ties to apparel and novelties. Sometimes, but not always, the goods are exclusive to a given catalog; catalogers may be exclusive direct licensees for an entire property as well.

Mail order is appropriate for sports, entertainment, publishing, art, corporate trademarks, music and all types of properties. In Germany and some other countries, mail order can account for a significant percentage of sales for a given licensed property.

The number of property-specific catalogs selling merchandise based on a single property or family of properties grew in the 1990s. NASCAR, Coca-Cola, Doonesbury, Elvis Presley, The Andy Griffith Show, Hershey's, Disney, Warner Bros. and Budweiser have all tested merchandise via dedicated mail-order catalogs. Some of these experiments turned into lucrative profit centers.

Licensors have also experimented with other printed direct-response vehicles, such as brochures for licensed merchandise included in the package for individual licensees' products. This can be an effective means of cross-marketing.

TELESHOPPING

Fashion designers and celebrities were among the first to try home shopping channels as a distribution outlet; personalities from sportswear designer Louis Dell'Olio to hair stylist George Caroll are among those who currently appear on home shopping shows to drive merchandise sales. Their success led licensors of other types of properties, including entertainment, sports, and corporate trademarks, to test home shopping as well, sometimes with strong results. QVC ran a Monopoly-themed show in 1999 that drove sales of 3,000 items, including a throw that sold out in one minute, while the same channel sold 130,000-plus units of Roots' Salt Lake City U.S. Olympic team beret in 2002, ranking as the top channel for this product.

Home Shopping Network, QVC and ShopNBC are the major tele-shopping networks. Smaller networks and transactional television programs (infomercials) also provide opportunities, as do short-form direct-response commercials; "Days of Our Lives" and other soap operas run short merchandise ads after their shows, sometimes publicizing the program's e-commerce site.

(See *Figure 8* [*page 74*] for a description of the three major home shopping networks.)

THE INTERNET

A growing number of licensors and licensees are attempting to sell merchandise over the Internet, either through their own sites or through third-party sites, as well as sometimes allowing their licensees to sell on their own sites or through independent operations. (Each licensor has a different strategy for what is allowable.) Most licensors' websites have some sort of transactional area featuring items like collectibles or t-shirts, often exclusive.

The Internet does not yet represent a significant channel for licensed product sales—it rarely represents more than 5% of total sales for a given property, and usually much less—although Amazon.com (which has set up dedicated shops for properties such as Harry Potter and The Lord of the Rings), eBay and others indicate the medium's potential. Several catalogers and bricks-and-mortar retailers effectively combine the Internet with their other channels of distribution, while entertainment companies and corporations have launched viable e-commerce areas within greater websites. As the number of online consumers grows and users become more comfortable with web-based shopping, this distribution channel promises to gain importance.

As of 2002, most licensors are at least experimenting with e-commerce. Some are testing a few products online before moving on to a wider retail strategy, as Cartoon Network has done with action figures based on its series Samurai Jack. Fashion designer Dollhouse sells its core product and encourages licensees to sell their branded products on apparel-related e-commerce sites. Sports leagues and events have authorized companies such as FanBuzz.com (now owned by ShopNBC) to distribute licensed apparel and accessories. Paws, Inc., licensor of Garfield, authorizes its licensees to sell on their own websites, as long as they feature a link back to the Paws site. Mattel's Hot Wheels and Barbie licensed computers are sold only through a direct-to-consumer website.

Online auctions are another growing area of Internet-based distribution, particularly for the major entertainment studios, which accept bids on original memorabilia and props used in the filming of popular movies. Most are accomplished through alliances between the studios and the major online auction sites eBay and Yahoo! Auctions. Marvel created a charity auction in which it and eBay offered 36 unique cars painted by guest artists to depict

Marvel Superheroes.

E-commerce is especially effective for properties that have fans scattered around the globe; too few people may live in any one city to make traditional sales there viable but, when aggregated on the web, the fan base is large enough to sustain a business.

Although not all customers are comfortable buying on the Internet, they do browse for information before heading out to a bricks-and-mortar store, so an e-commerce site often benefits a property indirectly by increasing customer satisfaction. The Internet also serves as a means to experiment creatively, promote properties and build consumers' relationship with a license, all at relatively low cost.

Licensed e-commerce success stories have included FANSOnly Network, an operator of collegiate online stores, which sold 38,000 items in 21,000 orders in one month (November 2001), through 72 official team shops.

OTHER

This wrap-up illustrates the main retail outlets that distribute licensed merchandise. Licensed products are not limited just to these channels, however: Pet supply stores sell leashes, bird seed and aquariums, all of which come in licensed varieties. Movie theaters have tested entertainment merchandise kiosks (with mixed success in the U.S., although this is a viable channel in some countries, such as Japan, where a Tokyo theater sold $15,000 worth of Doraemon merchandise at one all-night premiere). Fabric, paint, housewares, and airport stores, as well as other channels such as food service, are just a few of the potential outlets for licensed products. More nontraditional retail channels should arise as licensors and licensees look outside shopping centers for increased sales.

It should be noted that different licensors and licensees define tiers of distribution differently. A fashion designer may consider Bed, Bath & Beyond to be a nondesirable mass market outlet, while one of its licensees may consider it a key specialty account. An upscale brand may or may not find Home Depot to be an appropriate distribution outlet. During contract negotiation, licensors and licensees must be as specific as possible about where the licensed line in question may or may not be sold.

RETAIL EXCLUSIVES

As noted throughout this book, more licensors are forging exclusive deals with retailers. Retailers are looking to differentiate themselves, while licensors are looking for a strong promotional platform for new, classic and branded properties. Associating with a strong retailer helps attract licensees to a property and is, in fact, one of the key criteria potential licensees consider. And, licensors benefit financially; designer label Mossimo was in financial difficulties before forging its direct deal with Target; its income increased 10-fold almost immediately afterward. Direct-to-retail licenses also tend to benefit licensors promotionally, since retailers devote more marketing dollars to proprietary product lines.

After an exclusive, other retailers may be leery of carrying merchandise based on a property, since it is identified with one of their competitors. If the exclusive was successful, however, that track record will usually encourage other retailers to buy into the program when it becomes available.

Retailers often prefer not to take the role of direct licensee (as opposed to being the exclusive destination for merchandise supplied by licensees), since that is not the business they are in. Being a licensee causes logistical challenges, particularly in the area of inventory control and disposal. Yet they feel it is the only way to gain true exclusivity, so they demand these deals, despite the challenges. Margins also tend to be better with a direct license than when sourcing from manufacturers.

Manufacturers complain that they are being cut out with direct retail licenses, although the companies who would be the licensees otherwise often end up being the preferred vendors in an exclusive deal. They also claim retailers get a better deal on royalties and that their product quality suffers as they decrease their price to compete with retailer direct prices, while still being required to pay a higher royalty. When manufacturers do participate in an exclusive, it means a lucrative minimum order from the retailer. On the other hand, wide distribution can mean a many-fold sales increase over an exclusive, depending on the property and its position in its lifespan.

Some of the most high-profile retail-direct licenses include Martha Stewart with Kmart, Michael Graves and Todd Oldham with Target and mary-kateandashley with Wal-Mart. They can involve any type of retailer and any type of property.

Exclusives can take many forms. They can involve a whole category or categories of products:

- Christopher Lowell, a decorator with a show on the Discovery Channel, has a 1,000-SKU program at Burlington Coat Factory.
- Kmart is the exclusive retailer of Sesame Street children's apparel; this initiative accounts for 50% of the merchandise in its juvenile clothing department.
- Hot Topic had a year-long exclusive with art/character brand L'il She Creatures for a variety of apparel and stationery. The direct license was marketed under a Hot Topic private label brand in 350 stores.
- Sears had a six-month exclusive on Bob the Builder apparel and accessories, which were merchandised in Bob boutiques with nonexclusive books, toys, and videos.
- Callaway Golf and Nordstrom had a deal for seven years whereby the retailer was the exclusive manufacturer and retailer of branded apparel, footwear, and sun and skin care products under the Callaway brand.

- Retailer Gadzook's has a direct license with the Candie's brand for several apparel categories including swimwear.
- Products based on the magazine YM, including CD compilations, room decor and hair accessories, were tested and then rolled out in boutiques in 3,200 CVS drug stores as a means to launch a broader licensing effort.
- Martha Stewart's line with Kmart is exclusive for most categories in the mass market, but the licensor has upscale products under the Martha Stewart Signature line for the specialty tier as well. Products such as furniture, paint, floor coverings and fabrics are available in all types of relevant specialty stores.

Some exclusives encompass a single line of products, or even a single product:

- Purple Ronnie, a greeting card design, was licensed to U.K. retailer Condomania for an exclusive line of condoms.
- Payless ShoeSource is the exclusive retailer for Stanley licensed work shoes.
- The Disney Store sells Princess Best Friend Dolls, licensed to Lee Middleton Original Dolls, as exclusives in its online and print catalogs.
- National Geographic authorized Eddie Bauer as its exclusive retailer for travel accessories and Museum Company for exclusive stationery and gift items.

Exclusives can involve multiple geographic divisions or multiple chains owned by the same retailer:

- Products featuring the tween art property She's Charmed & Dangerous appeared in 100 concept shops in Federated Stores including Bloomingdale's, Macy's, Burdines, Rich's/Lazarus and Bon Marché.
- Toys 'R' Us was the exclusive, three-year, worldwide retailer for the relaunch of E.T. upon the film's 20th anniversary. A full range of merchandise in all categories was available at TRU chains including Kids 'R' Us, Babies 'R' Us, Imaginarium and the store's e-commerce site.
- Hennes & Mauritz (H&M) holds a Pink Panther junior's apparel exclusive and carries the same merchandise in its stores in Europe, the U.S. and elsewhere. The same is true of its other exclusive licenses.

Exclusives can be temporary and largely promotional in nature, sometimes as a means of launching a property before entering wider distribution:

- Spencer Gifts ran a Halloween promotion centered on Rocky Horror Picture Show, involving products, promotions and signage.
- Mervyn's ran a short-term Barney apparel exclusive, with prod-

uct supplied by Barney licensees Haddad and Celebrity, which included a signage-promoted wall and fixtures. The deal lasted for one season, after which the products rolled out to other retailers.

- May Company ran a five-month back-to-school promotion to launch Dora the Explorer merchandise. It held in-store events throughout its divisions, including Lord & Taylor, Filene's, Famous Barr, and several others.
- Nordstrom tied in with Fox's Olive the Other Reindeer, a book-based Christmas special, for an exclusive Christmas promotion that included merchandise such as plush, ornaments, and pajamas, and promotional elements such as signage throughout the store, property-identified gift cards and shopping bags, and visibility in the retailer's catalog.
- FAO Schwarz helped launch the PBS programming bloc The Bookworm Bunch with an exclusive promotion. It had a limited-time direct license to produce plush, and merchandised it in boutiques with nonexclusive licensed products and books.

Conversely, exclusives can be permanent, as is the case with Target's licenses with Ecko, Michael Graves, Todd Oldham, Cherokee and Mossimo.

Retail exclusives do not just involve bricks-and-mortar retailers; catalogs, teleshopping outlets and e-commerce sites are involved as well:

- Good Housekeeping-licensed bakeware, pantryware and small kitchen appliances were introduced through an exclusive on Home Shopping Network, then rolled out the next season to mid-tier and specialty stores.
- The Neiman Marcus catalog had an exclusive on a particular color of KitchenAid licensed cookware manufactured by Meyer.
- Art property the Katoufs is direct licensed to mail order company Spiegel for bed and bath items.

Some deals extend beyond the retailer's own stores, with the retailer acting as a wholesaler or participating financially in later wide distribution:

- Hot Topic was the exclusive retailer for the launch of product related to the comic book property Sandman. It has a single supplier for multiple categories, and receives a share of revenues from merchandise wholesaled to other retail chains after the promotional period.
- New York's Museum of Modern Art Store is the exclusive licensee for Frank Lloyd Wright frames, scarves, plates and textiles; it sells these in its own stores and wholesales them to other retailers such as Target.

There are a number of ways to structure exclusives. They can take the form of a direct license, an arm's length agreement supplied by licensees, a deal in which merchandise is sourced by preferred vendors of either the licensor or licensee, or some combination of the above:

- Cartoon Network joined with Brazilian department store Riachuelo to create Cartoon Cartoon corners in 70 outlets. Merchandise consists of products from licensees as well as the potential for Riachuelo to design its own exclusive items.
- Disney has forged direct-to-retail apparel; deals with a number of retailers in all tiers of trade around the world, including Tesco (U.K.), Kmart and JCPenney (U.S.), H&M (Sweden) and Pre-Natal (Italy). All Disney properties from films to ESPN are part of the deal, which is sourced by the retailer using Disney preferred providers.
- Scholastic and Toys 'R' Us jointly developed a line of Scholastic-branded educational toys, which are merchandised in boutiques in TRU stores.
- Joe Boxer apparel, accessories and all other categories are sold exclusively through Kmart within the mass and mid-tier channels. The licensor had to end some of its existing licensing agreements in order for the deal to go through.
- Target was the exclusive retailer of Eddie Bauer camping gear during a summer-long window. Licensee American Recreation Products was the supplier.
- Designer Alexander Julian has a broad exclusive with Lowe's for a variety of decorating and home building products. Most are supplied by licensed manufacturers; items such as paint are a direct license with Lowe's.
- Wal-Mart's mary-kateandashley deal is supplied by vendors selected by licensor Dualstar and its agent The Beanstalk Group; the retailer is exclusive but is not a direct licensee and does not pay royalties.
- Kohl's is the exclusive retailer for artist Warren Kimble in a number of categories. Many of Kimble's licensees are part of the deal; other products are sourced from vendors selected by Kohl's.
- Target sells exlusive scents for properties including Tricia Foley in the Country, B.U.M. Equipment, and Brambly Hedge. Private-label manufacturer Private Perfumery supplies the product.
- MTV granted Bed, Bath and Beyond a direct license for domestics that would appeal to college students living in a dorm. The retailer sourced the products through its own list of suppliers.
- Target launched its own Christmas property, Snowden, created by artist Nancy Carlson. Target owns all the rights, sells mer-

chandise and has created Christmas specials based on the character.

These examples are not an exhaustive list of options, but show the many variations retail-exclusive deals can take.

RETAIL BUYING

Creating and implementing licensed promotions and boutiques has become easier. Retailers know that concept shops and promotions drive licensed merchandise sales and even demand such activity before agreeing to support a license. Most major retail chains now have a structure in place to oversee licensed alliances, including an executive in charge of licensing and licensed promotions, who serves as the point person in the chain's dealings with licensors.

Typically, retailers purchase merchandise on a department-by-department basis (which made organizing licensed promotions a complex task until the late 1990s, when stores began hiring licensing specialists). Individual buyers have responsibility for one or more departments or for several products within one department. The smaller the retail operation, the more departments one buyer handles; mom-and-pop operations may employ one buyer for the whole store, while buyers for large chains are often responsible for just one category. (Small independent shops may utilize a purchasing company to serve as an intermediary.)

Buying structures vary from chain to chain or store to store. Normally, buyers of soft goods (apparel and domestics) do not purchase hard goods (toys, hardware, furniture and so on) and *vice versa*. Otherwise, a buyer for one chain can handle toys, gardening supplies and outdoor furniture while a counterpart at another chain buys toys, lunch kits, paper partyware and greeting cards.

A divisional merchandise manager (DMM) typically oversees several buyers and a VP or higher-level employee manages several DMMs.

TRENDS IN DISTRIBUTION

The licensing community has witnessed an ever more competitive retail environment since the late 1990s. Saturation has resulted from a combination of 1) more properties available, 2) less retail shelf space devoted to licensed merchandise, 3) the high failure rate of licensed properties, 4) the financial woes of the retail industry overall and 5) consolidation among retailers. Consequently, retail buyers are selective about supporting licensed properties and demand more promotional backing from licensees and, especially, licensors. As noted, many seek exclusive arrangements with licensors, whether long-term exclusive alliances, early promotional windows or unique product lines. They tend to prefer established franchises over new properties, although they continue to embrace properties they feel have the potential to be "hot."

Licensors and licensees cannot rely solely on tried-and-true promotional techniques. They must be innovative when creating retail promotions and creative when designing merchandise and graphics. Simply being associated with a license does not ensure a product's success.

Property owners and manufacturers are seeking new distribution channels and new markets for licensed goods, whether through the Internet, thematic retailing or entertainment experiences, cross-merchandising or cross-packaging alliances that earn them shelf space in new venues, or promotional alliances that expose the property to new markets and open doors for increased sales.

As retailers focus their efforts largely on classic properties, established corporate and fashion brands and potential blockbusters, steep barriers face proprietors of potentially successful — yet non-classic and non-homerun — licenses. Licensors need to consider niche distribution and unique promotional strategies in order to build a track record that will ultimately, perhaps, allow them to break into the mass market.

Of course, properties can succeed even if they do not try to be all things to all people. Lucrative licenses exist that target narrow market segments only. In fact, many observers believe that these niche properties will be more common in the future as general-audience properties find it difficult to succeed. And, niche properties inherently have that element of exclusivity that retailers of all stripes are seeking.

AVOIDING CANNIBALIZATION

Exclusivity is the best way to alleviate retailers' fears of cannibalization. But when a licensed property has distribution beyond a single retailer, this concern needs to be addressed. Licensors targeting several retail tiers at once typically authorize different products for each distribution channel. Upscale and mid-tier department and specialty stores sell direct-embroidered apparel, a relatively costly manufacturing technique, while mass merchants carry clothing featuring embroidered appliqués. Mass marketers offer plastic toys, while specialty and department stores distribute wooden playthings.

Alternatively, licensors can authorize unique designs for each outlet, so that a particular image or style is available only in one type of store. Some licensors, including the studios, corporate brand owners and the major sports leagues, have experimented with creating sub-brands, each targeting a different distribution tier or demographic group. While such a strategy can be effective, most licensors have limited their sub-branding activity to a few distinct labels, to avoid confusion in the marketplace and to portray a unified overall image.

Licensees are also concerned about their products being cannibalized by those of other licensees. The sure-fire way of dispelling licensees' worries is to grant a single manufacturer the right to sell a certain product or category to all distribution channels. This tactic is often not practical, however, since few potential licensees are capable of handling all channels or all products within a category adequately. (Also, licensors' objectives play a role;

property owners sometimes opt for several licensees in a category in order to maximize revenues from advances and guarantees.) Still, true exclusives, or at least some meaningful element of exclusivity, can eliminate the threat of cannibalization.

No matter what differentiation techniques are used, it is worthwhile to remember that the average consumer may not perceive the sometimes subtle differences that distinguish products in one channel from another. To a harried shopper, a $10 Pepsi t-shirt in Kmart is essentially the same as a $20 t-shirt with a slightly different design in a specialty store. These multi-tier strategies enhance retailers' and licensees' comfort level, however.

BARRIERS TO EXPANDING DISTRIBUTION

Many licensees and licensors of established properties look for ways to expand their distribution into new retail tiers, both traditional and nontraditional. Such expansion brings up several challenges for all parties involved.

In distribution channels where licensed merchandise is new — particularly in markets where independent stores dominate — both retailer and consumer demand is likely to be low at first as both groups get used to thinking of these stores as outlets for licensed products. This challenge sometimes causes licensors and their licensees to ignore an untapped distribution tier in favor of larger, established markets; they choose to wait until other companies have moved along the learning curve. Any independent store can still purchase licensed products, of course, but licensors and licensees may not feel it is cost-effective to aggressively target that segment until evidence develops of greater demand. Independent retailers, in turn, resent the lack of attention licensors pay them and complain of resistance when they try to order small quantities. (Some independent stores opt to stay away from licensed products altogether, as a means of differentiating themselves from mass market outlets.)

Distribution methods in various retail industries affect how easy it is to sell licensed products to those stores. Video rental, comic book shops and book stores buy their core product lines from a network of distributors. Retailers, especially small ones, are accustomed to buying all their products from their distributor rather than dealing directly with manufacturers, which is where they would need to go for most licensed merchandise. In these sectors, licensors and licensees should consider the feasibility of selling their licensed products through industry distributors rather than approaching retailers directly.

Another challenge is that many independent retailers do not have experience merchandising licensed products and must be educated on how to achieve maximum sales. They assume the products will sell themselves. For example, video store managers might display licensed plush in an out-of-the-way place or behind glass to prevent pilferage, reducing impulse sales. Similarly, movie theaters selling merchandise for the first time may put very little of it out on the lobby floor where filmgoers will see it.

A related problem is that many stores do not have space to display licensed merchandise adequately. Floor and shelf space is at a premium and is devoted to their core product lines. One solution is to provide space-saving and eye-catching displays already filled with merchandise. A bookstore owner may place a counter display full of licensed bookmarks near the register, but would not devote the time and effort to clearing shelf space for the same items.

Licensors and licensees must consider the purchasing habits of consumers in various distribution channels. Customers come to their neighborhood video store to rent films, perhaps carrying only the required $4.00 with them. Will they change their behavior to accommodate the availability of licensed products? Chains such as Blockbuster have shown that they will, at least in some markets.

Similarly, if the retailer sells low-priced items, such as trading cards or movie tickets, will shoppers purchase a much more expensive item such as a plush figure on impulse? For the licensed products to succeed, consumers will have to change their perception of these venues and alter their purchasing patterns. That may be a tall order in some channels.

Licensors need to figure out where consumers expect to see licensed merchandise based on their property. In some cases, it is beneficial for them to be surprised at a particular outlet—signifying that the licensor and its licensees have cut through the clutter—but they should not be dismayed by the placement.

Finally, licensors and their manufacturing partners must realize that an increase in channels will not necessarily increase sales; in some cases, a targeted program is best for the property. Too few channels, as a rule, is better than market oversaturation.

PART 2:
LICENSING STRATEGIES

CHAPTER 5:
STRATEGIES FOR LICENSORS

Every licensing program is unique and there is no "correct," step-by-step method of creating a licensing strategy. This chapter provides a framework within which licensors can make strategic decisions and outlines some of the issues they face when implementing a licensing effort.

Property owners should remember that licensing is a business tool, not an end in itself. Licensors must configure their licensing plans within the context of their overall marketing, advertising and promotional strategies. They should also outline their goals for the licensing effort — which will vary depending on the property and the licensor — before they make any other decisions. (See Chapter 1 for a discussion of possible objectives.)

DEFINING THE PROPERTY

A licensor increases its chances of successfully licensing a property if it first defines that property's characteristics. Manufacturers, retailers and, especially, consumers must be able to understand what the property stands for. Some of the factors to consider include:

- The property's brand attributes. Is it edgy, upscale, "fun," value-driven, educational, health-related, performance-oriented, "home-made," environmentally sound, "extreme," functional?
- The size of the target market and its demographic and psychographic characteristics. Demographic data include age, sex and economic level; psychographic or behavioral information focuses on where the target audience likes to shop, what they do in their free time and what sorts of products appeal to them.
- Specific property characteristics. These include the look of the logo and other graphic representations, color schemes, alternative logos and graphics, personality traits (for characters) and sample plot lines (for entertainment).
- Competitive properties. What other licenses target the same audience? How many are there and what are their characteristics?

It is interesting to note that demographic target groups have become more narrowly segmented over time. Whereas a property in the 1990s could be aimed at "children 6-11," or even simply at "children," it now is targeted toward teens, tweens, children 5-8, or preschoolers. Even preschoolers are more narrowly defined, with older preschoolers having separate interests from younger preschoolers. In addition, rather than fitting into neat groups, each property is identified specifically based on its own characteristics; some children's properties may be relevant to boys and girls 3-7 and others to boys 4-8. In general, age compression has brought the target demographic down for any given children's property; Barbie, for example, appeals to girls much younger now than it did originally.

Some properties are extended to target consumers outside their original fan base, either by design or due to the discovery of unexpected audiences. Both Powerpuff Girls and Blue's Clues have been featured on junior apparel for girls older than the core demographic for those shows (much older in Blue's Clues' case). SpongeBob SquarePants inspired products for college-aged males when it became apparent the show was of cult interest to this demographic. Hot Wheels was translated into products for nostalgic adults, such as automobiles and auto accessories.

It should be noted that the audience for a TV or film property, or the fan base for any type of property, is not necessarily the same as the core demographic that will buy licensed products. For example, boys love to watch Powerpuff Girls on Cartoon Network and make up about half the audience, but they do not purchase products and the licensing effort skews toward girls. Many properties have a multi-tiered strategy when it comes to demographic targets.

A number of properties are being positioned to appeal to specific ethnic groups. Some are targeted exclusively to a particular segment, while others are more mainstream but have elements that may appeal to a certain ethnic or religious group. Los Kitos and No Rodeo are Spanish-language comic strip properties that appeal to Hispanic consumers, while Nickelodeon's Dora the Explorer appeals to all kids but its bilingual themes make it especially relevant for Spanish speakers. Sports teams such as the San Diego Padres and the University of Miami Hurricanes have created secondary designs and slogans to appeal to Latin-American consumers. McGraw-Hill Children's Publishing's Landoll imprint translated several of its licensed children's book titles into Spanish.

The Rugrats property features Asian characters that may have potential in the Asian-American market; several licensees are making products incorporating these characters. The Showtime series Soul Food has led to products for African-American consumers, marketed through the show's website. Eyewear company Creative Optics licensed the Essence brand to appeal to African-American consumers.

Inspirational properties, such as those targeted to the Christian market or to proponents of "new age" spirituality, include Noah's Babies, a toy and giftware brand; PAX-TV, a broadcast network with a schedule heavy on inspirational programming (e.g., It's A Miracle); GodSpeaks, a series of billboard phrases; and VeggieTales, the home video franchise. The classic comic panel Ziggy targeted the inspirational greeting card and stationery market upon the character's 30th anniversary.

In addition to identifying specific property attributes and characteristics, licensors should also determine from the outset whether their property is essentially short-term or if it possesses the attributes to evolve into an evergreen. Most corporate trademarks and fashion labels will be around a long time; it is not worth the investment to launch such a line unless it is expected to last for years or even decades. Book properties and artists' images also have the potential to endure over the long term, as do niche properties with a steady collector base.

On the other hand, many films, television shows and musical groups are inherently short-term, at least as stand-alone properties. They appeal to consumers for one to three years (or even less), then fade out. Merchandise featuring The New Kids On The Block in 1990, for example, generated retail sales of $800 million, but the craze ended in about a year.

Some seemingly short-term properties can endure after they become outmoded as a fad, if the licensing and marketing plans supporting them reflect the transition from a short- to long-term strategy. Some fads are destined to burn themselves out quickly (Pac-Man, Rubik's Cube), while others (Batman, Garfield, Peanuts) survive faddish periods and—thanks to promotions, fresh merchandise, new media reincarnations and a focus on core categories—ultimately become classics.

Potential lifespan affects the licensing strategy. A property owner with a short-term license wants to maximize revenues during the property's life without worrying about its subsequent performance. Consequently, it will authorize every appropriate product category in all possible distribution channels from the beginning. The licensor and its licensees will make every effort to meet demand while it exists.

The proprietor's goal with a potentially long-term property is to watch sales increase steadily over time until they reach a strong, consistent level year after year. The licensor typically limits the product categories and distribution tiers initially to allow for later expansion, as well as taking steps to continually update the property.

Sometimes, in spite of the best efforts of the licensor to build an evergreen property, the market decides the property is a fad and sales take off. In that case, most licensors attempt to meet demand without oversaturating the market — rather than sticking to their original "classic"-style strategy — then refocus their strategy back to an evergreen one as the property's popularity inevitably falls.

Many licensees are not interested in inherently short-term properties such as music groups or standalone feature films, except as promotional opportunities. For merchandise, most will opt for properties with the promise of a long life, such as an entertainment property supported by multiple current and/or future entertainment vehicles or a consistently marketed corporate brand.

As mentioned earlier, licensors tend to position nearly all their properties, no matter what type, as "brands." Brands are entities that have built up a certain image in the eyes of consumers, attributes that are associated with that brand and no other. It takes years and multimillions of dollars to create and sustain a true brand. Although entertainment or music properties may endure and become multifaceted franchises, few become "brands."

CREATING A LICENSING STRATEGY

Components of a licensing strategy—which licensors should formulate within the context of their overall corporate strategy and objectives, and in keeping with the property's inherent attributes—include distribution, target products, timing, media and entertainment extensions, and promotional support.

DISTRIBUTION

The characteristics of a given property determine which retail channels to target. An upscale property fits naturally into the department and specialty store environment, while a short-term entertainment property will maximize sales if directed at mass merchants. Licensors of niche properties might aim for specialty shops, direct-mail catalogs, home shopping networks or the Internet.

Some licensors initiate multi-tiered programs, authorizing certain products for the mass market and other, more upscale merchandise for department and specialty stores, with products for each tier distinct. Playboy has a Club brand consisting of drinkware and bar accessories for younger consumers, sold through retailers such as Hot Topic and Urban Outfitters, and another called The Mansion Collection, sold through upscale department stores and utilizing more subtle designs.

Property owners must consider the geographic distribution of licensed merchandise. Consumers worldwide recognize the global corporate brand Coca-Cola or the former pop music group The Spice Girls. Such recognition dictates a worldwide launch strategy or, at least, a quick rollout of products globally. A television property's licensing effort depends on the international broadcast schedule for the series. Properties such as a minor league sports team or a regional college would follow a narrow distribution strategy focusing on their local area.

As noted, targeting or expanding into an inappropriate distribution tier can be harmful to a property. Designer Tommy Hilfiger's financial problems in the late 1990s were attributed by many observers to the company's overexpansion into too many distribution channels, particularly too much presence in the mass market. This reduced the label's cachet with the young urban consumers that were responsible for its early success.

PRODUCTS

The property's characteristics and target audience determine the appropriate product categories to license. If the typical customer has a low income, she might prefer a cotton t-shirt over a silk blouse. An educational children's property would fit better with an activity kit or science set than more frivolous products such as balloons (although nearly any item can incorporate educational elements). Properties with adult appeal would not drive more sales of plush or action figures, unless their target audience includes collectors, but a board game might be appropriate. A designer property with an upscale image might be perfect for decorative tabletop accessories but not keychains or plastic figurines. An ecological nonprofit organization would not license pollution-creating plastic toys; the Sierra Club encourages its licensees to use soy inks, vegetable dyes and other good-for-the-environment ingredients. The New York City Ballet licenses ballet shoes and leotards. An edgy entertainment property can be associated with products other licensors would not consider; the German character Pumuckl is featured on licensed toilet paper, something most property owners would shun.

One way to identify appropriate categories is to conduct focus groups or monitor websites that indicate what consumers want or what they believe makes sense for the property. Often the target audience will request certain products; Disney licensed its characters for checks and checkbook covers in 2001 after customers began to request that category more than almost any other.

It should be noted that the fit between a product or category and a property extends to the design of the licensed product itself. Many items are the result of "logo-slapping." That is, the licensed product is the same as its competition, except for the logo or artwork associated with the license. While in some cases a lack of lead time, high cost, or a short window of opportunity make creating truly unique products impossible, it is important to consider how to maximize the fit between product and property. In Jean-Paul Gaultier's perfume line, licensed to Beauté Prestige International, each item is distinctly Gaultier. His scent Fragile is encased in a snowglobe with a tiny figure dressed in a Gaultier couture gown; Gaultier designed the package. The advertising for the line also emphasizes the link with Gaultier, being cutting-edge and controversial, like his fashions.

Harley-Davidson licensed flashlights from Rayovac shine their light in the shape of the H-D logo; Lansky Brothers, the shop that provided Elvis with his clothes, is licensed to sell a line of men's apparel inspired by the King's tastes; Snapple licensed candy replicates the beverage flavors and, like the beverage, contains no artificial colors or flavors; Blue's Clues applesauce and pasta/cheese product are blue, which took significant product development time to create; Mothers Against Drunk Driving (MADD) sparkling ciders are non-alcoholic; MTV's Scooter Radio combines two products its core audience likes and remains true to the network's connection with music and teen trends; Hello Kitty toasters imprint the character on the finished slice; and Barbie children's eyewear comes in a hot pink case with a miniature set of glasses for Barbie.

Licensors also must consider the number of products to license. For a short-term, faddish property, it makes sense to authorize a wide range of products from the start, while preserving the longevity of a children's book property typically entails limiting the number of products initially and adding more as circumstances warrant. (A wider variety of items will sell during a property's peak compared to post-peak, when only the most relevant categories are viable.) If the goal of a corporate licensing effort is brand extension, the property owner is likely to begin by authorizing a few items closely related to the core product line and slowly adding other merchandise later if results from existing licensees suggest it would succeed.

Overall, licensors tend to grant rights for fewer total products than they did five to 10 years ago; Disney, for example, has stated that it wants to reduce its number of SKUs worldwide from 2.5 million to just a half million (including global and local merchandise). They hope to prevent oversaturation, want to focus on the best-performing categories, and believe lower total guarantee amounts are balanced by increased royalties from better marketing and reduced product development and administration costs.

Too many products can dilute the value of the property and reduce prices on licensed lines; NHL executives have admitted that when the league had an abundance of merchandise on the market, its products were used as loss leaders to attract customers into sporting goods stores, where they were then encouraged to purchase more profitable non-NHL items.

There is no single correct way to determine the number of products that make sense. There are more than 12,000 licensed Ford items available in all retail channels, while the HBO film Band of Brothers has resulted in one product, a Zippo lighter like those used in World War II.

How many licensees to select is another strategic question. Some licensors prefer to grant rights to a small number of licensees, each for a broad, exclusive product line sold through several distribution channels and geographic areas. Others opt for a large licensee roster, with each manufacturer producing a small range of products with narrow or no exclusivity. The former method allows more control over the property's image, guards against oversaturation and gives licensees more of an investment in the property's success; the latter brings in more revenues from advances and may be the only way to meet demand if a property ramps up quickly.

Neither the property type nor total expected sales levels are relevant to this discussion — at one point in the mid-1990s Pierre Cardin counted 840 licensees worldwide, while Bill Blass oversaw 70 in the U.S. and 70 internationally. Both had licensed merchandise sales of between $325 million and $350 million wholesale annually at the time.

The trend in the early 2000s has been for licensors to authorize fewer licensees, each of which are responsible for a wide product line. This is true even for sports and film licensors, which used to grant as many as hundreds of licensees for a single property. Property owners believe reducing the total roster of licensees encourages manufacturers to help build the brand and lowers the number of underperforming products on the market.

Licensors are also more often granting rights to a single licensee for multiple properties at a time, bundling several films in a franchise, several TV series on a network, or several brands under a corporate umbrella. New Line granted several licensees rights to all three Lord of the Rings films simultaneously; Nickelodeon has authorized Mattel and Jakks to produce playthings based on about a dozen of its properties.

Figure 9
TYPICAL CONTENTS OF A LICENSEE EVALUATION FORM

GENERAL COMPANY INFORMATION
Company name
Primary contact person
Name of person who provided information on the form
Addresses and phone numbers of headquarters and other locations
Number of years in business
Previous names of company, if any
Other companies operated by the principal of this company
    within the last five years
Corporate officers, owners and partners
Number of employees
Parent company, if any
Other names under which business is done
- subsidiaries
- labels
- brands

Top competitors

RECENT BUSINESS HISTORY
Annual gross sales volume for last three to five years
- in dollars
- in units
- by SKU
- by distribution channel

Annual net profits for last three to five years
Amount spent on advertising over the last three to five years
Description and history of manufacturing facilities, distribution facilities, sales
    force/organization, showrooms
Major competitors

COLLATERAL MATERIALS
Name of advertising, public relations, promotion agencies
Copies of price lists, brochures, promotional materials depicting the company's
    products
Audited financial results such as annual reports

RETAIL CUSTOMER INFORMATION
Three to five largest retail customers, sometimes by brand
- type of retail account
- address
- phone number
- name of buyer

Last year's wholesale volume with each top retail account
Summary of current distribution by % of sales volume in each channel, with
    largest customers in each

FINANCIAL AND CREDIT INFORMATION
Insurance
- type
- amount of insurance
- names of insurance companies
- policy numbers

Type of business (corporation, sole proprietorship, etc.)
Credit rating or other credit references

Continued Next Page

Figure 9 Continued

Bank references
- name
- address
- phone number
- contact person

Federal tax I.D. number

Litigation currently involved in, if any

OTHER BUSINESS INFORMATION

Description of quality control procedures

Description of in-house design and artwork capability

LICENSING HISTORY

List of current licenses held with the prospective property holder

List of current licenses held with other property holders
- contact information
- number of years held

Annual wholesale dollar volume of similar licensed products, if any

Reason for interest in prospective property

PLAN FOR THE PROPOSED LICENSED PRODUCT LINE

Trademarks to be used

Products to be made

Territory to be covered

Estimated manufacturer's price per unit

Product samples of similar products to those proposed

Retail accounts where licensed products will be sold

Timing of sample completion, production, product launch, shipping and other marketing dates

Collateral materials and promotional plans
- trade and consumer advertising
- in-store materials
- co-op advertising funds
- sales incentives

Trade shows where product line will be exhibited

Amount of advertising, promotion and merchandising funds

Materials (or drafts) showing products incorporating the property
- catalogs
- brochures
- advertisements
- price lists

Names and addresses of sub-contractors or manufacturing plants where each product will be made

Financial forecasts of gross sales and units for each line for two to three years (or the number of years proposed for the license)

OTHER

Any other information that will help demonstrate the licensee's ability to successfully market the product

Other trade contacts, in addition to retail, bank and licensor references

Note: Few licensee evaluation forms contain every element listed here, but all elements are contained in some forms. Exact contents of the evaluation form depends on the licensor's objectives.

Source: The Licensing Letter; EPM Communications

TIMING

A number of timing issues arise during the planning stages of a licensing effort. First, when is the appropriate time to launch the property? Most film licensors premiere licensed merchandise two to four weeks before the film's opening, hoping to make film-goers aware of the movie and increase its opening-day box-office take; a few prefer to tease the property by releasing select products several months prior to the film's premiere. (Most retailers as of 2002 allow film-related products only six weeks on shelves; in Europe, the opportunity is closer to four weeks.) The licensor of a corporate trademark might time its initial introduction to an anniversary, a consumer promotion or an important industry trade show.

Owners of television-based properties usually wait until the TV series becomes established in the ratings (at least the beginning of the second season) before they launch products; if merchandise reaches retailers too early and does not sell, store buyers are unlikely to give it another chance later. Some property owners encourage licensees of key categories such as publishing to market merchandise early, however, since these products help create awareness and increase the chance that the show itself will find an audience. If a television show is based on a recent successful film (especially one with a toy line in place), licensees may launch products day-and-date with the premiere of the show.

Introducing many products at the same time may make the biggest statement at retail, especially for an event-driven license or one that is already well known among consumers. The National Basketball Development League, a new minor league the NBA introduced in 2001, launched a full line of products in conjunction with the league's first games.

On the other hand, staggering introductions maintains the property's longevity and is a more effective way to test new strategies. A marketing-heavy retail exclusive may bring significant awareness to a property at its launch and allow it to build a track record upon which the program can build in later roll-outs.

Another timing issue that affects launch dates has to do with the roles of certain product categories, a few of which drive most licensing programs. Licensors of new fashion labels will often inaugurate the core apparel categories, which form the program's foundation, before focusing on secondary merchandise lines such as scarves, eyewear, hosiery, jewelry or footwear. A corporate property often launches with the brand-extension categories closest to the core brand (such as other food products for a food or beverage brand, leather accessories for a footwear brand).

For a children's action-entertainment property, the master toy licensee devotes significant funds to advertising, thereby encouraging sales of other merchandise. Meanwhile, products such as publishing, home video and videogames help establish juvenile entertainment properties because they enhance the child's interaction with the characters and storyline. These licensees are signed early and appear at retail closer to the property's debut than other categories.

Selling seasons also play a role in the timing of product introductions. For a fashion brand, it makes sense to debut a line at the beginning of a recognized selling season (spring, fall, resort or holiday), rather than at an off time when retailers are not buying much merchandise. Similarly, consumers can purchase as much as 70% of all toys based on a given license during the December holiday season, so premiering a toy line in January may not be optimal. More toy makers are experimenting with January or spring releases to break through the clutter, however, or with a limited selection available during the holiday and a greater roll-out the following spring.

Of course, for licensors of seasonal properties (those with short windows of opportunity tied to Christmas, Halloween or Easter), timing is even more critical. Products must be on store shelves six weeks prior to Christmas or at least three weeks prior to Halloween, for example, or they will lose significant sales opportunities.

Lead times — the time required for products to get to market — also affect a property's launch and rollout. Length of contract negotiations vary, as do requirements for product development and manufacturing (as little as three months for soft goods, as much as a year or more for hard goods). Imported merchandise takes longer to reach retail shelves than merchandise produced domestically.

Licensors must seek potential licensees far ahead of not only the products' introduction to consumers but also their debut to the trade. Licensees need to have products or prototypes ready to show to retailers at industry conventions such as Toy Fair in February or MAGIC (for apparel), in February and August. This adds another six months to the total time between signing the licensee and the products' retail appearance. (Most licensors and licensees present their lines and properties to major retail accounts prior to these shows, extending the lead time even more.)

Videogames, computer software, footwear, perfume, some food items and toys require some of the longest lead times and therefore are typically signed earlier than other categories, depending on the property, while apparel and paper goods can be added later and arrive at stores quickly.

Licensors, especially of entertainment properties, should keep in mind that the characteristics of the entire franchise affect strategic decision-making at the property's launch. Whether there will be subsequent home videos or television series might determine whether film-based merchandise is launched all at once or held back in favor of extending the property's life. A property that is recognized from previous media vehicles will lend itself to a different strategy than a brand-new property.

Finally, the age of the target audience plays into the launch strategy. A fashion or entertainment property for teens can often withstand the availability of a multitude of products at once (as long as there is no perception of oversaturation or overcommercialization), since they are inherently short-lived, while a preschool property associated with too many products may be viewed as undesirable.

Many licensors test products with their most avid target market before moving out to general retail. The cost of reaching this market is low and the chances of success are high, so it is a low-risk way to see if product licensing might be possible and, if so, to build an initial track record. Cartoon Network tested Samurai Jack figures on its website before expanding into retail merchandise; Gateway Computer sold cowhide-spotted computer accessories and stationery items first to employees and in its dedicated customer catalogs (developing most of the products through a single licensee rather than signing a full roster), before launching a broad licensing effort.

Timing—when to launch, when to expand and when to cut back—is not an exact science and can be one of the most difficult aspects of a licensing strategy to get right. The objective, with any program, is to balance demand and supply throughout the life of the property. The rule of thumb for a launch is to wait until consumer demand is evident; nothing can kill a property like having too many products on the market too early. Retailers are impatient with licensed merchandise that does not sell, sometimes giving it as little as three weeks to prove itself.

MEDIA AND ENTERTAINMENT VEHICLES

If a property will be around for a long time, licensors need to plan how to maintain awareness in customers' minds. For entertainment properties — and other types of properties as well — one method is to create new entertainment and media vehicles. These include books, comic strips, comic books, films, sequels, home videos, television series, Internet entertainment series and interactive games.

Not only do these entertainment extensions help retain the interest of the property's existing customers, they also enlarge the audience. The re-release of the Star Wars trilogy in 1997 brought many new fans to the property, including children of people who experienced the original releases starting in 1977. The publication of a series of original novels in the early 1990s was even more instrumental in rejuvenating the property.

Entertainment support can be extensive throughout the life of an entertainment property. The Japanese children's character Doraemon has been supported by 23 feature films, a Doraemon-painted race car and other themed sports events, more than 60 compilation comic books and short stories (the property started as a comic strip in a magazine in the 1970s), and 1,800 hours' worth of animated television.

These types of entertainment extensions help sell more licensed product and more core product. When the PBS TV series based on the Clifford the Big Red Dog books went on the air in fall 2001, monthly sales of the original books doubled, while sales of licensed merchandise (exclusive of books and videos) reached more than $100 million at retail in six months. Extensions also give licensors and licensees the opportunity to launch more merchandise; manufacturers associated with the first Lord of the Rings film planned to introduce additional merchandise upon the debut of the home video and DVD versions of the movie.

Non-entertainment licenses that have used media or entertainment to freshen their properties include retailers, celebrities, magazine titles and fashion designers that have lauched music CDs or magazines to extend awareness. For example, Cosmopolitan magazine issued music CDs containing music that appeals to its readers, while Martha Stewart released a CD containing spooky music to be played as trick-or-treaters come to the door on Halloween. Fashion brand FUBU created a whole division for music and other media called FB Entertainment.

Some entertainment licenses are being introduced as multimedia properties, rather than starting in one medium and moving on to others. Jimmy Neutron: Boy Genius, a Nickelodeon property, was planned for Internet, TV, film and other media from the beginning.

PROMOTIONAL SUPPORT

Promotions prolong the life of all types of properties; some promotional activity is associated with the core brand, while other activity is directed specifically at the licensed products. Promotions surrounding entertainment properties are often associated with the introduction of a new product line or entertainment vehicle or with a significant anniversary. Other opportunities arise simply because there is a natural fit between the property and a promotional partner, as illustrated by a 2001 effort in which Homer Simpson of The Simpsons served as spokescharacter for Pentium processors; ads showed what would happen if the normally dim-witted character had a Pentium chip in his brain.

Sports properties are often promoted in conjunction with championship or All-Star games; being in a bowl game can significantly increase sales for licensed collegiate products and is a good hook for promotion. Fashion labels benefit from extra marketing activity at the start of a new season or to celebrate a new style, or when the designer wins a high-profile award. Promotions for corporate properties can be tied in with advertising that backs the core brand or with an anniversary of a brand, product or advertising icon. Artists may promote a new group of designs, an award or images donated for charitable purposes.

Promotional activity can be broad and frequent. To continue the Doraemon example cited above, that property has been the focus of tie-ins with phone, toy, chemical, transportation, food, retail, theme park, publishing, insurance, auto, photography and banking companies, among other partners. All the media and promotional activities based on a property work together to keep the property fresh and in the forefront of consumers' minds, and to increase the audience's or fan base's personal connection with the property.

Promotional activity is especially important to extend the life of a property that has experienced a faddish period and is on the decline. 4Kids Entertainment planned tie-ins with companies such as Rexall Sundown (vita-

Figure 10
SAMPLE GRID FOR FINANCIAL FORECASTING
PRE-SCHOOL ENTERTAINMENT PROPERTY

PRODUCT CATEGORY	YEAR 1	YEAR 2	YEAR 3	YEAR 4	YEAR 5
Accessories	$0,000.00	$0,000.00	$0,000.00	$0,000.00	$0,000.00
Apparel	$0,000.00	$0,000.00	$0,000.00	$0,000.00	$0,000.00
Domestics	$0,000.00	$0,000.00	$0,000.00	$0,000.00	$0,000.00
Housewares	$0,000.00	$0,000.00	$0,000.00	$0,000.00	$0,000.00
Infant Products	$0,000.00	$0,000.00	$0,000.00	$0,000.00	$0,000.00
Music/Video	$0,000.00	$0,000.00	$0,000.00	$0,000.00	$0,000.00
Publishing	$0,000.00	$0,000.00	$0,000.00	$0,000.00	$0,000.00
Stationery/Paper	$0,000.00	$0,000.00	$0,000.00	$0,000.00	$0,000.00
Toys/Games	$0,000.00	$0,000.00	$0,000.00	$0,000.00	$0,000.00
Videogames/Software	$0,000.00	$0,000.00	$0,000.00	$0,000.00	$0,000.00
Other	$0,000.00	$0,000.00	$0,000.00	$0,000.00	$0,000.00
TOTAL	**$0,000.00**	**$0,000.00**	**$0,000.00**	**$0,000.00**	**$0,000.00**

STEP 1: Find historical sales figures for comparable properties. Make sure you know if the figure is for retail or wholesale and for what time period.

STEP 2: Estimate the lifespan of your property, and determine what sales levels it will be able to generate once the program gets under way, in comparison to the historical examples.

STEP 3: Based on step 2 and your anticipated growth rate, fill in total expected retail sales for each of years 2 through 5 in the bottom line of the spreadsheet.

STEP 4: Estimate what percentage of total retail sales is likely to be attributable to each product category targeted. Apply these percentages to the total retail sales for each year to fill in the blanks for likely retail sales for each product category.

STEP 5: Figure out wholesale sales by applying average retail markups for each product category using the formula:

WHOLESALE = RETAIL X (1 - MARKUP)

If markup is unknown, use 50% (e.g. wholesale is approximately half of retail), a good rule of thumb.

STEP 6: Apply average royalty rates for each product category to the wholesale volume in each category to determine royalty income. Use average royalty rates in Chapter 7 if exact rates are unknown. Add up royalty income for all product categories to determine total royalty income for each of years 2 through 5.

STEP 7: For year one, estimate total advances likely for each category, given the number of licensees and products planned. Year 1 income is from advances only.

Source: The Licensing Letter; EPM Communications

mins), Kellog (cereal), and The Learning Company (software), among others, to keep interest strong for Pokémon after it had peaked.

On the other hand, a promotion can serve as a departure point for a new property. The little-known comic book character Jingle Belle tied in with the online retailer WickedCoolStuff.com for a holiday promotion that featured the first licensed Jingle Belle merchandise.

Chapter 12 discusses promotional activity in more detail.

FRESH DESIGNS AND PRODUCTS

No matter how many media events or high-profile promotions surround a property, licensed goods will not perform well over time if they remain the same year after year. Adding new products to the merchandise mix is a critical way to keep a property alive. Many fashion labels start with apparel and accessories, then expand into home furnishings or personal care products; children's book characters with videos, CD-ROMs, music, plush and publishing, then board games, apparel and accessories; corporate trademarks with collectibles based on nostalgic advertising images, then apparel; artists with stationery and gifts, then tabletop items or domestics. These additions encourage repeat purchases, bring in new customers and provide opportunities for advertising and promotions.

Even within existing product lines, it is essential to add new designs each season. Licensees need to update apparel, accessories and footwear to reflect fashion trends; introduce new toy items so children can add to their collections; and develop home furnishings to incorporate seasonal colors. Any category can become stale if not enhanced by new designs. Disney Consumer Products introduced new apparel in 2000 that used Mickey Mouse's head as a design element, among other novel approaches, a departure from previous treatments that portrayed Mickey as a character.

CO-BRANDING, CROSS-LICENSING AND SUB-BRANDING

Another method of extending a property's life is to introduce it to new audiences through cross-licensing (combining more than one property on a single item) and co-branding (linking two properties or brands, typically a licensor's and a licensee's, on a single item). This approach targets the customers of both properties and perhaps encourages some fans of one to become fans of the other as well.

The differences between cross-licensing and co-branding can be subtle. Both are wide-ranging in terms of the properties involved. Examples of cross-licensed products include:

- Coca-Cola and the Andy Warhol Foundation combined for a cross-licensing program with merchandise featuring Warhol's artwork depicting Coca-Cola bottles.
- Chevrolet and Betty Boop joined together for a program whose images consist of Betty interacting with Chevrolet "muscle cars."

Co-branded products treat the licensee's property or brand as equal to the licensor's:

- Designer Paul Frank, with the character Julian, and Warner Bros., with Tweety, both entered into co-branding agreements with Sanrio in which Sanrio stationery and gift items feature both its own Hello Kitty and Frank's or Warner's characters.
- Barbie has been the focus of several co-branding deals; one product features Barbie in a McDonald's restaurant.
- The NBA and clothing manufacturer FUBU created a co-branded line to appeal to young urban consumers, who are fans of both properties. FUBU also licensed the character Fat Albert for a co-branded line.
- The Got Milk? campaign, from the California Milk Processor's Board, is cross-licensed with the "milk mustache," owned by Dairy Management and MilkPEP. Their advertising campaigns are co-branded with licenses including The Simpsons, SpongeBob SquarePants, Alfred E. Neuman (of MAD Magazine), the Three Stooges and others.
- Rugrats vitamins are co-branded with both the Rugrats and the Centrum name. Centrum gives the product credibility as a health item, while Rugrats gives it kid-appeal.
- Best Foods licensed Nestlé for a co-branded line of peanut butter featuring both the Nestlé and its own Skippy logos.
- Hasbro licensed the Eggo Waffles brand for an Eggo Waffles Easy-Bake Oven.
- Jeep-licensed mountain boards feature the Jeep name as well as the licensee's name, MSB. While this is not typical for Jeep licensed products, the MSB name is important among consumers in the snowboarder market.

Creating a sub-brand, like co-branding and cross-licensing, can achieve the goal of extending a property's audience. Timex has several sub-brands, including Expedition and TMX. Each has its own licensing effort, targeted at a specific demographic group.

SELECTING LICENSEES

After creating their overall licensing plan, licensors can select licensees within the context of the program's strategic direction. Potential licensees fill out a licensee evaluation form that covers many of the points discussed below; the information helps licensors screen the applicants. *Figure 9 (page 95-96)* outlines the basic contents of a typical application, although it should be noted that actual forms vary in length and depth depending on the licensor's desire for specific details. (Licensees sometimes initiate the licensing relationship, but the process thereafter is the same.)

On occasion, licensors ask potential licensees to submit a proposal or fill out an application as a first step in the process. While this method might save time for the licensor, it is not a common-sense way to proceed. Licensees need enough information to be able to create a reasonable proposal that is good for them and for the property. There should be a certain amount of give-and-take and information-sharing between the licensee and licensor before the licensee fills out the application or creates a proposal to submit.

It is also important that licensors understand their licensees' businesses before committing to a particular category or to specific licensees within that category. Many licensors do not take the time to really research what their licensees need from a licensing deal or what benefits and risks licensing holds for them. The best deals spring out of a relationship between a licensee and licensor that understand each other's objectives and business strategies.

CRITERIA FOR SELECTION

Licensors evaluate potential licensees against several criteria before ultimately deciding which manufacturers to add to a property's roster.

The Product Line

Licensors should ensure that the products proposed by the prospective licensee fit with the property's strategy and are compatible with its characteristics. Considerations include the product's design, the materials used in its manufacture, its quality and the way the property is incorporated into it. It also helps if the proposed licensed products have some unique characteristics that will make them stand out in the marketplace. Many property owners request samples of items similar to those proposed.

The Potential Licensee's Track Record

Does the licensee have experience manufacturing and selling products similar to the proposed line? Licensors should examine these items and others the licensee has produced. Were the design and product quality up to the licensor's standards? If the licensee has experience marketing licensed products, what were the results?

Manufacturing

Licensors should determine whether manufacturing will be done in-house or through a subcontractor or sublicensee and whether the products will be imported. Many property owners recommend paying a visit to the manufacturing facilities. If a third party will handle production, the licensor should demand as much information about that company as possible to ascertain that it is capable of satisfactory work. Licensors should also make sure the licensee or its affiliates can meet expected demand.

Distribution

With few exceptions, a licensee's existing relationships with retailers and the strength of its sales force are important considerations for licensors (although if a product is strong enough or the fit between product and property appropriate enough, distribution may follow). At the same time, red flags should pop up if past experience shows that a potential licensee may approach unauthorized distribution channels (e.g., selling to Kmart for an upscale brand or exporting when it has domestic rights only).

Long-Term Capabilities

Licensees should be capable of introducing new, innovative and fashion-forward product lines each season. Some property owners look for manufacturers that can expand into additional product categories if initial merchandise sells well.

How Many Other Licenses Does The Manufacturer Hold?

Does the licensee intend to treat the property as one of its primary brands or does it maintain a stable of licenses? Fashion licensors often prefer the first alternative, since they seek a significant advertising and promotional commitment from their licensees. On the other hand, entertainment licensors that view advances as a primary objective may opt for a licensee that pays the required advance, even if it stockpiles the license and does not produce merchandise. (This is becoming less common; entertainment companies often view licensed products as more valuable in a marketing sense than for straight revenue-generation, although both are still important goals.)

Marketing Plans For The Property

Some licensors, especially from the fashion, art and corporate trademark sectors, desire licensees who will actively promote the brand; some may require this type of marketing support. A licensor of a short-term entertainment property may consider this factor less important, although in many cases licensees' (especially toy companies') advertising is critical to the program and a prerequisite for other licensees to sign up. Many licensors also demand their licensees be willing to contribute a fee or a percentage of sales to a central marketing fund administered by the licensor.

Financial Strength

Is the company financially stable? Specifically, does it have the cash flow to achieve all it proposes as far as marketing and manufacturing the licensed line? Licensors demand bank and credit references to help them evaluate a manufacturer's financial status.

Reputation As A Vendor

Licensors ask potential licensees for retailer references to determine if the manufacturers' retail customers value them as vendors. Important factors include whether the licensee delivers products on time, maintains a reputation for quality products, builds strong long-term relationships with retailers and provides responsive customer service.

Sales Forecasts

The manufacturer's sales forecasts for the proposed products should be in line with the licensor's expectations. They should also be realistic given the track record and manufacturing and marketing capabilities of the licensee.

What Is The Potential Licensee Willing To Pay?

The willingness to pay desired royalties, advances and guarantees is usually not the sole criterion in the selection process. In cases where all else is equal, however, one licensee's willingness to pay more may help the licensor decide. For short-term entertainment properties, price may be one of the most important considerations, especially if revenues are the licensor's primary goal and/or several manufacturers are competing for the license.

Increasingly, the payment structure for a license is viewed as a total package, with royalties and other monetary payment balanced by marketing support, product development investments and other licensee contributions that will help the line succeed. While the licensor wants the optimal total package, the final deal has to be one with which the licensee can live given its sales forecasts for the line and its overall financial situation.

Personnel

A good relationship between the licensee's and licensor's staffs will help the partnership succeed. The licensor should feel confident that a potential licensee will communicate any problems and that its employees will treat the licensor's assets with care.

Systems and Tracking

Licensors are increasingly looking for licensees that have systems in place to track the success of the licensed line. Sophisticated licensees closely monitor sales by channel, geographic region and other criteria, which helps them respond to the marketplace quickly and devote their resources properly. Not only is such a licensee better positioned for success, but it will be able to give licensors the detailed distribution and sales reports they desire to make their own programs more effective.

Ethical Issues

Certain intangibles and business philosophies also come into play. Some licensors are looking for licensees that do not exploit Asian workers, for example; the University of Iowa is one licensor that has canceled well over 100 licensing contracts due to human rights violations, failure to disclose specifics about their business or not signing the institution's conduct code. Various colleges and universities are on a similar mission, as are some licensors from other sectors. Kathie Lee Gifford, in her apparel deal with Wal-Mart, has seen the negative ramifications that human rights issues can bring to a property. Other ethical issues may also come into play as part of the licensee selection process.

LICENSING VS. IN-HOUSE PRODUCTION

Some licensors eschew licensing altogether in some or all categories in favor of in-house production. Small markets, a category's or company's financial picture and other factors may determine that producing an item in-house—i.e., sourcing it internally, perhaps buying merchandise from a vendor outright, instead of licensing—is more viable than a traditional licensing structure.

Footwear brand LUGZ originally produced its apparel in-house and was satisfied with its sales levels. Yet it ultimately turned to licensing as a means of gaining expertise from companies with a long track record in the apparel industry; it felt its clothing sales would never expand beyond a certain level without this added know-how. Toy maker Fisher-Price launched a branded apparel line that it handled in-house at first and sold via direct-response channels to maximize its control over the initiative. It was manufactured by sister company Mattel Direct.

Several fashion labels, from Robert Stock to B.U.M., have opted for 100% licensing, while others such as Quiksilver prefer in-house control. The latter has purchased entire subsidiaries in new categories rather than licensing those products out to third parties.

LICENSEE PRESENTATIONS

When selling a property to potential licensees, licensors should outline all the elements in their licensing strategy clearly. This includes offering a synopsis of the property and its characteristics, an estimate of the size and attributes of its target audience and a description of graphic elements. A style guide, supplemented by other reference materials, shows licensees the logos and other elements available and presents some possibilities for product development.

Key selling points include the property's record of sales, either for the core product line or existing licensees' merchandise; ratings or theatrical box-office figures; any known interest from retailers (an increasingly important factor); advertising and promotional plans; and proposed media vehicles. The more professional and well-thought-out a licensor's presentation to potential licensees, the greater its chances of generating interest.

RETAILER PRESENTATIONS

Although licensees typically bear responsibility for selling licensed products to stores, licensors are increasingly called upon to make presentations to retailers as well. They may meet with retail executives nine months or so before the introduction of the licensed merchandise, to presell the property and smooth the licensees' path, or join their licensees on sales calls. Increasingly, they are meeting with retailers well in advance of the property's launch, even before signing a single licensee, to arrange exclusives or at least gauge their support. (This is especially true for entertainment properties, but is important for all sectors.)

Backing from a leading retailer can be the most important determining factor in attracting quality licensees. It can also dictate who the licensees will be, as some retailers participating in exclusives demand that their preferred vendors be added to the roster, or at least suggest partners with which they have a good relationship.

It is important that appropriate retail executives attend licensors' sales presentations. The chain's licensing point person is the key contact, but several buyers, managers and marketing executives may be involved in the decision-making process and all should hear the pitch. In addition, licensors and licensees — whether meeting with retailers together or separately — should be sure to deliver a consistent message about the property.

Because the retailer is such an important part of the licensing equation, many licensors and licensing agents have at least one executive on staff who is charged with servicing retailers on a full-time basis. This person should have retail experience and be able to identify and address retailers' needs.

Licensor-provided promotional support — including point-of-purchase materials, prefabricated displays and co-op marketing dollars, often partially financed by licensees' contribution to a central marketing fund (CMF) — helps encourage retailers to back a license; factors such as these are nearly as important as the attributes and track record of the property itself.

ADMINISTERING THE LICENSING PROGRAM

Creating and implementing a licensing program is only the first step. Licensors or their agents must still administer it on a day-to-day basis. Most observers recommend hiring at least one full-time person for this task (or sometimes many more, depending on the specifics of the program) if the licensing effort is being handled in-house. Some licensors, particularly in the corporate arena, rely on executives from other departments to add licensing to their job description. In these cases, licensing tends to drop to the bottom of that person's list of priorities.

Day-to-day adminstrative duties include approving products at various stages of the design and manufacturing process, not just for the first line of merchandise but for everything developed under the licensing agreement; collecting royalties and monitoring quarterly royalty statements; seeking out and counteracting infringement; announcing new initiatives to licensees and retailers; and, especially, keeping lines of communication open on an ongoing basis. It is essential that licensors relay any changes in the property or its strategy — promotional time frames, movie release dates, concert tour schedules, injuries to athlete endorsers, brand advertising schedules, design changes, marketing themes — to both licensees and retailers. These developments may greatly affect their businesses and the more time they have to react, the better they will be able to resolve any problems.

Product approvals are a time-consuming and important part of the daily administration of the licensing program. Each new product in the line is approved, as dictated in the licensing contract and by the licensor's need to maintain control of merchandise quality. The approval process varies by licensor, but typically requires okays at least at the concept stage (drawings or models), the pre-manufacturing stage (prototypes) and at the manufactured stage (final samples). In some categories, materials must be approved, such as fabrics or embroideries for apparel. Some licensors have five or more steps in their required approval process, each defined according to their own parameters.

Continually refreshing a property is another part of the administrative process. This entails creating style guides (on CD and/or in print) each season, sometimes with interim style guides for specific reasons. Back-to-school product linked to a property being launched or introduced in a new form for the Thanksgiving/Christmas/Hanukkah holiday season, may need its own style guide to allow back-to-school licensees to create merchandise coherent with the holiday products yet not divulging too much in advance.

The computer, the Internet and e-mail have streamlined many of the administrative details associated with licensing. Database management increases efficiency in marketing to the trade and consumers. Licensor websites allow licensees to peruse images, while e-mail can be used to transmit camera-ready artwork. E-mail also eases communication, especially with overseas partners, since it reduces language and time complications. Licensors can post any changes to the property or any information that affects the licensing program on their websites, or send e-mail alerts or newsletters to their partners. E-mail is also effective for initially soliciting potential licensees in new categories.

Of course, automation does not replace the need for face-to-face meetings, which account for an enormous amount of time but are a necessary part of a program's administrative requirements. Meetings with international agents, meetings with licensees (individually and in "licensee summits"), attending conventions, visiting licensees' and potential licensees' offices and factories, and traveling to retailer headquarters are just some in a long list of meetings that make up a licensor's week.

The number of people a licensor must devote to administering the program depends on what business the licensor is in, whether an agent is involved with the program, how many properties are licensed, and other factors. An artist may handle all licensing solo or with one additional person; a corporate licensor may have two to 10 people devoted entirely to licensing; an entertainment studio may have a staff of dozens.

Setting up a full-time staff dedicated to licensing signals a property owner's commitment to licensing as a business tool. Licensors, especially in the corporate sector, must decide where this department fits within its overall structure. Do licensing staffers report to marketing or to the brand managers? Are they considered support for the product development team? There is no universally accepted organizational placement for a licensing department, but these questions must be answered at the corporate level.

FINANCIAL FORECASTING

Predicting licensing income is not easy, given the vast number of variables with which a licensor must contend. This has become even more true as the financial aspects of licensing deals become more complex and flexible. (See Chapter 7 for more on royalties and other money matters.)

Financial forecasts depend on the strategic decisions outlined in this chapter. The property's target audience, the number of products available, when those products are introduced, how fast the program rolls out and the property's total expected lifespan all play a role in determining a license's financial value over time, as does the timing of advance and guarantee payments and expected royalty flow. The assumptions used in creating a financial forecast should parallel the property's planned strategy.

One reasonable way to start estimating potential revenues for a property is to analyze retail sales levels generated by comparable licensing programs. A mass-market fashion brand might be compared to Sasson or Bonjour, a children's book property to Clifford, Curious George or Arthur, or a food/kitchen-related brand to Pillsbury.

It is not easy to find retail sales figures on most properties, especially if they are not "homeruns." Licensors can start by researching whatever numbers are widely available through an online search of relevant citations in consumer and, especially, trade magazines. *Women's Wear Daily* publishes estimates for women's apparel labels, *Playthings* for toys and entertainment, *Sporting Goods Business* for sporting goods brands and leagues, *HFN* for home-related brands, and *Gifts & Decorative Accessories* for artists. *The Licensing Letter* also includes such information.

The licensor can then compare the potential of its property with the sales generated by similar properties, trying to be as realistic as possible. Most new properties are not "the next Mickey Mouse" or "the next Pokémon" or "the next Coca-Cola"; the expected revenues for a given licensor's property are likely to be a fraction of the totals for properties about which retail sales figures are widely circulated.

To estimate annual royalties, the licensor divides retail sales figures in half to estimate wholesale volume. Retail margins vary, but halving retail levels to arrive at a wholesale figure is an accepted rule of thumb if actual margins are not known. (For a wholly mass-distributed program, margins of 10%-20% are more realistic; thus, multiplying retail sales by 80%-90% will result in a wholesale estimate.) Multiplying wholesale sales by the average royalty rate (see Chapter 7) gives the licensor an estimate of royalty income.

If a licensor forecasts that its property will reach $50 million in annual retail sales, wholesale sales would be about $25 million. Assuming a royalty of 7%, annual revenues to the licensor — before agency commissions — would be $1.75 million. Revenues for the first year of a property are not indicative of eventual sales; a licensor can count on advances and possibly guarantees, but royalties are more likely to start accruing a year or two later, depending on the timing of the launch and the length of the product-development process.

Estimating a property's economic potential is not a science. The point of coming up with a reasonable forecast is to help the licensor determine if launching the program is worthwhile and/or to help garner financing. The process may also highlight areas in the licensing strategy that need rethinking. Forecasting best-case, worst-case and realistic scenarios is a good idea, since it will offer a glimpse of the implications of each. It should be noted that being too optimistic in forecasting raises unrealistic expectations and can make a property seem to be a failure—and to be a failure in the eyes of licensees and retailers who planned for higher levels—even if it generates strong total sales. Expectations must be in line with the nature of the property and not with successful competitive properties that may have different attributes.

Figure 10 (page 101) provides a sample format and procedure for forecasting licensing revenues; the product categories, number of years and other specifics will vary depending on the property.

Total royalty revenue for a property may be split among various partners. Property creators may share with studios on an entertainment property, for example, or there may be several underlying rights holders, depending on the history of the property. This will be discussed further in Chapter 7.

USING A LICENSING AGENT

For new licensors, agents offer instant expertise: They can negotiate contracts, recognize fair royalty rates and identify the best licensees and product categories. They can also help a licensor develop a strategy based on their experience of what works and what does not. Agents make sure licensors get paid, push through timely product approvals, help create designs and stylebooks and assist with most of the duties the licensor would otherwise have to do in-house. Agents also maintain contacts within the industry, which is attractive to new licensors. Licensing is a business of relationships; it takes time to develop working partnerships with potential licensees.

Most licensing agents receive approximately 35% to 40% of all royalty income — although commissions range from as low as 15% (rarely, for well-established programs) to as high as 55% — including advances and guarantees. Many agents that handle corporate trademarks require an upfront fee to demonstrate good faith and pay for expenses in the event that the property owner decides not to go ahead with its licensing plans, but agents' income in most other sectors is dependent primarily on licensing revenues. An increasing number of agents, particularly in the corporate sector, charge retainers of several thousand dollars (typically $3,000 to $20,000) per month. Some agents add fees for consulting outside the scope of the licensor-agent agreement or for additional duties such as PR or creating a style guide (the latter on a cost-plus basis).

The cost of retaining an agent is balanced by the licensor's ability to avoid hiring a full-time, in-house licensing staff, or can at least reduce the size of that staff. A good agent is also likely to bring in more revenue than an in-house licensor could, especially if new to the business. If setting up an in-house licensing operation overseen by at least one full-time manager costs $250,000 for the first year and an agent charges a commission of 25% for its services, a licensor would have to generate royalties of at least $1 million (about $10 million in wholesale sales of licensed merchandise at a 10% royalty) for the cost of the agent to exceed the amount required for the in-house division:

$$25\% \times \$1 \text{ million} = \$250,000$$

In this hypothetical scenario, if expected royalties are less than $1 million, it is more cost-effective to retain a licensing agent. (Of course, costs vary widely.) Neophyte licensors often rely on an agent to launch the program and maintain it in its early years, then take it in-house after it is established.

Contracts with agents usually cover a period of two to three years, often with an option to renew if the program meets performance criteria. Most licensors retain agents on an exclusive basis to handle all categories, but some hire them to handle certain categories, while taking responsibility for others in-house or through a master agent. Binney & Smith retained Nancy Bailey & Associates to handle its Crayola brand, which already had numerous internally administered deals, for expansion into personal care, food and children's home furnishings.

Licensors that decide not to use an outside licensing agent typically cite their need for more control over their licensing effort. In addition, since agents have many clients—which often are competitors, particularly in the case of art or entertainment agents — conflicts of interest can present themselves. And, as more agents diversify, for example representing both licensees and licensors (see the section on the changing role of the licensing agent, which follows), the opportunity for conflicts can grow.

SELECTING A LICENSING AGENT

A number of directories, including the *EPM Licensing Letter Sourcebook*, list licensing agents and the properties they handle. Licensors use a range of criteria to select the one that is suitable for them.

Licensors of corporate trademarks would probably not opt for an agent focusing on sports or entertainment, since typical licensing tactics for those properties differ from those for a corporate program. While the mechanics of licensing are the same from one property type to another, strategies and contacts usually vary. Similarly, an agent that manages mostly short-term properties is not a good match for a licensor that envisions slow, steady growth for its brand. Licensing agents are increasingly specialized, focusing solely on art or corporate properties, for example, but there are some full-service agents. In any case, their experience varies.

Most licensors consider an agent's track record a good indicator of future performance. Licensors should feel free to talk to the agent's present and past clients about their relationship with the agent and about what strategies the agent recommended. Personal relationships are as important between licensors and agents as they are between licensors and licensees. Does the agent forthrightly answer the licensor's questions? Offer adequate support services? Communicate openly? Does the agent's way of doing business fit with the licensor's? If a licensor's intuition warns against a particular agent, it is usually good advice to explore other options.

Some licensors evaluate agents, in part, based on the number of properties they represent. Certain agents handle a stable of properties. They keep a relatively large staff and have experience with different types of clients. They most likely have built relationships with a variety of companies throughout the business and maintain economies of scale by presenting several properties at once to appropriate licensees.

Other agencies handle one or just a few properties. They may have a small staff or operate a sole proprietorship. These companies are able to devote a large percentage of their time to servicing their clients and their income depends on the success of each client's licensing effort.

There is no right or wrong way to choose an agent; the licensor's objectives determine which criteria are most important, while the agent's proposal, including costs and how it would handle the property, dictate whether there is a fit.

THE CHANGING ROLE OF THE LICENSING AGENT

As the market for licensed goods becomes more competitive, with more properties and less shelf space, the role of the licensing agent has evolved from one predominately of sales to one of brand management. Agents are increasingly asked to forge and maintain retail relationships, aid a property with marketing support and help gain distribution, among other tasks.

Meanwhile, as more licensors have opted to maintain their licensing activity in-house—particularly in the entertainment sector—rather than using an agent, traditional agents find themselves competing with the major studios and networks. As a result, they have had to change their businesses, adding consulting services, for example, becoming producers or coproducers of entertainment themselves (and thus becoming licensors in their own right), or becoming licensees as well as agents. There are fewer entertainment licensing agents in business today than 10 years ago; several agents have been purchased by corporations or studios, leaving fewer true independents. Most independent licensing agents specialize in the corporate or art sectors.

The Beanstalk Group, a leading corporate agency, is an example of how agencies are coping with the changing market. It has added a management consulting division; represents licensees for property acquisition as well as acting as an agent for corporate brand owners; purchased a portion of the advertising specialty company Ha-Lo, making it a licensee (such as for die-cast vehicles tied to the 20th James Bond film); and became a subsidiary of The Ford Motor Company.

Competition among agents has become so great that some are paying fees to licensors to secure the right to represent their properties. Fees can range from $10,000 to $1 million, depending on the property and the rights sought. This type of deal is not the norm, but examples have been on the rise around the world, particularly in the entertainment sector.

In corporate licensing, independent agents are working more often with brand managers within the licensor's company. These executives are starting to view licensing as a tactic, like PR and advertising, to support the brand, rather than as a low-priority afterthought.

CHAPTER 6

STRATEGIES FOR LICENSEES

Licensing is just one facet of a manufacturer's marketing strategy and should fit logically and comfortably within its overall business plan. Some licensees acquire a stable of properties in the hopes that a few will be homeruns, while others depend on one or a few licenses for a significant portion of their revenues over the long term. Others opt to do no licensing.

Many of the issues facing licensees are interrelated with those facing licensors, which are outlined in detail in Chapter 5.

SETTING OBJECTIVES

Licensing, as a marketing tool, can provide a manufacturer with a number of very different benefits, as discussed in Chapter 1, depending on the overriding corporate strategy. A licensee should think through its objectives for acquiring a license before deciding which properties to target or whether licensing is the right solution at all. The company's specific goals will dictate appropriate properties to evaluate and eliminate others from consideration.

If a licensee's objective is to attract a reliable pool of customers, it might opt for a property that has a measurable collector base — such as Elvis Presley, Star Trek or Campbell Soup — that it can count on to purchase new products. If it wants to gain the equity of a name its target customer has long recognized and valued, it might select from one of a number of corporate trademarks, fashion brands or classic characters that appeal to the same audience. If it wants shoppers to associate its merchandise with "fun," it might choose a Saturday morning cartoon or a film property such as Austin Powers. If it wants to increase sales dramatically over a short period and does not mind taking a risk, it might decide on a potentially blockbuster movie.

In any case, the property should offer a good fit with the licensee's products, in terms of demographic target, corporate philosophies and goals of the partners, and other factors. In addition, the licensee should not be afraid to say no if the financial parameters, or any parameters, do not make sense. Manufacturers should not risk more on a license than they can afford to lose.

WHAT LICENSORS WANT FROM THEIR LICENSEES

In order for a manufacturer to sell itself as a potential licensee for a given property, once it decides a specific license fits its goals, it must first understand the licensor's objectives.

Many licensors desire distribution, first and foremost. They want to sell products through as many appropriate retail channels as possible and they depend on their licensees to achieve this. Most expect potential licensees to have existing relationships with major retailers *before* they acquire the license. While some manufacturers hope to use a license as a point of entry into new distribution channels — and this is possible in some cases — it is more common for property owners to select a licensee because of its existing retail customer base.

As retailers' prominence in the licensing equation has grown, they have begun to have a say in which licensees are selected for a given property, especially when they help launch the property with an exclusive promotion and/or sales window. Manufacturers that have forged the best relationships with those retailers have the advantage over other companies.

Licensors seek manufacturers with the ability to create products that fit with their property's image in terms of price, quality, design and value and look for unique, fashion-forward products that reflect consumer tastes. They may also desire licensees with enough manufacturing capacity to allow them to expand into other categories if initial merchandise is successful.

Many licensors prefer, or even demand, licensees that are willing and able to commit to their brand and support it with advertising, promotion and sales activities. They want to know how important the licensed line will be relative to the manufacturer's other products and whether the licensed line will be emphasized on sales calls to retailers.

Such a commitment can be costly for a manufacturer. For a large line of home furnishings based on a designer name that is new to that category, the licensee's marketing investment can reach seven figures and the cost of getting the product to market can be hundreds of thousands of dollars more.

Licensors are also looking for monetary compensation from licensees, through royalties, guarantees or advances. Money is rarely the exclusive reason for selecting one licensee over another, but it certainly is one component of the decision.

The importance to the licensor of each criterion varies depending on its objectives. An entertainment company with a brand-new animated series or film may depend on advance money to help greenlight the production; a licensee's willingness to pay upfront will be a point in its favor. The owner of an established fashion brand may count on advertising and promotional contributions by licensees and would prefer a manufacturer that intends to treat the license as one of its primary brands and help build brand equity over the long term. The size of the guarantee would be secondary in this case. One of the main concerns of a corporate trademark licensor is the integrity of its brand; it may value the licensee's ability to create high-quality products above all else. The licensee's distribution network may be the deciding factor for an artist who has little ability to market products to major retailers and would rely on the licensee to do so.

Licensees may ask: If licensors want significant promotional dollars, large advances and guarantees and/or huge distribution networks, can a small company with limited resources become involved in licensing? In some cases, yes. A new licensee may be willing to commit to a large number of SKUs (stock-keeping units, the identifying numbers assigned to all retail products) within its category, in lieu of a high advance or guarantee. If a property owner is looking primarily for an extensive product presence at retail and can open doors for a licensee, it might give the nod to a small manufacturer willing to commit to a wide range of items over a large licensee who will pay but not ensure the same number of products.

Similarly, small licensees that lack a mass-market distribution network may be best positioned to sell to a particular retail niche. They might be willing to get on board early with an unproven license (thus helping the licensor meet its objectives of gaining exposure for the unknown entity). While the last option can be risky — there is no guarantee the property will be successful — the licensee's payments to the licensor are likely to be lower than for an established property, at least until sales take off.

A potential licensee might offer a unique product or design that fits exceptionally well with a given property, making it attractive even without significant marketing funds or distribution. Bedding and loungewear company Blue Moon was awarded a license, its first, for Roy Rogers based on its designs; the deal opened up new distribution channels for the company. A new company, HoneyTree, was able to acquire a license with Disney for Winnie the Pooh by proposing plastic Pooh-shaped squeeze bottles of honey, something that fit perfectly with the property and stood out from the competition.

LOCATING POTENTIAL PROPERTIES

Attending trade shows is one way to find out what properties are available for licensing and what products are licensed. An annual exposition sponsored by the International Licensing Industry Merchandisers Association (LIMA), held in June in New York City, is a showcase for licensors of many property types. It is helpful for locating entertainment and character, corporate trademark, artist, celebrity and a few sports licenses; some sectors, such as fashion, are not well-represented. Browsing this show will give licensees a good overview of the properties available in a given year and who handles them, as well as facilitating initial contacts with licensors and agents. Several similar, but smaller, expositions are springing up in other territories, including Europe, Latin America and Asia.

At industry trade shows, manufacturers sell their wares to retailers. These conventions are useful for licensees that want a sense of which properties are being licensed for specific categories. If a manufacturer is interested in fashion licensing, a staff member could attend one of several apparel-related trade shows held throughout the year, such as MAGIC. Trade shows exist for every industry; most trade publications list upcoming exhibitions, many of which highlight licensed products. In any year, there are well over 100 exhibitions of interest to the licensing community in the U.S. alone, as well as an increasing number of international shows. The Appendices at the back of this book list some of them.

Trade journals are also good sources for news about licensed properties. Licensing publications focus exclusively on this type of information, but nearly all consumer product-oriented trade magazines cover recent licensing developments within their industries and sell advertising to relevant licensors and/or licensees. For example, in a publication for the sporting goods industry, such as *Sporting Goods Business* or *Sporting Goods Dealer*, editorial coverage and advertisements contain licensing-related information on apparel, sports equipment, sports accessories, caps and footwear based on professional sports leagues, colleges, sports events, sporting goods brands, fashion labels, corporate trademarks (such as gun brands), and outdoors-related nonprofit groups. (See the Appendices for some of the licensing publications and journals covering consumer products categories where licensing is a factor.)

Another way to find out who handles specific properties is to peruse one of the licensing industry directories published by EPM Communications and other companies (see the Appendices). These books list agents, licensors and licensees, as well as the properties with which they are associated, and are updated annually. Joining a licensing organization such as LIMA and/or a trade group serving industries touched by licensing is also a way to generate contacts.

EVALUATING PROPERTIES

Potential licensees benefit from discovering as much as possible about a given property, including:

- the past sales history, if any, for other licensed products based on the property. Methods of determining such figures, in addition to information from the licensor, include TRSTS reports (a toy sales ranking from the NPD Group) or similar research for other categories, as well as trade magazine articles.

- the popularity of the property itself. Several measurement mechanisms exist, such as Nielsen ratings for TV shows, box-office receipts for films, and sales and market share figures for properties that are consumer products brands (e.g., Adidas).

- consumer awareness of the property, gauged by survey data such as Cartoon Q (research conducted by Marketing Evaluations), proprietary information such as focus group results or similar research.

- the specifics about the property itself. It is enlightening to read scripts, find out who the stars are in entertainment productions, peruse books or magazines on which properties are based, and examine advertising for fashions or corporate brands.

- artwork available. The property's visual look has to appeal to the licensee's customer base and look good when adapted to the licensee's specific products. Some properties may be very popular but do not translate well to 3D products, for example, or there may not be enough artwork available to create a whole home furnishings range.

Some licensors ask potential licensees to submit proposals for a licensed line before they open discussions and give them the particulars listed above. Manufacturers should demand as much information as possible about the property so they can decide whether they want to pursue the license and can submit a proposal that makes sense for them and for the property. If they are unable to get this information without creating a proposal first, perhaps the license is not right for them.

DEMOGRAPHICS

The demographic, psychographic and behavioral characteristics of the property's target audience — age, sex, income level, shopping habits — should match those of the licensee's customers. This is among the most important criteria to consider; creating a product tied to license that is not a good fit with the licensee's target consumer will not only lead to failure but may harm the company's image with its core customer.

FIT BETWEEN PROPERTY AND PRODUCT

The combination of the property and the product should make sense. A deal between NASCAR and WD-40 for licensed automotive lubricants and other aftermarket products represents a conceptual fit; many other properties would be out of place in this category. Foot massagers and shoes both fit well with the Dr. Scholl's brand, but hair accessories do not. Cosmetic accessories and hair-care products make sense for the Revlon brand; furniture does not. Plush toys are appropriate for Madeline; action figures are probably not. Keychains are a likely product for South Park; diamond jewelry is not. These examples seem to be common sense, but many licensed product lines have failed because they lacked a good fit between property and product. Some licensees conduct focus groups or other research to determine if their customers perceive a match.

CONSUMER AWARENESS

One of the benefits of licensing is the instant consumer awareness some properties bring to a manufacturer's product line; this is often the licensee's key objective for acquiring a license. The licensee should evaluate each property in terms of whether the company's target market is aware of it and likes it. If a manufacturer is considering a corporate trademark or fashion label, its customers should know the label exists and value its attributes. An older female target audience may not be as aware of an extreme sports brand as a younger male consumer would be. A brand-new TV property may lack consumer awareness; on the other hand, an extensively hyped film develops name recognition among many consumer segments even before it is released. An Internet or music property may be unknown to the general public but hot among a desirable consumer segment.

INTEREST FROM OTHER LICENSEES

Some manufacturers wait to sign on with a property until other key licensees are already on board. This gives them confidence, in part because it means the property will benefit from increased marketing support. Licensors often find that once the first three to five licensees are solidified, the rest follow easily.

While this may be a common sense way to do business in some situations—a children's backpack maker may want to know there is a major toy company linked to an entertainment property before it is willing to commit—it is not always viable. In some cases, the fit between a product and property makes sense regardless of whether other manufacturers are associated with the license. Waiting to ascertain other companies' interest may make a licensee lose a good opportunity.

PROMOTIONAL SUPPORT

Most licensees (and the retailers to which they sell) view the licensor's marketing plans for a property — whether packaged goods or retail promotions, fast food tie-ins, advertising, websites, events or sponsorships — among the most important factors in deciding which license to select. Some properties maintain built-in awareness, as discussed above, but virtually all require at least periodic boosts from marketing exposure.

Of course, a licensee cannot rely only on the licensor for exposure; it is responsible for marketing its own product line. Its products also get a boost from other licensees' promotional efforts in support of their merchandise.

MEDIA AND ENTERTAINMENT SUPPORT

Licensees look for current and planned vehicles such as magazines, books, video and PC games, TV series and specials, films, webisodic series, home videos and music CDs that will extend the life of the property and keep it fresh. These types of awareness-generators are most often associated with entertainment properties, but extend to nearly all property types. Magazines launch music CDs, musicians appear on television or create film soundtracks, artists create children's books, and corporate properties authorize books or direct-to-video productions. All of these help maintain and strengthen exposure for the property.

RETAIL SUPPORT

Licensees look at what major retailers are aligned with a property before signing on. These initiatives, whether involving guaranteed purchases or, more likely, an exclusive promotional window, add to the property's consumer awareness level and a licensee's sales potential. Even in the case of a retail exclusive promotion in which a licensee does not participate (perhaps because another company is the retailer's preferred vendor or because its category is not part of the deal), the increased exposure as a result of the promotion may make the property attractive for the licensee as products roll out beyond the exclusive. In the case of an entertainment property, some licensees are more interested in who the retail partner is than in what media vehicles are planned; this is a big change from five to 10 years ago.

IMAGE

Potential licensees need to be sure that the brand image of a property —

the way customers perceive it — is one with which they want their products and company associated. Sometimes these images are not constant; an agreement with a well-known celebrity could seem beneficial one day and controversial the next. An upscale brand may change its strategy and start distributing low-priced products, thus diluting the brand in the eyes of consumers and the licensee. A sport's image may go up and down depending on whether there is an exciting playoff race or an impending strike. It pays to carefully consider a property's image and remain aware of how it may change over time before committing.

VISUAL APPEAL AND FRESHNESS

As noted earlier, no matter what the licensee's goals, the property should look good on its products, whether a blouse, plate, gift box or chair. The graphic design of logos, characters and supplemental artwork should appeal to the licensee's customers and be appropriate for its merchandise. An animated character that allows some flexibility of design might be more appropriate for a t-shirt than an approved photograph of the star of a popular live-action TV program. Some licensors are willing to allow the licensee to experiment with different designs while others require rigid adherence to a limited range of visual options; the former may be more desirable to many licensees. The licensor's ability to keep the imagery fresh — such as through seasonal redesigns, annual holiday-themed art and/or frequently updated style guides— is also a key selling point for a property.

LIFESPAN

Manufacturers should consider a property's likely lifespan before acquiring it. A licensee treads a fine line between meeting demand while a license is strong and avoiding inventory surpluses when popularity falls off. This is one of the biggest challenges for short-term, "hot" properties such as a music or film license; market oversaturation can kill the property permanently and wipe out a licensee's profits. Thus, the property's anticipated lifespan — and its likely rates of growth and decline — affect inventory and production decisions. Short-term properties may not be appropriate for products that require major retooling, are capital-intensive or require significant investments in product development. In general, the appropriateness of a short- *versus* long-term license depends on the licensee's objectives. Although most licensees (and retailers) now prefer potential classics (and licensors try to extend the lives of their properties indefinitely), one is not inherently better than the other and there are opportunities, especially on the promotional side, for short-term licenses such as films.

TIMING

The launch and expansion strategy for a licensed property should coincide with the licensee's plans. Negotiations with the licensor must begin in time for contract negotiation, product development and prototypes to be complete before the licensee begins to sell to retailers. In addition, the property's launch date should make sense for the licensee's category. A manufacturer of Halloween costumes or back-to-school products might think twice before acquiring rights to a standalone spring movie license (or one from the previous holiday season); demand may fall off long before August. The same is true for a toy line, where 50% or more of sales typically occurs in the fourth quarter.

Some licensors and licensees agree to test their product lines (either as a test for the property overall or specifically for that line) in a limited way prior to rolling out. This short-term test period minimizes risks for both partners in the equation. Stride Rite licensed a new and relatively unknown property, Kooties, from Fineline Properties, for a holiday test period in 50 stores. If the 2001 test was successful, the shoe company had the option to expand the deal into a two-year licensing agreement.

RIGHTS

The licensee should know exactly what rights the licensor owns and is authorized to grant. In auto racing, several different licensors — drivers, sponsors, auto makers, governing bodies, racetracks — may all control part of the package of rights that the licensee wants. In the entertainment industry, acquiring a film license does not automatically guarantee the use of the actors' likenesses or voices, or of the music in the film. Corporate trademarks may be held or claimed by more than one licensor (as was the case in the relaunch of the Indian Motorcycle brand) or rights to a similar trademark may be held by different licensors in different categories (as is the case with the Field & Stream name). (See Chapter 8 for more on rights.)

LEGAL PROTECTION

The licensee is paying for the right to utilize a unique, legally protected — trademarked and/or copyrighted — property on its products. This protection ensures that other companies cannot market merchandise that is confusingly similar to the manufacturer's licensed line. If a property is not adequately protected through trademark or copyright registration in all countries where the products will be sold, the licensee may lose sales to infringers and have little or no recourse. Therefore, manufacturers should make sure that trademarks and copyrights are in place — or at least in progress — before signing a licensing agreement.

EXCLUSIVITY

Some licensors grant exclusive rights, while others authorize nonexclusives. Some allow very narrow exclusivity, such as — to cite an extreme example — granting a licensee the right to make baseball-style caps, in cotton, adjustable, with a button on top, in two colors, with one basic design, for U.S. only, to be sold in department stores only. That may be fine for a licensee that feels the property is valuable enough to justify such a narrow grant of rights, but other licensees might decline the license unless they receive the exclusive rights to manufacture all headwear worldwide. Most agreements fall somewhere between these two situations.

Sometimes "exclusive" deals are a matter of semantics. Mattel was the exclusive master toy licensee for the first Harry Potter film in 2001, for example, and held rights for most toy categories. Yet its competitor Hasbro, through various subsidiaries, was licensed to create items for the toy trade such as trading card games, novelty candies and electronic playthings.

There has been a rise in exclusive agreements as licensors move more toward a brand management strategy, preferring one strong licensee in each broad category over several smaller licensees making fewer products each. Yet there are occasions where certain products are better handled by a smaller licensee. In general, too many manufacturers selling items linked to a given property to the same retailers leads to oversaturation, resulting in lower prices or placement in markdown bins.

In the European Union, there are few true exclusives except in the case of rare pan-European deals. "Exclusive" licensees in each country cannot be prevented from distributing into other EU nations.

PREMIUM RIGHTS

Licensees can increase sales by acquiring rights to sell products as premiums as well as at retail. In addition to generating incremental revenues, receiving the rights for both types of distribution prevents the possibility of the two channels cannibalizing each other. Some retail licensees, such as major players in the toy industry, will not sign a licensing agreement unless they have the rights for both premiums and retail merchandise. In other cases, granting both types of rights to one licensee is not feasible. Many companies that sell to retail stores lack expertise in premiums, while many premium companies do not maintain relationships with retailers (or have distinct divisions targeting each channel). Promotional partners also have their own preferred providers through which they source their premiums.

Advertising specialty distributors are licensed for products sold through corporate incentive or fundraising catalogs and to supply promotional partners' gift needs. Typically, they source licensed product from official retail licensees first, then supplement their offerings with unique items they source internally, in cases where items are not already available. Sports and events licensors tend to be active in the ad specialty market.

COMPETITION

Manufacturers should look not only at the details of a property itself but also at the property's competition. When several very similar properties are on the market at the same time, it can dilute the value of each, especially those that came on the market riding the coattails of a successful property by emulating its attributes. For example, after the success of Pokémon in 2000, a raft of anime properties, particularly those for younger children that involved monsters and collecting, as Pokémon does, came on the market. Although each was distinct, situations like this may cause confusion in the marketplace, both among retailers and consumers.

LICENSOR'S BUSINESS PLANS

Licensees want to be sure that a licensor is not overextended, handling too many properties or involved with more promotions than they can manage. Manufacturers should be confident, through an analysis of the licensor's total business, that the property owner can deliver on its promises.

PAYMENT STRUCTURE

The royalty rate, guarantee and advance should all be acceptable to the licensee given the benefits it is gaining from its association with the property. Furthermore, if a licensee is undecided between two properties that meet its objectives equally, then a comparison of royalty/guarantee/advance packages will be an important tie-breaker. Some licensors are willing to negotiate the relative weight of the three payment components, such as lowering the advance in favor of a higher guarantee and/or royalty rate. In general, payment structures are becoming more flexible, with graduated royalty rates based on performance, more cross-collateralizing of multiple properties, and more give-and-take possible. (See Chapter 7.)

Some licensees tend to accept high guarantees or higher-than-desired royalties so they do not miss out on what they perceive will be a hot property. They often live to regret it when the license does not pan out or does not generate enough sales to recoup the high costs of the license. Licensees should not be afraid to say "no" if a deal entails too much financial risk or not enough potential benefit. No matter how good a property looks, a too-high guarantee or other financial risk should make a licensee walk away.

Golden Books (later bought by Random House) severed its 70-year licensing relationship with Disney, according to the company, because the terms Disney wanted to negotiate would not allow the financially strapped Golden to make a profit. The break came despite the fact that Disney licensed titles accounted for $35 million in sales, more than 15% of Golden's total revenue.

The licensee should evaluate all the characteristics of the license before focusing on payment. A manufacturer should assess the property first, and be certain it is the right match for its products, before negotiating the financial package.

MINIMIZING RISKS

Any licensing arrangement is potentially risky. Some properties drive success for licensees in virtually every category while others fizzle out across the board. Even the most successful programs include a few manufacturers with underperforming product lines; conversely, a handful of licensees can do well with a property considered a failure overall.

Ensuring an appropriate fit between the property and the product is a key means of minimizing risk. If a property is popular, but does not match a product's demographics, brand image or product design, the licensed line will probably fail. The property and product should be more than just a good theoretical match. The execution — the way the property is integrated into the product — must offer a competitive advantage over similar merchandise in the same category. Simply tacking on a logo or character will usually not work (although time and financial constraints may make that the only option in some categories). In general, the product must have some reason for incorporating the property. Perhaps a scarf or plate benefits from a design that only a license can provide or a videogame acquires a unique element of play value through its association with a property. A licensed Volkswagen electronics line incorporates design elements of the VW Beetle and is immediately recognizable as associated with that brand; other licensed electronics are indistinguishable from competitive products except for the logo.

The product itself also has to be something consumers want. A licensed property cannot drive sales of merchandise that has no appealing attributes besides being associated with that property, but it can add incremental sales to an item that stands alone as a good product. A license may convince a child to purchase a toy if he or she likes the TV series or film on which it is based, but if the toy isn't fun to play with, demand will not last long. A corporate logo appearing on a product that consumers do not want will not make them purchase it, no matter how much they respect the brand. Negative word of mouth could, in fact, harm the entire property. On the other hand, a good licensed product can still sell, even after a property's widespread popularity fades.

Finally, the licensee's own marketing efforts minimize risk and enhance the success of a licensed product line. Most successful manufacturers emphasize the licensed line in sales calls, advertise to the trade and consumers and encourage their entire sales force to get behind it. Properties do not necessarily sell themselves; licensed lines need the same amount of attention that a manufacturer's own brands receive. Licensees should not rely only on the licensor's promotional backing; manufacturers know their own channels better than licensors do and can provide them with the support they desire.

FINANCIAL IMPACT OF LICENSING

It is difficult for manufacturers to forecast the economic impact of acquiring a license. Potential licensees should consider the following points when trying to determine the financial potential of a proposed licensing deal.

ADVANCES AND GUARANTEES

Since advances are paid upon contract signing, rather than as sales accrue, and are nonrefundable, a licensee may feel that a given property is not worthwhile if it requires a prohibitively high upfront payment.

Most guarantees are required minimum payments and can be a significant financial burden to licensees, if sales do not reach expected levels. (In rare cases involving nonexclusives, guarantees may simply be performance benchmarks rather than required minimums.) See Chapter 7 for details on royalties, guarantees and advances.

As noted earlier, licensees should only accept rational payment structures. The licensing business, especially in the entertainment/character sector, has become guarantee-driven rather than royalty-driven, which moves more of the risk to the licensee from the licensor.

MARGINS AND PRICING

Royalties are tied to actual sales and affect a manufacturer's gross margins. The impact can be either positive or negative, depending on the industry; if a license can command a premium price, margins are likely to increase, but if licensed products are sold at the same price as generic or in-house-designed merchandise, margins will narrow (see Chapter 7). If a license squeezes margins, can the licensee still compete with other companies in its industry? Will quality suffer? If a royalty requires the manufacturer to charge higher wholesale prices to the retailer, will this adversely affect sales? Licensees should answer these questions before signing up for a property.

Manufacturing and shipping are variable costs that accrue as the products are produced and delivered and also have a potentially significant impact on margins. They may rise or fall compared to a generic product when a license is involved; for example, manufacturing costs may be higher as a result of changes made to incorporate the license into the product. These and other variable costs should be added to the royalty to determine the total per-unit impact of the licensing deal.

VOLUME

In some cases, manufacturers may feel that lower margins and per-unit profits are a worthwhile tradeoff for the increased volume generated by the license. The licensee should also consider, however, whether similar sales gains can be achieved some other way without negatively affecting margins. If so, a license may not be the best option.

INVESTMENTS

Licensing agreements require investments outside of payment for the license itself. Retooling, product development and marketing costs associated with launching the licensed line all become sunk costs if the line fails. A licensee should examine whether it can afford these expenditures, as well as any guarantees and advances, in the event that a worst-case scenario occurs.

Manufacturers should consider whether they are likely to recoup these investments, as well as how long it will take to reach the break-even point, both in terms of earning out the guarantee and recovering other costs associated with the line.

INVENTORY CONTROL AND FORECASTING

Hot licenses cause demand to ramp up quickly, resulting in inventory shortages. While short-term sales will be strong, lags in filling orders could damage the licensee's relationships with retailers and shoppers. On the opposite end of the spectrum, supplying too much product before demand is strong will kill a property.

A more important inventory concern related to licensing, especially for hot or faddish properties, is the possibility of market oversaturation if demand falls precipitously after its peak. A large inventory surplus can lead to major losses for the licensee, which will have to dispose of the inventory at reduced prices or at a loss and absorb the cost of shipping products back from retail stores (if they are returnable). These costs are considerable and can wipe out profits generated during the peak of demand.

Closely monitoring demand and supplying retailers conservatively can alleviate some of this risk, but licensees should consider whether their business can withstand such a situation before entering into an agreement for a property with a potentially short lifespan. Both too much demand and too little can have negative ramifications.

In general, tying in with licensed properties makes sales forecasting difficult. Even for a classic or a brand, it is hard to determine how fast—or if—a particular product line will take off and how long it will succeed. For licensees linking with numerous entertainment properties, such as major toy companies, sales can rise and fall significantly from one quarter to the next, causing jitters among top management and investors.

ADMINISTERING THE LICENSING PROGRAM

As for licensors (see Chapter 5), administering a licensing program requires a significant amount of time, expense and human resources from the licensee's staff, depending on the number of licenses held and the number of products in each licensed line.

Some licensees delegate the adminstration of the licensing effort to an employee that already has other duties, such as a product development or marketing person or the president. Companies with several licenses or a single-property program that accounts for a large percentage of their business typically hire at least one staff member that is devoted to licensing full time.

A dedicated person makes it easier for the licensee to keep up with all the licensing-related tasks that accumulate: keeping track of changes to existing licenses; monitoring current and future licenses as they become available, to see if they have potential; ensuring fresh designs under the license each season; meeting with retailers about the licensed line; meeting with licensors; sending samples and concepts to the licensor for approval; meeting with other licensees and attending licensee summits; attending licensing and other conventions; going with sales reps on sales calls for licensed lines; and many other duties.

LICENSING CONSULTANTS

Many companies, especially those that maintain a stable of licenses and/ or do not have a full-time person on staff to seek and evaluate properties, retain a manufacturer's representative or a licensing consultant that focuses on serving manufacturers. These specialists represent licensees in evaluating properties, staying on top of what licenses are available, negotiating agreements and developing strategies. They provide value by offering years of experience in licensing and a multitude of business contacts. In addition, they serve as the client's full-time eyes and ears in the business, which is especially important for companies without an in-house licensing executive. Some may assist in the day-to-day administration of the program after deals are signed.

Licensing consultants vary in terms of how they are paid. Some require a flat retainer, some receive an advance against a commission (averaging 1%-2% of net sales of the licensed lines) and some demand a retainer plus a percentage of net sales. Working with a licensing consultant is often more cost-effective than hiring a full-time in-house employee or dedicated licensing staff.

RETAILERS AS LICENSEES

As noted and discussed in more detail in Chapter 4, retailers are more often becoming direct licensees for long-term private-label lines or for certain products within an exclusive promotional window. Retailers' criteria for evaluating properties are similar to those outlined for licensees in this chapter. Specifically, they look for properties that will place their stores at the top of shoppers' minds, appeal to their core consumer, increase store traffic and sales (both of the licensed line and other products), and differentiate them from their competitors.

They are also concerned with details such as the financial deal they can forge—they increasingly have the lion's share of negotiating power vis à vis licensees and licensors—and about the specifics of sourcing the licensed products (from licensees, their own preferred vendors or through internal sources). More on the financial aspects of direct-to-retail licensing is included in Chapter 7.

PART 3:
THE DETAILS

CHAPTER 7:
MONEY MATTERS

The basic structure of compensation for most licensing relationships involves a royalty per unit of merchandise sold, a minimum guarantee payment against royalties and an advance, all of which are interrelated. Flexibility and creativity are possible in the negotiation of licensing deals; for example, many partners are structuring agreements to include graduated royalties and guarantees tied to performance benchmarks.

THE BASICS

The basic unit of payment is the royalty, around which advances and guarantees are structured. Royalties, advances and guarantees vary depending on a number of factors and all are negotiable.

ROYALTIES

The royalty percentage most commonly falls between 5% and 14%, but can be as low as 1% or as high as 20% and beyond. Royalties are typically applied to the manufacturer's selling price (not the retail price) of each item sold, less allowable deductions. If a manufacturer sells 1,000,000 licensed t-shirts to a retailer at $5.00 per shirt and its agreement with the licensor calls for a royalty of 5%, the payment to the licensor would total:

$$\$250,000 = (1,000,000 \text{ units} \times \$5.00 \times 5\%)$$

GUARANTEES AND ADVANCES

The minimum guaranteed royalty, or "guarantee," is the minimum amount the licensee agrees to pay the licensor at the end of each year or contract period regardless of sales. It limits the licensor's risk and encourages the licensee to do whatever it can to succeed with the licensed line.

The guarantee is charged against royalties. If royalty payments over the period covered by the guarantee *exceed* the guarantee amount, the licensor requires no further payments because the guarantee has been met. If total royalty payments over the period are *less* than the guarantee amount, the licensee owes the licensor the difference between the guarantee and actual royalties at the end of the period.

Guarantee amounts differ depending on the deal, but they usually equal a percentage (often about 50%) of expected royalties over the guarantee period. Continuing with the example above, suppose the t-shirt licensee estimates it can sell somewhere between 250,000 and 300,000 units. After a negotiation, the licensee and licensor agree to base the guarantee at half of expected sales, using the midpoint of the range:

$$1/2 \times 275,000 = 137,500 \text{ t-shirts}$$

By applying the 5% royalty rate to this base sales forecast and assuming a manufacturer's selling price of $5, the partners would fix the guarantee amount at $34,375:

$$\$34,375 = (137,500 \text{ units X } \$5.00 \text{ X } 5\%)$$

If the licensee sells only 125,000 shirts over the period covered by the guarantee, it will owe the licensor $2,750, the difference between actual royalties and the guarantee amount:

$$\$34,000 - (125,000 \text{ units sold X } \$5.00 \text{ X } 5\%) = \$2,750$$

If the licensee records sales high enough that actual royalties exceed the guarantee — more than 137,000 units — it has met the guarantee and owes the licensor no further money. Sales of 300,000 t-shirts, for example, would generate royalties that exceed the guarantee by approximately $41,000:

$$\$41,000 = (300,000 \text{ units sold X } \$5.00 \text{ X } 5\%) - \$34,000$$

Guarantee amounts are subject to negotiation and vary depending on licensees' and licensors' objectives. They can be as low as about $350 (for some artist-licensed items) and as high as $20 million (for a long-term videogame, toy or publishing deal) or higher. (Some agreements do not require a guarantee at all.) Licensing executives report that guarantees most commonly fall into the $10,000 to $50,000 range across all deals, but many deals are much higher: In the early 2000s, a publisher reportedly paid $1 million for all rights to a preschool property, a health and beauty product marketer more than $250,000 for the rights to a film property, a toy company $1 million for rights to create plush figures based on the Salt Lake Olympic Committee mascots, and a toy company $35 million for a high-profile feature film.

In certain cases, licensors require high guarantees — often because of short-term accounting and financial goals, especially for public companies in the entertainment field, or because demand allows it — that are unrealistic in that licensees will never recoup them. Too-large guarantees also encourage market oversaturation, which is harmful to the property, licensor and licensee. Many licensees agree to these figures, however, even though it is unlikely sales will justify them. In other words, the business, especially in the entertainment sector, has become guarantee-driven rather than royalty-driven, although the pendulum seems to be swinging back. As of 2002, the business's recent weak performance has made these unrealistic minimums common, as licensors become more willing to share risk.

It should be remembered, in any case, that licensees can always pass on a deal for which guarantees seem too high. A realistic guarantee should be based on rational sales forecasts from the licensee, given its distribution structure and sales force capabilities, not on factors such as how much investment in the property a licensor wants to recoup or a minimum requirement from a corporation's top management.

The main purpose of the guarantee is to ensure that the licensee makes its best effort to sell the licensed merchandise and that it compensates the licensor anyway if it does not. During the contract period, the licensor cannot sign other licensees for the same products (unless the agreement is non-exclusive), regardless of whether the licensee does anything with the prop-

Figure 11
AVERAGE ROYALTY AND RANGE OF ROYALTIES
BY PRODUCT CATEGORY
2001

PRODUCT CATEGORY	AVERAGE ROYALTY	RANGE
Accessories	7.4%	5%-10%
Apparel	8.4%	7%-10%
Domestics	7.4%	5.5%-9%
Electronics	8.2%	5%-10%
Food/Beverages	7.1%	4%-10%
Footwear	8.0%	6%-10%
Furniture/Home Furnishings	8.7%	7%-10%
Gifts/Novelties	8.9%	5%-12%
Health/Beauty	8.7%	8%-10%
Housewares	7.7%	6%-10%
Infant Products	8.2%	5%-10%
Music/Video	8.7%	8%-10%
Publishing	8.7%	7%-15%
Sporting Goods	8.4%	7%-10%
Stationery/Paper	8.3%	6%-10%
Toys/Games	8.6%	7%-10%
Videogames/Software	8.5%	8%-10%
OVERALL AVERAGE	8.4%	4%-15%

Note: Ranges are typical reported ranges. Royalties can fall below or above these ranges within a given category.
Source: The Licensing Letter; EPM Communications

erty. Thus the guarantee.

The licensee must pay the guarantee if the merchandise underperforms, even despite its best effort and even if the property as a whole is a disappointment. Many licensees argue that the licensor bears responsibility for the failure of the property overall, but they owe the licensor the guarantee all the same. In rare cases, licensors may forgive a guarantee for a product line based on a flop, usually in lieu of a more favorable deal with a future property. The unpaid portion of the guarantee might carry over to a future property, or the guarantee for that future property may be lower than normal to compensate for the unreasonably high guarantee on the first property.

Licensors typically require a portion (such as 25%) of the first year's guarantee as an advance, payable upon contract signing. In the case of a low guarantee, the licensor may require the full amount in advance; at other times the advance may be a token payment of a few hundred dollars. If the advance is very large, licensors may allow licensees to remit half the advance upon contract signing and the remainder in a series of payments every six months, rather than as a single lump sum upfront.

In some cases, a licensor might lower or waive an advance in return for a higher guarantee or royalty rate, especially if it wants to encourage the licensee to spend upfront on product development or marketing.

FACTORS AFFECTING ROYALTY RATES AND GUARANTEES

Royalty rates vary, as *Figure 11* (*page 133*) shows. The law of supply and demand plays into the royalty asking price. A property that many licensees desire, such as Star Wars, can command royalties of 14% or higher. On the other hand, properties that are not in great demand, such as a new syndicated television show, bring in lower rates because the licensor has more to gain by attracting licensees than the licensee does from signing on. The same phenomenon occurs for all property types; an established fashion brand yields a higher price than a newly launched, little-known label.

In the most competitive sectors, such as children's apparel brands or contemporary artists — there are hundreds if not thousands of art properties vying for licensees — royalty rates tend to be lower and more consistent than in the entertainment field. Within any segment, however, properties more in demand attract higher royalties than other, similar properties.

Distribution also plays a role in determining royalties. Licensors receive lower royalties from manufacturers who sell to mass merchants (due to lower prices), but sales levels compensate for the smaller per-unit income. Average gross margins within the licensee's industry influence royalties as well. The margin, usually stated in the form of a percentage, is the licensee's gross profit per unit divided by its sales price. Gross profit is the manufacturer's sale price minus the cost of goods sold (the unit cost).

Companies that operate in industries associated with low margins, such as food manufacturing (where a licensed product based on a famous chef would garner royalties of 2%-5%), cannot cost-effectively acquire a license if the royalty rate is too high. The royalty would slice margins even more, creating a competitive disadvantage for the manufacturer (see Chapter 6). This situation is particularly true for industries where licensed products are sold at the same price as non-licensed items. In the case of children's domestics or paper school supplies, for example, manufacturers' selling prices are nearly equivalent for licensed merchandise and products designed in-house. Manufacturers that have to pay a royalty face higher unit costs — and consequently maintain lower margins — than their competitors:

Example 1: If margins in a certain licensee's industry average 50% and licensed merchandise cannot command a premium price at retail, a 10% royalty lowers margins from 50% to 40%, reducing profit by 20%. For example, if the manufacturer's selling price for a nonlicensed item is $10, and the cost of goods sold (the variable unit cost of each item sold) is $5, the margin would be 50%. If the same item is licensed and still commands $10, a 10% royalty ($1 per item) is added to the cost of goods sold, increasing it to $6 and reducing margins to 40%. This example, as well as the others in this chapter, assumes that the cost of goods sold for generic and licensed items are approximately the same (which is not always the case).

Example 2: If industry margins are 20%, the same situation outlined in Example 1 would cause margins to decrease to 10%, a 50% drop in gross profit. For example, at a manufacturer's selling price of $10 and a cost of goods sold of $8, the gross margin is $2 or 20%. But with a 10% royalty ($1 per unit), the cost of goods sold rises to $9 per unit, cutting margins in half to $1 per unit.

Consumers of some products, such as alarm clocks or hair-care appliances, view a license as a competitive advantage and will purchase a licensed product at a higher price than its generic equivalent. Manufacturers' selling prices can in turn be higher without complaints from retailers. In this case, licensees maintain or improve their margins by associating with a license. The licensee can in essence transfer the entire royalty to retailers, who pass it along to their customers:

Example: If a manufacturer sells a generic (nonlicensed) item to retailers for $10, the customer would pay $20 for that product at retail, assuming a 50% markup. (The retail markup is the difference between the retail and manufacturer's selling price, divided by the retail price.) If the item is licensed, the manufacturer pays a 10% royalty on the manufacturer's selling price of each item. By increasing the price to the retailer to $11.11, the manufacturer can still net $10 per item after paying the royalty:

$$\$10 \text{ net} = \$11.11 - (10\% \text{ of } \$11.11)$$

As the wholesale price increases to $11.11, the customer's retail price rises to $22.22, assuming the same 50% markup. This is the ideal situation for licensees, but they can only accomplish it in industries where consumers will pay more than 20% extra for a licensed versus a generic item.

⋅⋅⋅

Licensees' and licensors' objectives also affect royalty rates, guarantees and advances. Some entertainment licensors seek high advances to help pay for or greenlight a production, but may accept a lower royalty rate in return for more upfront funds. A licensor may offer a lower royalty rate to attract a licensee to an unproven property or to gain its commitment to a longer contract. A corporate or other licensor may have a strict policy regarding advance or guarantee minimums; some will not accept deals below $5,000, for example, and others not below $100,000. High guarantees, if they do not match the licensee's objectives or capabilities, can be detrimental to a program, however, since they can lead to overshipping and sales totals that do not meet expectations (even if high).

A licensee that desires a broadly defined exclusive typically pays a higher royalty rate and/or guarantee, since it is preventing the licensor from earning income from other manufacturers in the same category. Some licensees lower their guarantees by promising to present more SKUs to retailers. This commitment benefits licensors by increasing the chances that more products end up on retail shelves, which can be a greater boon than high guarantees, depending on the property.

Since every licensing agreement is unique, negotiations between licensee and licensor can result in any number of royalty-guarantee-advance combinations. Some property types are more negotiable than others — entertainment and artists' contracts diverge significantly, while major league sports deals tend to fall along similar lines.

Royalties, guarantees and advances are often divided into pieces that are tied to different products or different geographic areas within an agreement, to ensure that the licensee puts equal effort into each product or territory. Rather than being able to earn out the entire guarantee with one product or area, ignoring the others, the licensee must meet its guarantee for each category or territory separately.

GRADUATED ROYALTIES

Increasingly, licensors and licensees forge deals in which royalties are adjusted as licensees reach various milestones throughout the life of the property. These hurdles are written into the contract and are intended to protect the licensee if the licensor's predictions of performance do not come true, much as guarantees protect licensors. Essentially, licensors and licensees share more risk in the early days of the agreement. Most licensors and licensees have embraced graduated royalty plans based on sales milestones, although some complain that such a systems requires more paperwork since sales have to be monitored more closely.

In a graduated royalty deal, a licensee might pay an 8% royalty for the first X number of units sold, 9% for the next X units and finally 10% for all units above that level. Guarantees and advances are tied in as well; the lower the advance and guarantee, the lower the level at which a higher royalty takes effect. A few licensors have experimented with lowering the royalty rate as sales increase, on the theory that the promise of higher margins (due to the lower royalty rate) provides an incentive for the licensee to sell more.

In another type of benchmarking structure, one corporate licensor authorizes guarantees each year at either the same level as the previous year or 50%-60% of the previous year's royalties, whichever is higher. Guarantees are raised only if royalties are high enough to warrant it. (All the licensor's deals are long-term pacts.)

Benchmarks may be tied to the performance by the property or the fulfillment of promises by the licensor rather than to licensees' sales. The licensor of a brand-new hour-long syndicated television series may promise that the show will be available in 80% of U.S. households at the launch date. At the time it is negotiating with licensees, however, the show has only secured 65% coverage. A licensee is interested in the property but feels it is too risky at current coverage levels. The licensor may offer a lower royalty and/or guarantee in the first year as an incentive. The partners then agree upon higher payments in subsequent years, providing that exposure reaches certain milestones. If the show becomes a hit, the licensee will end up paying appropriately high royalties, but the downside is minimized in the risky early months. Other measurable milestones could include Nielsen ratings for a TV series or sales of toys based on the property. Licensors might look for a higher royalty if a show moves from once-a-week airings to five or six times per week.

Conversely, the licensor may incorporate specific "negative" milestones into a contract, such as requiring the licensee to pay a penalty if it misses a crucial deadline (e.g., a product introduction or delivery date). If a selling season is short, a late delivery would critically affect sales and harm the property, so the licensor wants compensation.

Graduated royalty deals can be complex. Sales can be measured either in dollar terms or in units; there are many other variables, such as geographic boundaries or distribution channels, that may be involved in the final math.

FREE GOODS

Some licensed merchandise is royalty-exempt, including products distributed free or sold back to the licensor. Examples might include samples used in the selling process; merchandise distributed in-house by the licensor or licensee, such as for employee premiums; and products sold to the licensor for resale (e.g., an on-campus college bookstore that carries the institution's licensed merchandise; the university is the licensor and the retailer). The contract typically caps royalty exemptions and/or distribution of free goods.

In other cases, licensed products may be sold at a discount to affiliates of the licensor or licensee, in which case the royalty rate may differ from that for normal retail transactions. These sales may be subject to a royalty exemption or reduced royalty since the purchaser is a sister company, or they may require a full royalty on the discounted price or even a higher royalty to compensate for the reduced price. The structure of compensation for free and discounted goods is a matter of negotiation.

ALLOWABLE DEDUCTIONS

Royalties are most often based on the "net sales price," which means the manufacturer's selling price less allowable deductions. Licensors authorize very few deductions, but in some cases may grant:

- Cash or volume discounts to retailers
- Returns (in product categories such as publishing where items are sold on a returnable basis), often including a reserve for returns of about 10% to 20%
- Freight

Since these reduce the total royalty, licensors typically limit allowable deductions to a maximum of about 2% to 5% of the first billing amount. Some observers believe that more and more expenses will become part of the definition of allowable deductions in the future, but these are the current standard. Depending on the specifics of a given deal, others may be added. Determining allowable deductions can be one of the most difficult points during negotiations for both partners.

ADVERTISING ADJUSTMENTS AND MARKETING FUNDS

Increasingly, licensors require licensees to participate financially in marketing the property, beyond advertising their own product line. Licensees often view the properties they acquire as a long-term investment and are willing to consider paying into a central marketing fund (CMF) or providing other marketing support.

The practice of establishing a CMF started with fashion labels, corporate brand-extension programs and some sports properties, but now licensors of nearly all other property types, including entertainment, are instituting similar structures. In fact, it is becoming the norm for many licensors, at least in North America, where failure to commit to a CMF contribution can be a deal-breaker. (The practice is not universally accepted in countries outside the U.S. and Canada, although it is on the rise in some nations, such as in northern Europe.) Agents (including international subagents) are sometimes required to pitch into the fund as well.

For a long-term corporate licensing deal, the amount spent on marketing fund contributions, plus the licensee's own marketing support, can exceed guarantee levels in a given year.

Licensees' contributions toward marketing can assume several forms:

- Licensors may require licensees to pay an additional one-half to three percentage points on top of the royalty rate, with 2%-3% becoming standard. This money goes into a licensor-controlled central marketing fund—the licensor typically matches licensees' contributions—earmarked for TV campaigns, retail promotions, co-op advertising with retailers and other efforts on behalf of the property. This is the common CMF structure.

- Licensors may allow a licensee to deduct a point or two off its royalty rate if it spends the equivalent on co-op advertising with the retailers to which it sells. For example, an apparel brand demands a 5% royalty from its licensees, but the licensee can deduct up to 1% of that if it spends the equivalent on co-op advertising with its retail customers, subject to licensor approval.

- Licensors may require licensees to devote a certain percentage of total licensed volume to advertising. A fashion label requires its licensees (which can number in the hundreds) to devote 1%-2% of total volume toward their own advertising in support of the brand. This demand can translate to several millions of dollars in collective advertising expenditures worldwide.

Some licensees are not willing to participate in a CMF, arguing in part that this type of advertising is a licensor's obligation to begin with. They also do not like that the licensor controls how the fund is implemented and are leery that they cannot track whether its use specifically aids their product line. They are willing to spend on advertising or marketing, and would be willing to donate more than the amount required for a CMF, but only if it goes toward a specific promotion in which they are involved.

Some licensors demand an additional contribution to an art fund, similar in structure to the CMF, whereby licensees help finance the continuous creation of new images to keep the property fresh over time.

ROYALTIES APPLIED TO THE RETAIL PRICE

There are times when the royalty rate is based on the retail rather than net sales price. Book publishing is one example; publishers traditionally pay their authors royalties calculated on the retail price and they often compensate licensors the same way, though even then there are exceptions to take discounting into account. In some international territories, such as Japan, royalties are conventionally paid on retail.

Royalty percentages are normally lower in such cases, adjusted so that income is roughly comparable to what it would have been if the typical rate was calculated on the net sales price.

DIRECT-TO-RETAIL DEALS AND RETAIL EXCLUSIVES

Royalties can be based on retail prices when there is no manufacturer's sales price, such as when a retailer or cataloger is the licensee. As noted, these direct-to-retail deals are on the rise, as are retail exclusives. Payment for these types of arrangements can be handled in a number of ways.

- The retailer acts as the licensee, paying a royalty to the licensor, and sources the products by purchasing them from its preferred vendors. The royalty can be based on the retail price or on the vendor's sales price (e.g. the retailer's cost) and can be a percentage or a flat fee per unit sold (or purchased). The rate is lower when calculated on the retail price rather than wholesale, since the base price to which the royalty is tied is higher. (In general, direct-to-retail royalties tend to be lower than for a typical licensing deal, due to the retailer's negotiating power and the promotional value of the exclusive.) A direct royalty structure must take into account factors such as shrinkage and markdowns, which affect the definition of the retail price.

■ The retailer purchases products from its own or the licensor's preferred vendors (licensees), who pay the royalty to the licensor on each item sold. The retailer is not part of the royalty stream, although it may pay the licensor a fee or provide value through in-kind contributions such as signage or advertising.

■ The payment structure may be a combination of the above.

In addition to the royalty, the partners need to negotiate who handles the costs of packaging, in-store signage and other facets of the alliance. Licensees or vendors, retailers and/or licensors may be responsible for all or a portion of each facet, depending on the deal. Martha Stewart's agreement with Kmart, renegotiated in 2001, called for the royalty rate to be based on retail (instead of wholesale as previously) and moved responsibility for developing packaging and signage to the licensor.

F.O.B. PRICING

When a licensee sources a product from overseas, it sometimes sells to retailers through an F.O.B. (freight on board) arrangement. This means that the retailer buys the item when it is still in the country where it was manufactured and is responsible for shipping it back to the U.S., as well as customs and ground transport. The F.O.B. price charged by the licensee is significantly less than for products delivered to the retailer's door, since much of the cost is transferred from the licensee to the retailer.

Since the invoice amount is less for an F.O.B. transaction than for a traditional sale, licensors adjust the royalty upward (often by four percentage points or so) so their income is equal to what it would have been if the products had been imported and delivered by the licensee.

F.O.B. rates are becoming increasingly important as more licensed products are sourced overseas. Licensing agreements typically specify both F.O.B. and net sales royalty rates, depending on the licensee's current (and potential) practices with regard to invoicing their retail customers.

FLAT FEES

Rarely, licensees will pay a flat fee per unit, such as $.75 to $1.75 for each videogame sold, in lieu of a royalty percentage. This is primarily done to simplify accounting, if prices are not consistent, or if a product or service is free to consumers.

Multimedia software licensees, who utilize a number of different properties within one product, may pay flat fees for content that is required but not central to the production (e.g., remitting a few hundred dollars per year to a publisher for the use of reference book content in a CD-ROM). If the CD-ROM is branded under a licensed property name (e.g., Cosmopolitan or Barbie), the licensee pays a traditional royalty.

Licensors that authorize the use of their properties within an online service or web portal may receive a flat fee per customer use, as might licensors who authorize the use of their properties in a digital greeting card.

ROYALTIES TO MULTIPLE PARTIES

There are cases where a licensee must pay royalties to more than one licensor for a single product line. Normally, the total royalty is higher than for a solely owned property, but each individual licensor's cut is lower than usual.

DEVELOPERS, INVENTORS AND AUTHORS

In the videogame industry, a manufacturer must deal with several parties: the licensor for the right to use a trademark (such as a celebrity, a film or a sports property); Nintendo or Sony or another videogame hardware maker for the rights to make a game for a certain platform (e.g., PlayStation); and sometimes a third-party game developer for the right to employ a particular game architecture. Each of these entities demands a royalty.

Toy manufacturers may pay a royalty of about 5% to a toy inventor as well as a royalty to the licensor of the trademark on which the game is based. Similarly, a publisher might pay an additional royalty (or sometimes a flat fee) to a recognized author of a licensed book (unless the writer is on the licensee's or licensor's staff or is working under a work-for-hire contract), as well as to the trademark owner.

It can sometimes be difficult for a toy manufacturer to afford a royalty to both a trademark owner and an inventor. As a result, it may forego pairing an inventor's creation with a license, linking the property instead with a toy that has been marketed before under another license or in a generic version. While the extra creativity brought by an inventor may be the extra element that causes a licensed product to succeed, this match may not occur due to cost considerations.

Manufacturers of multimedia software may owe royalties and/or fees to many parties involved in the creation of the product. These include licensed property owners, developers, publishers, writers, owners of film clips, photographers, musicians or music copyright holders, and graphic designers.

CROSS-LICENSING AND CO-BRANDING

Cross-licensing occurs when a manufacturer acquires the rights for multiple licensed properties and combines them on one product. If each of two properties, say a character and a sports league, normally commands a 10%-12% royalty in the relevant category, the licensee might pay a total of 14%-16% for the cross-licensing rights, with 7%-8% going to each of the licensors.

For an action figure in the likeness of a recognized athlete in uniform,

---

the licensee would typically pay a lowered royalty to both the league and the player or players association, totaling 17%-20%, higher than the royalty to either party alone but less than double.

In rare cases, a licensee might have to pay the full amount to each licensor, doubling the royalty. Generally, however, if both licensors like the product concept, they will allow the licensee to earn a profit on the product line, while still providing each of them with a lucrative income stream.

Sometimes cross- or multiple licensing agreements can get complicated. A manufacturer who wants to produce auto-racing merchandise usually pays a 5% royalty to the driver, 5% to the owner of the team/car, 5% to each sponsor, and 2%-4% to the car manufacturer, as well as royalties to NASCAR or another governing body, other third-party partners, and various promotional fees totalling about 20% or more. A licensee of an art-themed card or board game may have to pay royalties to several artists, estates and museums. A chess set with figures of nostalgic baseball players could entail royalties to Major League Baseball, baseball publications who supply artwork or logos, and 32 players (one for each piece), via their agents or players associations, for a total royalty again of about 20%.

SUBLICENSING

Some contracts allow licensees to sublicense third-party manufacturers for certain categories or territories (always with the licensor's approval). For example, a licensee may hold rights for all apparel and accessories for a brand, with permission to sublicense leather goods, eyewear and footwear.

In general, the licensor and licensee split proceeds from sublicensing agreements. The division of royalties varies; the licensor might receive anywhere from 25% to 75% of the amount paid to the licensee from the sublicensee, although a licensor's cut of less than 50% is rare. Percentages can vary by category as well. One sporting goods brand licensor receives half of the proceeds from a sublicensing deal in apparel, 75% from backpacks, sportbags, cologne and writing instruments, and 70% from other categories, all through a single master licensee.

BUNDLING AND CROSS-COLLATERALIZATION

Licensors are increasingly apt to grant rights to more than one property within the context of a single agreement, such as several films or a film and a television show within the same franchise, or several unrelated trademarks under the same corporate umbrella. In many cases, each product line under the agreement is tied to a distinct royalty and guarantee.

Sometimes, however, licensors will allow licensees to cross-collateralize the revenue streams, meaning that if one portion of the agreement is weak, the licensee can make up for that with other properties under the same agreement, rather than being responsible for separate guarantees for each facet of the line. This structure allows licensors and licensees to share the risk more equitably and is intended to aid the objectives for the overall franchise or corporation rather than forcing each product line to perform separately. It spreads the risk over a whole portfolio of properties and reduces the chance of oversaturation of product related to one component of the franchise, thus harming the other components.

Cross-collateralization usually does not work unless the properties are related in some way and have the same or similar ownership (including all rightsholders). They also tend to be more likely in categories with expensive and long product development processes, such as videogames and toys, and mostly in the entertainment sector where multiproperty franchises are common. Recent examples include Activision acquiring global rights for both Stuart Little and Stuart Little 2 from Sony, for Nintendo software platforms, and several licensees purchasing rights for all three Lord of the Rings films simultaneously from New Line.

SUPERROYALTIES

A superroyalty is an experimental method of preventing licensees from distributing product outside the scope of their agreement without terminating the agreement. For example, a licensor that is worried about potential oversaturation might add several percentage points to the royalty on products where more than a certain number of units are sold during a set period of time; if more products are distributed than the pre-agreed cut-off, the licensee owes the higher royalty on the units sold after the benchmark is reached. Or, it might penalize a European licensee for shipping outside of its contractual region. European Union law dictates that licensors cannot prevent such cross-border shipping within the EU, but licensors can make it less attractive to licensees (and agents) by charging a higher royalty for such activity. The royalty is high enough that it is perceived as a penalty worth considering.

INGREDIENTS

Brand-extension deals within the food and beverage industry (and some others) may involve the buying and selling of ingredients as well as the typical financial arrangements associated with licensing. For example, a co-branded citrus-flavored baking mix would probably involve the purchase by the licensee of the flavor ingredient, as well as the rights to the brand name. The terms of these deals vary, but usually involve quantity purchases at a favorable rate. The licensee and licensor must understand each other's businesses, including, in some cases, commodity pricing (in which case the actual price varies daily but the partners must agree to a reasonable flat price in advance).

MULTIPLE SHARE HOLDERS

In addition to the royalty streams that are agreed upon by the licensor (or its representatives) and the licensee, there are a number of distinct negotiations on the licensor's side regarding the division of revenues among the partners who hold a share in the property. An entertainment property, for example, might involve various underlying rights holders, broadcast distributors and networks, and coproducers (possibly including the licensing agent), as well as the talent and other creative participants. Other property types may also have multiple ownership issues, although the situation is most common in the entertainment/character sector.

There is no set method for the division of royalties. The percentages are based on various factors, including each partner's investment in the property and their role in creating or distributing it. The division of licensing and merchandising income is often part of a larger division of revenues; for an entertainment property these revenues would include money from sales to broadcasters (both first and subsequent runs) at home and internationally, home video and other key ancillary rights. In addition to each partner's share of revenues, the parties need to decide whether each receives its portion as it comes in or after the recoupment of expenses.

Each partner's share of merchandising royalties may also be connected either to worldwide revenue streams or to specific geographic regions. For example, German broadcaster SuperRTL had distribution rights for the television series Oggy and the Cockroaches in its home territory and reportedly received 30% of merchandising revenues that accrued in that region.

EQUITY AGREEMENTS

In rare cases, typically involving large licensors, long-term agreements and numerous product categories (typically representing a large share of the licensee's business), a licensor might take an equity stake (usually in the form of stock or stock options) in a licensee as part of the compensation package for the licensing agreement. This allows the two partners to share more equitably in both the risk and the reward and gives each an increased incentive to make the line succeed.

Warner Bros. received stock options for Mattel as part of its Harry Potter deal, as did Walt Disney in its deals with Hasbro and Golden Books, both for multiproperty agreements. Lucasfilm accepted stock warrants from Hasbro and Galoob (later acquired by Hasbro) as part of the payment for the Star Wars license. The licensor can end up with options or warrants for significant stakes in the licensee, with known instances ranging from 5% to 20%.

While most publicized examples have been in the entertainment/character sector, other property types are involved in such agreements as well. For example, the NFL took an equity stake in Reebok as part of their partnership in which Reebok became the NFL's exclusive sidelines licensee.

In rare cases, a licensee or agent might take equity in a licensor. 4Kids Entertainment, which represents Pokémon for merchandising, broadcast and home video outside Asia, acquired 3% of The Pokémon Company, the property's licensor, as part of its deal.

PAYMENT FOR NON-RETAIL LICENSING AGREEMENTS

Non-retail licensing agreements vary in how payment is structured:

- Use of a licensed property in advertising might involve a flat fee or a percentage of the total media buy.

- Promotions could call for a single flat fee, a separate fee for each promotional element, a combination of flat fees and premium royalties, or no fee. In the last case, payment takes the form of a tradeout in which the licensee provides something of value other than cash— such as advertising or point-of-purchase signage — in return for the rights to the property.
- Promotional premiums could entail a flat fee per unit or a percentage (often 10%) of the cost of the premium. Supplying premiums could also be part of the overall fee or a tradeout for the promotion, without a separate payment.
- Licensed restaurant or arcade operators may owe a percentage of total food and/or merchandise sales, often with an additional licensing fee.
- Internet content distributors may pay a flat fee per download or page view, or a percentage of the user fee if the content is distributed on a pay-per-view basis.
- A service provider, such as of an educational course, a travel tour or a camp, would typically pay the licensor a cut of the fee paid by the participant, possibly with an additional flat fee for the use of the trademark.
- A slot machine provider might pay a royalty on the sale of the machine to the casino (usually at a cost of about $10,000 per machine) or could owe a percentage of about 5% of the machine's take (in which case the casino typically gets the machine for free).

These are just a sampling of the many types of compensation packages that are possible for non-retail agreements. Payment for promotions will be discussed further in Chapter 12.

FLEXIBILITY

As noted throughout this chapter, licensors and licensees have become more flexible regarding the payment structures for licensing deals. While the basic royalty-guarantee-advance structure remains the foundation, many variations make their way into the final contract. The adage that everything is negotiable is truer today than ever before.

Part of this emphasis on flexibility hinges on the difficult times the business has been enduring, which spurs partners to try new means to succeed. Licensors with the most in-demand properties can still afford to force licensees to agree to their terms, but as a rule flexibility and negotiation are the bywords in most deals.

As a property's performance and exposure rise or fall, adjustments can be made to royalty and guarantee rates. Cooperative marketing efforts or additional services provided by either the licensee or the licensor could affect the royalty rate. Deals surrounding a property that does not meet expectations early on can be adjusted for the long-term good of the property and

the partners, while guarantee amounts and payment deadlines can be renegotiated to take schedule changes (e.g., delayed movie releases) into account.
Royalties can vary by distribution tier, customer, property, product, territory
or other elements.

In general, the riskier the property, the more creative the deal.

CHAPTER 8:
PROTECTING YOUR RIGHTS

Legal protection is what gives a property its intrinsic value. Licensees are paying for the right to associate with a unique property—one that cannot be copied legally—that will give them a competitive advantage. A licensor should therefore ensure that it has cleared its property for use and protected it for use, before attempting to license it out. Fully registering a property in all territories where it will be marketed gives the licensor the legal means to battle infringers and counterfeiters, but is also costly for a global licensing effort involving many categories.

Nothing in this chapter or book should be construed as legal advice. A licensor should consult with its attorney — preferably one with expertise in licensing — regarding any legal matters.

TRADEMARKS AND COPYRIGHTS

Establishing trademark rights is the primary tool for protecting a property that will extend into licensed merchandise. Most licensors also supplement their trademarks with full copyright protection of graphics, text and other creative aspects related to their logos, characters and designs.

TRADEMARKS

A licensor can trademark words, brand names, depictions of characters, phrases, symbols, designs — or any combination of these — that identify and distinguish the goods of one company from those of another and that consumers are not likely to confuse with marks already in use or reserved for use. There are some exceptions; a company cannot trademark place names unless combined with other words (Minnesota Golden Gophers) or logos (the word Minnesota graphically depicted in conjunction with a portrayal of the Gopher mascot), for example, or terms that describe a product (The Green Book).

In the U.S. and other countries, trademark rights are based upon the first use of a mark on or in connection with goods and services. Before adopting a mark as the basis for a licensing program, a licensor should determine that the mark is not likely to be confused with another that is already in use or covered by an intent to use registration (discussed below). This can be determined by searching trademark registration records, industry directories and publications, and other sources. There are several companies that conduct trademark searches at a cost of about $400-$600 per search; results should be reviewed by an attorney to determine how to proceed.

Assuming the search does not reveal any conflicts, the licensor should proceed to register the mark under the appropriate classifications. (The PTO lists a total of 34 classes for goods and an additional eight for services.) If the licensor has already started using the mark itself or through a licensee, it can submit an application for registration based on that use. If not, it can submit an application based on the "intent to use." In some coutries, including the U.S., a licensor may apply for registration based on an existing registration in another country.

Companies can renew their trademark registrations in perpetuity, as long as they exploit the marks in each classification where they are registered. They can also register marks in additional classifications as their use expands. More than one classification can be listed on a single application for registration, but there will be a separate fee for each classification listed.

All products and printed matter featuring the trademark should be marked as follows:

- The ™ symbol indicates that the property owner considers the brand or depiction to be a trademark not to be infringed upon; it does *not* signify that the trademark has been registered with the Patent and Trademark Office.

- The ® symbol means that names, depictions and so on are registered as trademarks with the PTO; it can appear *only* beside registered marks.

The licensor's style guide should outline the correct way for licensees to identify each element of the property.

Trademarks must be registered in each country separately, as required by the laws of each of those countries. Most licensing executives recommend starting the registration procedure in each region approximately a year and a half before the launch of the licensing program.

In some countries, whoever registers a trademark first owns it, even if it is a well-known global brand. A proactive approach to international trademark registration not only helps protect against and battle infringement but also stops unauthorized parties from legitimately usurping a licensor's marks.

Cost Versus Protection

Each trademark registration requires a fee (which is $325 per class in the U.S.). Attorneys fees for assisting the licensor through the process can run in the $1,000-$2,500 range. The more registrations, the better protection, but costs mount quickly. A trademark owner can:

- separately register various depictions, names, slogans and logos associated with one property;

- register each mark under various classifications. A typical children's licensing program comprises about a dozen classes, such as clothing, footwear, headgear; games, playthings, sporting articles, Christmas decorations; and paper, cardboard and goods made from these materials, including printed matter, stationery and playing cards;

- register its marks internationally, typically at least in Canada, Europe, Australia and Japan, where most international licensed product sales occur, as well as countries where piracy is likely. This basic roster totals about 25 territories.

The costs of registering multiple depictions in multiple classifications in multiple countries add up fast. Licensors and their legal counsel must weigh the need for adequate protection versus the reality of budgetary constraints. Licensors may delay some registrations or combine some elements under one registration to reduce costs. (It is worth noting, as well, that registering and exploiting too many marks could dilute the value of the most important ones.)

Trademark protection and enforcement differ from country to country. Some regions have strong laws, but do not enforce them; some have weak or no laws covering trademarks; and some have strong laws and strong enforcement (the registration procedure tends to be lengthy in these territories). In general, laws are improving, as is enforcement in some territories, but there is a long way to go. Licensors should be aware of the particulars of each country's trademark situation before entering the market.

Registration Procedure

Property owners register their trademarks with the Patent and Trademark Office (PTO) of the U.S. Department of Commerce (703-308-HELP; www.uspto.gov).

Within about three months after filing an application, a PTO attorney reviews it. If the PTO refuses the application, the licensor receives a letter explaining why. One common reason is that the proposed trademark is confusingly similar to an already-registered mark. Others might be that the mark is not used as a trademark, is merely ornamental or decorative, or is merely descriptive of the goods on which it is used. The licensor has six months to respond with arguments as to why these objections should be overcome.

If the application is approved (or the initial refusal is overturned), the PTO publishes the proposed mark in its weekly publication, *The Official Gazette*. Anyone who believes the proposed trademark damages one of its own marks has 30 days to respond. If someone opposes the registration, the PTO's Trademark Trial and Appeal Board schedules a hearing to resolve the conflict.

If there is no opposition and the licensor applied for registration based on actual use or amended its application during the review process to establish actual use, a registration certificate will issue about 12 weeks after *The Official Gazette* publishes the mark. If the licensor applied for registration based on an intent to use, a Notice of Allowance will be sent to the licensor, and the licensor will have six months to either use the mark on the designated goods in interstate commerce or file an extension. If it uses the mark and files a Statement of Use that the PTO approves, it will receive a PTO-issued Certificate of Registration.

Quality Control

Quality control, by means of the product approval process, is not just essential to the marketing of a licensed brand, it is also critical to trademark protection. All merchandise marketed under a given trademark must be traceable to a single source, which, in the case of a licensed brand, is the licensor. If licensees market products that stray from the rest of the line in terms of color, design, logos, quality or marketing materials, consumers may not realize their connection with the core brand. Third parties could argue in court that the licensor relinquished its trademark rights since the licensed products are not clearly identifiable with the core property. So-called "naked licensing" (licensing with no attempt to monitor the quality of products) could result in the loss of trademark rights.

COPYRIGHTS

Unlike trademark protection, copyright is valid upon creation. The copyright owner does not technically have to publish or exploit the design or image, known as a "work," to protect it against infringement. For maximum legal remedies, however, most licensing executives suggest registering the work with the Copyright Office of the U.S. Library of Congress (202-707-3000; www.loc.gov/copyright).

Copyright applies to original works of authorship, such as graphics, music and written works. A creator cannot copyright names, titles, short phrases and slogans, ideas or anything in the public domain, but he or she can copyright the design of a logo or a lettering style associated with a name.

The copyright in a work is owned by the individual(s) who created the work, unless it was created as a "work made for hire" or "work for hire." A work for hire is defined as such if it is created by an employee while performing his or her job responsibilities. (Independent contractors such as freelance writers or designers do not automatically give up their rights to a property they create for a licensor. If the licensor intends to hold the copyright for their work, freelancers must sign a work-for-hire agreement stating that the licensor holds the rights.)

Before registering the copyright in a work, a licensor should confirm that it is the copyright owner. If the work was created by an independent contractor or otherwise does not qualify as a work made for hire, the licensor should obtain an assignment of the copyright from the creator(s). Similarly, a licensor should require assignments from all licensees who add new material to a licensor's copyrighted works in the course of modifying designs for licensed products. (More on this later in the chapter.)

Copyrights registered in the U.S. are valid in all countries that are parties to any of several international copyright conventions or have signed bilateral copyright treaties with the U.S., which means virtually all major markets for licensed merchandise. There are about a half dozen copyright conventions, the major ones being the Berne Convention and the Universal Copyright Conventions of Geneva and Paris.

Licensors strongly recommend the use of a copyright symbol (©) or other copyright notice (Copyright © 2002 by EPM Communications, Inc.) in conjunction with copyrighted works, although technically this is optional. The date used is the year the designs are first distributed, if the product is for sale.

Unlike trademark registrations, which licensors can renew indefinitely, copyright protection expires after a time, whether the owner and/or its licensees are using the property on products or not. For copyrights registered as of January 1, 1978, the term is the author's life plus 70 years, or, in the case of a work-for-hire (registered by the company that commissioned it rather than by the author), 95 years after publication or 120 years after creation, whichever comes first. The rules vary for works created prior to January 1, 1978, depending on whether the work was ever published or whether a renewal registration was filed.

New copyrights can be registered for similar but different depictions of the expiring properties. However, any new copyright will apply only to the new elements added to the initial work, and will not extend the term of copyright in that initial work. In addition to copyright protection, graphically depicted characters and other artwork and designs may be eligible for trademark protection, which will not expire a long as the work continues to be used as a trademark.

PUBLIC-DOMAIN WORKS

Once copyrights expire, they enter the public domain. Anyone can then utilize the property without charge or permission. Essentially, the public, rather than the creator, owns the work. Trademarks can also fall into the public domain, but only if the owner abandons the mark through nonuse, permits the mark to become the generic name for the products with which the mark is used, fails to take action against others who infringe on the mark, or fails to exercise sufficient control over the quality of products used and sold by licensees. The yo-yo is a classic example of a former trademark that returned to public-domain status, becoming a generic description of a certain type of toy rather than a brand name.

As noted earlier, trademarks can safeguard properties even after copyrights have run out, if diligently exploited and enforced (and preferably registered). Trademarks protect the characters of Beatrix Potter even though many of the copyrights expired in the mid-1990s. Graphic representations, names and logos associated with Peter Rabbit and other characters are still available for licensing and secured against infringement by unauthorized parties. The text (which is not covered by trademark protection) is in the public domain, but trademarked elements are safe for licensees to consider.

FEES AND PERMISSIONS

Incorporating public-domain creative works into products occasionally requires fees and permissions, not because anyone owns the rights but because access is limited. A work of art painted two centuries ago is definitely not protected under copyright law anywhere in the world, meaning that a company is within its rights to take a photograph of it for use on merchandise. If the original work rests in a museum that restricts photo-taking and no other known or accessible photos of the work exist, however, getting the museum's permission (and paying it a fee) may be the only way to acquire reproducible images of this painting.

Photographs of public-domain works are protected by copyright and their use requires a fee to the photographer or other rights holder. A manufacturer that created a series of posters featuring actors who were famous for portraying mafia characters did not pay a royalty to the licensors of the shows and films in which the actors appeared, since the characters were not identified by their association with a property or character name, but did pay a royalty to the photographer who shot the images.

LICENSING PUBLIC-DOMAIN EVENTS

Publicly owned events can also be the focus of one or more licensing programs. Licensors — often governmental bodies or associations but sometimes unrelated third parties—create a logo and slogan for the event, which then identifies "officially" licensed merchandise. A licensor cannot trademark the event itself, since it is in the public domain, but it can protect a unique logo inspired by the event.

Of course, any number of parties can establish their own trademarked logos, while other, nonlicensed companies can create merchandise based on the event, as long as they do not infringe on one of the protected properties. Therefore, some public-domain events result in a crowded and confused marketplace, diluting the value of any one property.

The millennium, for example, inspired several licensing efforts in the late 1990s, each with its own positioning. They included Year 2000, Class of 2000, Times Square 2000, The Millennium Bug and Y2K. Similarly, the 1992 500th anniversary of Christopher Columbus's discovery of America prompted several licensing efforts, sponsored by the U.S. government, the Spanish government, an association of Italian-Americans and other groups. The 100th anniversary of the Statue of Liberty, the 50th anniversary of World War II and the 25th anniversary of the first man on the moon all sparked licensing programs.

RIGHT OF PUBLICITY

A licensor can protect celebrity likenesses, signatures and names — on behalf of the celebrities themselves or their estates if they are deceased — through trademark registration. There is also a body of law collectively known as the "right of publicity," which governs the right of famous people to control the use of their own name and likeness in commercial endeavors. Rights of publicity vary on a state-by-state basis, with California (home of Hollywood), Indiana (home of CMG Worldwide, a leading representative of celebrities and estates) and Tennessee (home of Elvis) among the leaders in developing strong laws. Most states and countries do not explicitly offer such protection.

Much of the so-called right of publicity relies not on statutory (written) law, but on common law (developed through judicial precedent). In general, trademark protection is clear-cut and allows for better security of celebrity properties than the right of publicity, depending on the jurisdiction.

MULTI-LICENSOR PROPERTIES

Identifying a property's ownership can be complex when several rights holders are involved in the development of a property. Each owner may have a hand in the licensing program, particularly with regard to product approvals and royalty income.

This situation holds especially true for entertainment properties. A television show, for example, may be based on a book or comic book. The producer may copyright and trademark new made-for-TV elements while the original property owner (who could be the author, the illustrator, the publisher or some combination) retains rights for pre-existing elements. Either the creator, publisher or TV producer (or a combination) may handle the licensing effort for the show. The program may also involve syndication companies, broadcast or cable networks, licensing agents, stars and/or other creative staff, as well as international agents, producers and networks.

In a simple example, licensing and promotional rights for the Spider-Man film released in 2002 were handled by a joint venture between Sony (which distributed the film) and Marvel (which owned the underlying comic book rights). The two firms shared revenues from the venture and split licensing responsibilities, with both companies handling publishing, Marvel selling for toy, apparel, accessories, collectibles and gift rights and Sony retaining the rest of the categories.

Fortunately for licensees, one of the rights holders typically acts as the "point person" for the licensing program, becoming the manufacturer's main contact. No matter how rights, responsibilities and rewards are divided up behind the scenes, the licensee works primarily with one party on a day-to-day basis.

NEW PROPERTIES DEVELOPED BY LICENSEES

Within the context of a licensing agreement, a manufacturer may create a new property that is, in turn, licensable. A t-shirt maker might design a new image based on the original property, a book publisher or author might come up with a new character or a videogame publisher might realize a new "look and feel." The new property incorporates elements of the original and either the original licensor or the licensee (or both) may trademark or copyright the new entity and benefit from merchandising revenues.

As the licensing community focuses more on partnership and on creativity in introducing licensed products that stand out from the competition and appeal to consumers, these types of situations arise more frequently and can become a sticking point in negotiations.

Disney and Square Co., an interactive game maker, co-own four characters that were developed for a title called Kingdom of Hearts that was part of the Disney license. The new characters interact with Disney's classic characters such as Mickey Mouse. Disney is the lead licensor on the new characters, but both companies share in revenues from products featuring the four co-developed properties.

Licensing contracts should specify details about the ownership of newly created entities within the context of the licensing relationship, prior to the development of such properties, especially if such a situation is likely to occur. (See Chapter 9 for more about contracts.)

LIKENESSES

Licensing agreements that involve live performers (e.g. sports, entertainment, music) bring up the question of likeness rights and approvals. Licensees often desire the rights to a film or television show only if they can incorporate the images of major stars into their product lines.

Observers point to the unavailability of the talent's likenesses as one (but not the only) reason for the poor performance of certain film properties; key actors did not want their images on products, which limited manufacturers to items featuring logos or other graphics. Consumers did not embrace certain categories of product as they might have if actor likenesses had been involved. Even when actors allow their pictures to be associated with products, they may be very picky about *how* the items portray them, making it virtually impossible to survive the product approval process. Recent products based on the classic TV series The Brady Bunch lack the image of the family's father, a key role on the show, because the actor's estate will not allow his image to be used on products.

There are situations in which actors give up the right to approve their likenesses when in character. In most cases, however, top-billed stars will have some say over the use of their names and images, if they allow their use at all. Licensees should ascertain upfront which actors' likenesses are available and what the talent's likely reaction to merchandise will be. Some manufacturers and promotional partners even recommend that prospective licensees have their lawyers look over relevant portions of the contract between the studio or producer and the talent, if possible. People interpret contracts in various ways and some licensees feel more comfortable getting their own counsel's opinion on the implications of the actor's contract on the licensing relationship. Meanwhile, licensors should communicate honestly with licensees when any approval problems arise.

While a contract between an actor and a studio may explicitly grant the use of his or her likeness, the studio may back off from that requirement if the actor has second thoughts. Its desire is to keep big-name stars happy with an eye toward future relationships and/or their participation in film-related publicity.

ACQUIRING RIGHTS FROM MULTIPLE RIGHTS HOLDERS

Some products incorporate several properties, as discussed in Chapter 7. A pack of playing cards might feature a different celebrity or the work of a different artist on each of the 52 cards, requiring rights to be obtained for each entity. Similarly, a licensee might have to go to several individual universities to create a nationally distributed line of collegiate merchandise. Licensee Acclaim had to acquire rights to three announcers and 35 boxers for a videogame title.

A *New York Times* article noted that a company pursuing permissions for a five-second clip of *Star Wars* to be used in a CD-ROM product had to work with nine parties: the rights holder for the movie (Lucasfilm), actors, the Screen Actors Guild, stunt performers and coordinators, the director, scriptwriters, the musician's union and a music publisher. In a case like this, licensees can make their job easier by selecting a group of properties handled by one agent or licensor, as long as this does not compromise the marketability of the product line.

BUNDLING RIGHTS

In some cases, licensing agreements involve a bundle of different types of rights. A licensee of a corporate mark might want not only a trademarked brand name and copyrighted logo designs, but also certain of the licensor's proprietary, patented technologies. A licensee of a home fashion label might need not only the rights to the brand name but also to patented designs. Licensors should clearly specify in their contracts which rights they are granting, while licensees should ensure, before entering into a deal, that each desired facet of the property is fully protected by the appropriate method and available for their use.

Licensing agreements also increasingly include a bundle of rights to different but interrelated trademarked and copyrighted properties, especially in the entertainment/character sector, as was discussed in Chapter 7. These deals usually involve properties that are part of a single franchise, such as a film, its sequels and subsequent television series. They most commonly, but not always, involve long-term licensees holding rights for several products and geographic regions. Nickelodeon granted Mattel the rights to virtually all of its TV, film and brand properties across a wide range of toy categories.

GEOGRAPHY

Rights holders of a single property may be different from one region to the next. An entrepreneur in one country may register a well-known global mark before the worldwide rights holder does so. In many territories this makes the entrepreneur the legitimate property owner; global and usage rights do not take precedence over registration in these regions.

In the case of entertainment properties, various coproducers and financial partners may hold ownership rights and licensing rights in their home territory. Canadian studio Nelvana holds rights for the TV series Medabots around the world, except in Asia and Italy, where rights were already assigned before Nelvana came on board.

This type of situation can be a barrier to creating a coherent worldwide program. In 2001, U.K.-based HIT Entertainment purchased rights to the character Pingu from three rights holders, ZDF, Swiss TV and Telepool, all in the German-speaking territories. The company explained that the fragmentation of ownership had been a barrier to global licensing; the property had achieved popularity in only a few countries, such as the U.K. and Japan.

MUSIC

As mentioned in Chapter 2, music licensing encompasses several distinct areas outside of merchandise. Sound-chip products and entertainment vehicles such as home videos, television series, music CDs and electronic media may need to license music clips or performance rights, for example, in addition to or instead of acquiring trademark rights. The basic types of music licensing include:

- Performance rights. These govern live and recorded performances of music such as those heard on the radio, theme songs and background music on television or home video, supermarket music and music in nightclubs, among other incidences. Rights are cleared through organizations including ASCAP, BMI and SESAC, which represent the songwriters and composers and grant blanket licenses on an annual basis that allow the use of all the songs they represent.

- Dramatic rights. These govern original works such as music from operas, ballets, and Broadway shows that are performed on stage or in other live situations. Licensees deal directly with creators or their representatives.

- Mechanical rights. These are granted by music publishers, respresented in the U.S. by the Harry Fox Agency. Mechanical licensing governs audio-only recording such as on a CD or audiotape or over the Internet. The mechanical royalty rate is 8 cents for songs of five minutes or less and 1.55 cents for every minute thereafter, as of 2002.

- Synchronization rights. Also granted by publishers via Harry Fox, these govern uses of music in combination with visual images, such as in motion pictures, television series, videos, DVDs and electrical transcriptions (e.g. on computer chips and in novelty items such as greeting cards). Rates are negotiated on an individual basis.

PHOTOGRAPHIC DEPICTIONS

Photography is a copyrightable expression of an idea. Its most straightforward use in licensing is when product licensees acquire an image from a photographer such as Ann Geddes, paying a royalty. A more complex issue is the need to license photographic representations of copyrighted or trademarked objects (or public domain objects, including artwork) from the photographer who holds the copyright on the photo. In other words, a licensee may have to pay a fee or royalty to and acquire rights from the photographer of an image it wants to use, in addition to forging a licensing deal with a trademark owner such as an artist or museum.

Conversely, a photographer cannot license photos of a trademarked or copyrighted property without the permission and participation of the rights holder of the property depicted. The estate of the Three Stooges won a court case in 2002 against a photographer that had been selling t-shirts and prints featuring his photos of the Stooges. The court found that, based on the celebrities' right of publicity, the photographer should not be allowed to capitalize on the Stooges' notoriety without the permission of their estates.

PARODY AND ARTISTIC EXPRESSION

Some artists and online entrepreneurs use copyrighted or trademarked images in their creations as they attempt to parody or make a comment on issues they feel are comedic or important. Licensors carefully monitor such uses and often claim them as violations of their rights. For example, a property owner would sue an Internet porn site that featured one of its characters committing a lewd act, even if the user claimed it as a legitimate expression. Licensors often win these cases; the key is whether the court finds that the usage creates confusion among consumers. That is, viewers might think the licensor had something to do with the site's creation or that it is official or endorsed.

Sometimes the artist wins the battle, however. Mattel sued an artist for copyright infringement when he used Barbie in a photo exhibit. The doll was shown in "crude" and "misogynistic" ways, according to Mattel. Yet the court in the initial trial found that the artist's depictions fell under the realm of free speech protection. Mattel planned to appeal, stating that the display caused confusion among viewers, who might think Mattel supported the usage.

ELECTRONIC RIGHTS MANAGEMENT

New technologies have opened up new issues regarding rights for electronic products (not just electronics *per se* but also merchandise in other categories, such as toys, which increasingly feature electronic components). Many licensors are creating rights management systems that allow them to grant rights to music, video, voiceovers and other elements of properties, for toys, advertising and videogames, all of which can be transmitted and ordered electronically.

The growth of the Internet and corporate intranets have also given rise to the phenomenon of electronic rights management of imagery. A licensor can post tens of thousands of available images on its website for licensees to browse; once the partners forge a deal, licensors can ship camera-ready artwork via e-mail or password-equipped licensees can access it on a secure portion of the site. Paws, licensor of Garfield, has been one of the active players in this area, as have several art-specialist licensing agencies.

Two companies, Corbis and Getty Images, have been leading players in purchasing digital rights to artwork, including many museum-held paintings. They are in the business of licensing the rights to these images, as clearinghouses, for editorial and commercial use. These types of companies reduce photo research time, a development of value to licensees in many categories. (Agency Global Icons represents both companies to the licensing community, as of 2002.)

Licensees are more frequently seeking sound clips and other electronic components of a license to add to their products. They should realize that music and other rights can not necessarily be acquired from the primary licensor; other parties may hold rights to certain facets of a property. The licensee's key licensor contact can help determine where the licensee needs to go for these rights, sometimes serving as a clearinghouse for various subsidiary rights.

[Electronic media have also allowed style guides to be created electronically and to be distributed on CD or over the Internet. Much of the approval process can be accomplished electronically, although licensors still need to view samples at some points in the process. Negotiations can proceed in large part online as well, to supplement face-to-face meetings. All of these innovations have cut significant time from the product development process and the licensing process as a whole.]

VALUE OF RIGHTS

While rights of ownership are intangible, they are also valuable. Placing a monetary figure on them can be difficult and is often based on a combination of anticipated revenue streams and the hard-to-measure yardstick of "goodwill." Yet there is no question that the monetary value of owning a trademarked or copyrighted property is significant. In 2001, Disney paid an estimated $340 million, according to published reports, for 25 years' worth of rights (including new media rights) to Winnie the Pooh, representing the remaining time until the property's copyrights expire. Many character franchises, corporate trademarks and sports entities are valued in the tens or hundreds of millions of dollars.

CHAPTER 9:
CONTRACTS

The licensing contract ensures that both parties — the licensor and the licensee — agree to their respective roles and responsibilities. Many licensors have developed a standard boilerplate (a contract containing the clauses the licensor wants), but the specific points in a deal are virtually always negotiable. The licensor typically prepares the initial version of the contract, but this can vary; in the case of book publishing, it usually works the other way around. As licensing deals become more complex, there is more negotiation of the terms in the boilerplate—how much depends on the licensor and the property— but it remains a first step for discussion.

Both licensors and licensees should consult attorneys specializing in licensing before entering into an agreement. This book should be construed not as legal advice but as a guideline and overview.

MAJOR POINTS IN A LICENSING CONTRACT

The items outlined here are not necessarily in the same order that they would be in a licensing contract and are certainly not in the language of a legally binding agreement. They are intended as plain-English descriptions of the major deal points.

GRANT OF RIGHTS

The grant of rights is the core of the agreement. It outlines the properties, products, territories, distribution channels and price points allowed for the licensed line.

Description of the Property

The contract should clearly specify which elements of a property or properties the agreement covers, including trademarked names, graphics and logos. Does the contract refer to the Disney family of classic characters or Goofy alone? All Coca-Cola properties or just a group of nostalgic advertising images? An artist's entire body of work or simply a single series of related works? Describing the property and its elements explicitly prevents confusion later.

As more licensors look to reduce their number of licensees to prevent oversaturation, more contracts cover a greater number of properties. In some, each property may be tied to its own guarantee amount or royalty rate; in others, the properties may be intertwined. Licensees of all three Lord of the Rings films are governed by the terms of a single agreement and view the entire series of movies as a single, interrelated franchise.

Products Manufactured, Sold or Distributed

The document should describe the products covered by the agreement, specifying designs, materials and sizes. These details serve to distinguish the products under the contract from any similar items manufactured by other companies tied to the same license.

In addition to product descriptions, the licensing contract outlines whether the licensee has the right to *sell* the licensed products, the right to *manufacture* them or the right to *distribute* them (or a combination). The right to sell implies that the licensee can offer products imported from overseas, manufactured by domestic subcontractors or produced in-house, directly or through a distributor. The right to manufacture means the licensee will make the products without sublicensing or subcontracting. The right to distribute means the licensee sells the products of other licensees to a specific retail or mail-order channel or within a defined geographic region, or in a different form (e.g., home video for a theatrical film).

Many grant all three rights to a single licensee. Kate Spade, the accessories designer, granted Estée Lauder the right to manufacture, market, distribute and sell health and beauty items, such as cosmetics and fragrances, under the Kate Spade label.

Licensors retain the right to approve any sublicensees or subcontractors. The subcontracting manufacturers or sublicensees are associated with the licensor and its assets; in order to maintain maximum control over the property, the licensor must be able to reject any proposed companies it does not consider appropriate for the job.

Distribution

The contract outlines the distribution channels to which the licensee can sell. This ensures that two licensees' distribution rights do not overlap and that upscale brands do not find their way into mass market outlets. The agreement could authorize sales to department and specialty stores, mid-tier retailers, mass-market channels, direct mail only, a single direct-mail catalog, home shopping, the Internet or some combination of these. Which distribution channels the licensor grants depends on its strategy for the property and the capabilities of the licensee.

Since distribution channels overlap—some chains are considered mass by some and mid-tier by others, for example—it is essential to adequately define each channel as it applies to a given agreement. Some licensors have created a list of dozens of narrowly defined channels that they add as an appendix to their licensing deals to help make clear what rights are being granted.

Licensors typically reserve the right to approve any distributors the licensee intends to employ as intermediaries between themselves and retailers. These companies are associated with the property, just as the manufacturer is, and any negative actions on their part reflect poorly on the licensor. Some property owners bar the use of distributors.

The agreement should specify whether the licensee can sell its products through retail outlets only, as premiums only, or both. Retail licensees sometimes want the rights to distribute premiums in their product category, since free or inexpensive premiums from other companies that are similar to their products can cannibalize their sales. On the other hand, the licensees' capabilities may dictate the authorization of separate licensees for premium and retail distribution. Another alternative is to grant premium specialists the right to distribute only items sourced from retail licensees. Licensors often retain the right to reject corporate customers that want to purchase premiums based on their properties. These companies are associating themselves with the property, albeit indirectly, and could harm it and the licensor's image with any missteps.

E-commerce sales over the Internet represent an area of concern for licensors, who do not want unauthorized websites to dilute the value of their properties, merchandise to enter countries where trademark issues might apply, or licensees to compete with one another, among other issues. Property owners take different approaches with regard to distributing over the Internet: Some allow licensees to sell over their own sites and/or third-party e-commerce sites; some allow licensees to sell to bricks-and-mortar retailers that also sell via e-commerce, but not on their own sites; others reserve all e-commerce rights for themselves; and yet others look at each situation on a case-by-case basis.

Geographic Territory

The contract should delineate the geographic areas where the licensee will sell the products, whether it be the U.S., Canada and Mexico; a single country such as France; or the entire world. A deal can allow distribution in just a small region of the country; Famous Fixins was allowed to sell Dale Earnhardt beef jerky in the southeastern U.S. initially, with plans for a future product roll-out. Agreements, as a rule, explicitly state that licensees cannot knowingly sell to retailers or intermediaries that might distribute the merchandise outside the approved territory.

Licensors are prohibited from restricting licensees geographically within the European community, no matter what their grant of rights says. Of course, licensees who proactively do so are unlikely to work with the same licensor in the future. Licensors also take steps to prevent unwanted distribution, such as imposing a superroyalty on licensees who sell outside their territory's borders, or financially penalizing sub-agents that grant rights to licensees that violate their contracts.

Categories such as toys, fragrances, footwear and interactive games typically are granted worldwide rights (with distributors handling territories in which licensees do not have adequate coverage), because of the long lead times and high investment in product development. In other categories such as apparel and stationery, worldwide deals are rare but not unheard-of; the NHL signed Nike Team Sports to a worldwide sports apparel and headwear deal.

Exclusivity

Some agreements define exclusivity broadly. Reebok is the sole on-field supplier and has rights to most apparel categories in North America for the

NFL, as well as 10-year rights for all NBA, WNBA and National Basketball Development League on-court apparel. Activision acquired rights to the film Minority Report for all current and future console, handheld and PC gaming platforms for five years. Disguise acquired all Marvel characters (current and future) for costumes, accessories and masks in a long-term deal.

Others interpret exclusivity narrowly, such as the hypothetical example of caps made of cotton, featuring one or two graphic designs, an image on the front of the cap only, a button on the top and adjustable sizing. Most deals fall somewhere between this extreme and complete worldwide exclusivity. Licensors can limit the grant of exclusivity for designs, distribution channels, geographic areas, sizes, manufacturing materials or any number of other criteria.

If the agreement is nonexclusive, the contract should state this fact; this includes deals in the European Union, where parallel imports dictate that no exclusive involving a single country is truly exclusive.

Rights To Newly Created Properties

The contract should outline who will own rights to new properties that may be created by the licensee within the context of the licensing agreement. These could include new logos, characters or designs. The partners should agree upon an ownership split upfront if this situation seems likely.

Advertising And Promotion Materials

Property owners normally grant their licensees the right to use the property in advertising and promotional materials supporting the licensed products, subject to the licensor's approval.

PAYMENT AND AUDITING PROCEDURES

The contract should fully outline and explain all matters relating to payment.

Compensation

The major elements of compensation include:

- The royalty rate, including any adjustments in the rate as the property reaches specific milestones in sales or exposure.
- The minimum guarantee against royalties. The contract should also state whether the guarantee is a required payment (the most common situation, especially for exclusives) or simply a performance benchmark upon which renewal depends (for some nonexclusives).
- The amount of the advance and when it is due (usually in full upon contract signing).

The document should outline the payment schedule for all of the above. Licensors usually ask for quarterly royalty statements, with payment due within 30 days. The outstanding portion of the guarantee, if any, is typically payable at the end of the year or contract period.

The agreement describes the method of royalty reporting, including whether licensees must break down reports by SKU, by geographic area or by retail channel or account (or any other measurement) and which specific information they should report (e.g., units sold, dollar sales, invoice amounts, allowable deductions taken, returns). These breakdowns help licensors keep track of sales along important variables, allowing them to fine-tune the program.

Other payment-related issues contained in the contract, depending on the situation, include:

- The licensor's cut of the licensee's revenues from sublicensing agreements.
- The royalty rate for samples or other free goods, if any, as well as a limit on the amount of royalty-free goods allowed. Discounted goods sold within the licensee's or licensor's company or to affiliates may also demand a special royalty, which the contract should detail.
- The fact that all outstanding royalties and any still-owed portions of the guarantee must be paid upon termination of the contract.
- What penalties the licensee will charge for late royalty payments (e.g., 1% to 2% per month overdue).
- What items, such as freight, returns and cash discounts, can be subtracted from sales totals before the royalty is applied, along with the authorized cap on such deductions. (Other selling, manufacturing and distribution costs are rarely deductible.)
- Exactly how licensees should calculate the royalty, including whether it is based on an F.O.B. or retail price or on cost.
- Penalties or "superroyalties" for overshipping or distributing outside the authorized geographic territory. (Alternatively, the contract may contain production limits or other methods of preventing oversaturation.)

Definitions

The contract should define all terms that might be confusing, particularly when they relate to royalty payments. One common example is the term "net sales." Most agreements call for licensees to pay royalties on net sales (usually the invoice amount less certain allowable deductions), but, since the term can be ambiguous, the document should explain its meaning clearly, as well as other terms such as "samples," "free goods" or "discount goods."

Auditing Procedures

Licensors retain the right to audit the licensee's books, which the contract should state. It should also include specifics about how compliance reviews will be carried out. (They are often handled by an outside company that specializes in royalty compliance.) For example:

- what prior notice should be given to the licensee?

- how often can the licensor audit the licensee's books?
- how long after termination of the contract can the licensee request an audit?
- how long must a licensee keep its books relating to the agreement?

The contract should also specify the penalty in case of any discepancies or nonpayment (including extra penalties for each month overdue and required interest payments) and whether the licensee must pay for the audit, as is usually the case, if discrepancies surpass a certain level (e.g., 5% of royalties owed).

Some licensors reserve the right to audit in the case of suspected overshipping or overmanufacturing (in cases when the contract dictates production or distribution limits), as well as for accounting discrepancies.

As part of the auditing procedure, licensors also reserve the right to make copies of relevant materials in case of future need (as in court).

PRODUCT DEVELOPMENT AND APPROVALS

Licensing contracts outline the procedure and time frame for product development and approvals. While licensees typically are responsible for product development, there may be cases when the licensor takes on much of the early work, such as creating the concepts, with licensees assuming duties just prior to manufacturing. The contract should outline the division of labor.

It should also outline the steps and timing involved in the approval process. Clauses should include the number of samples the licensee must send the licensor for approval; the time within which the licensor must approve or disapprove (e.g., within 10 days of the receipt of samples); and the stages in the manufacturing process where approvals are necessary (e.g., conceptual models, preproduction samples, production samples and/or finished samples, as well as additional points within the production process, if any). Licensors approve promotional and advertising materials and packaging utilizing the property, as well as the licensed product line.

Each licensor's requirements for product approvals varies, and the contract should contain definitions what constitutes each point along the approval process. There should be no confusion regarding how the licensor defines "the concept stage," for example. Licensors with more than the common three benchmarks in the approval process should be particularly concerned with these definitions, since they may identify the stages differently than licensees are used to.

The agreement should state whether the failure of the licensor to approve within the given time frame signifies approval or nonapproval. Most licensors prefer that their failure to approve constitutes nonapproval, since this ensures that products will not slip through the cracks and be approved accidentally. Licensees, on the other hand, would rather treat a lack of response by the licensor as approval, in order to reduce potential delays. A strong approval process benefits both parties, however.

If the licensor does not approve a product initially, it gives the licensee a certain period (such as 30 days) to remedy the problems. Failure to respond within the contract-specific time frame could be grounds for termination. Licensees may demand that licensors provide a reason for any nonapproval.

Licensors often reserve the right to inspect the licensee's production facilities as part of their quality control procedure.

TERM OF THE CONTRACT

The contract should state the term, or duration, of the agreement. Two to three years is the average, but this varies depending on a number of factors, such as how long the licensee and licensor have had a mutually acceptable relationship, what type of property is involved and the licensee's history. Some deals are valid for as little as six months and some for a decade or more, depending on the circumstances.

There has been a movement toward deals of five, rather than three, years in special situations, such as where many products are involved and/or sales are likely to be high, when the property constitutes a large portion of the licensee's business, or in a renewal situation. Recent five-year deals include Hasbro's and Action Performance's agreement with auto racer Jeff Gordon for toys and collectibles; Disney's with its long-time European publishing licensee Egmont, a renewal deal encompassing 20 countries; and Fila's with its Japanese master licensee Kanebo for footwear and apparel expected to reach $1 billion at retail. Action Performance renewed its deal with auto racer Jeff Gibbs for seven years in 2002 (subject to certain performance standards).

Limited-term licenses (in the six-months-to-a-year range) are appropriate in cases such as special events, limited editions, promotional premiums or seasonal properties. Guarantees typically are due upfront, and the royalty rate may be higher than for a longer-term deal.

Contracts should specify the effective date of the agreement (the date the relationship officially begins).

Termination and Breach

Most licensing relationships will end eventually. The finish can come in an amicable parting when sales run their course; when the parties disagree or one of them violates the contract terms; because of a change in ownership; when one of the parties did not meet specified performance criteria; when the line failed; or because the parties were unable to agree on renewal terms.

The agreement should outline what types of behavior would consititute a breach of contract. These could include failure to meet crucial production schedules, failure to meet a product introduction date or a first sales date, failure to continuously sell the merchandise, failure to earn out the guarantee, failure to pay royalties, selling products where not allowed by the contract, or bankruptcy. A licensor may reserve the right to terminate one aspect of the agreement (such as a single geographic area) if that facet is weak but the rest of the relationship strong. Some licensors institute financial penalties before resorting to termination, depending on the severity of the breach.

All rights to the property revert to the licensor after the contract terminates. Many agreements provide that either party can end the relationship for any reason upon 30 to 60 days' written notice.

The agreement should clarify what happens *after* termination. The licensee must pay any outstanding royalties or guarantees. The parties should agree on what is to be done with remaining inventory; a manufacturer may be granted 60 to 90 days upon termination to dispose of excess merchandise (nonexclusively, so the licensor can seek a new licensee), after which the manufacturer cannot allow any products to reach the market. Licensees must pay royalties on sales of these surplus items, although they may be low since the products will probably command a reduced price.

The contract should also outline what happens to molds, tools, dies, screens and camera-ready art, if not worn out. A major manufacturer may keep molds as valuable, and sometimes reusable, assets (a toy company may reissue the same action figure with different paint as a generic or under a future license); it may subsequently negotiate to sell or lease them to the licensor or a future licensee. (Obviously, it cannot use them for unauthorized merchandise.) In most cases, however, all existing materials specific to the license are sent back to the licensor.

Upon termination, there may be outstanding financial issues that need to be resolved. When fashion label Nautica and licensee Genesco ended a 10-year footwear licensing relationship in 2001, Genesco owed Nautica a cancellation fee. That and other costs of winding up the licensed business cost Genesco close to $3 million that year.

Options

Many licensing agreements contain an option to renew, which reduces risk for both parties—allowing them to maintain a good arrangement but exist amicably if things are not working—and emphasizes the potential for a long-term partnership. For example, a two-year agreement might contain an option for a third year. The possibilities range from an automatic renewal, if certain performance criteria are met, to no contractual option. The licensor may grant the licensee a first look at the licensor's next property or the right of first refusal on it.

If the licensee decides to renew under the option, the partners typically renegotiate royalties, guarantees and other terms of the agreement, such as adding categories or territories.

Contracts must be renewed periodically, not just to incorporate ongoing changes as the relationship evolves, but for trademark protection. A perpetual license between a licensor and licensee may lead to claims of "assignment in gross," which could result in the licensor's loss of rights to the trademark.

INDEMNIFICATIONS AND INSURANCE

The licensor indemnifies (protects) the licensee against third parties that dispute the licensor's ownership of the property. The licensee indemnifies the licensor in the case of lawsuits that result from injuries or deaths caused by the licensed product.

While the licensee is responsible for any suits of this type brought against it, the licensor — which often has deeper pockets — may be held responsible as well. For that reason, the indemnification is typically backed up by insurance, such as $1 million each in personal injury and product liability coverage. These sums may be higher in categories where lawsuits are common, such as food or toys.

Most companies already carry insurance or maintain a risk-management program (if they operate in industries where insurance is prohibitively expensive or difficult to acquire). Licensors usually demand they be named on the licensee's policy as a coinsured party and that they be informed of any changes to the licensee's insurance or risk-management program during the term of the agreement.

OTHER PROVISIONS

Some of the potential contractual terms outlined in this section are typical of virtually all deals, while others are optional. They include, in no particular order:

- Warranties on the part of the the licensor that it owns the property and has not granted the same rights to other licensees. It also warrants that properties covered in the agreement do not infringe on other trademarks.
- A statement that the agreement does not constitute ownership of the property by the licensee. (In other words, the manufacturer is renting, not purchasing, the rights.)
- A schedule dictating the products' introduction to the trade and specifying the date of initial merchandise shipments.
- Warranties on the part of the licensee that it will make its "best effort" to market and distribute the products under a schedule specified in the agreement. (There may be financial incentives and penalties to back up these promises.)
- Warranties that both parties have the authority to enter into the agreement and to live up to their responsibilities.
- Provisions that licensees must mark products and collateral materials with appropriate trademark and copyright indicators. Licensors usually require licensees to use specific labeling to ensure consistency among all licensed products. They often require manufacturers to source the labels or hangtags from a specified supplier.
- Statements regarding which party has the right to take legal action against an infringer, if counterfeiting occurs, as well as who

must pay for such an action and which party receives the rewards, if any. (Normally the licensor takes responsibility for combatting knock-offs, but there are occasions when the licensee may want some participation in anti-infringement efforts, such as when a licensor decides not to pursue a counterfeiter or if the licensed line in question represents a significant portion of the licensee's business.)

■ Provisions allowing the licensor to approve any changes in ownership of the licensee, and *vice versa*, including large financial investments or an outright sale. Such changes of ownership, if not satisfactory to the licensor, may be grounds for termination of the agreement. (Warner Bros. chose not to keep its Cartoon Network licenses with Golden Books when the latter was acquired by Random House in 2001.) The rise in consolidation among licensors and licensees makes this an important clause.

■ A clause stating which state's laws apply in the case of a dispute and a provision outlining how the parties will resolve disagreements (e.g., through arbitration).

■ A mention that licensees may, with the licensor's permission, change the products from how they are outlined in the agreement (due to market changes), but that royalties and other provisions of the contract continue to apply to the altered goods.

■ A provision noting the licensee's acknowledgment that the property has its own "goodwill" value, which is owned by the licensor.

■ A statement from the licensee agreeing that the brand has acquired "secondary meaning." This is applicable to descriptive brand names; that is, where the name suggests the product (as opposed to being a made-up name). Trademarks normally do not cover descriptive names. If a name has "secondary meaning," however, it is considered more than a simple description, but rather distinctive to the merchandise with which it is associated. Such a brand can be registered as a trademark.

■ A provision known as "licensee estoppel," in which the licensee acknowledges that the licensor's properties are valid trademarks. This clause bars the licensee from disputing the trademark's validity at a later date.

■ A statement that the licensee cannot assign any of the rights granted in the agreement to other parties.

■ A statement that the licensor is not obligated to market, sell or support a property. This may lower the value of the trademark over time and is something licensees should question.

This is not an exhaustive list. Both licensees and licensors, in association with their attorneys, may demand that a contract include further points, depending on the particulars of the situation. A licensor might reserve the right to consult on the licensee's business with regard to a property, for example, particularly if it is a key licensee accounting for a large portion of the property's sales. This is not a standard clause, but has been incorporated into some specific licensing contracts.

EXPANDING A LICENSING CONTRACT

The partners in a licensing agreement may expand or extend their deal for any number of reasons. A successful licensee may, before the original contract period is over, add distribution channels (including the Internet), increase the number of products in its line, extend the range of sizes or expand into new geographic areas as yet unfilled by the licensor. In some cases, the licensor may incorporate these changes as amendments to the original contract, while in others it may draw up an entirely new agreement. The former situation usually allows new products to reach the marketplace more quickly, but is not always practical. Expanded agreements come with new compensation provisions, which must be outlined in the new document or appendix.

Another expansion situation occurs when a licensor offers a related, but separate, property to an existing licensee. Warner Bros. may allow a Bugs Bunny licensee to sell items based on Marvin the Martian (both are part of the Looney Tunes family of characters). The National Basketball Association may grant an NBA licensee the rights to create additional merchandise incorporating the insignias of the WNBA, the women's basketball league.

The licensee may reserve the right, as part of the original contract, to expand into new areas if the initial products succeed. This type of deal requires the licensor to keep those categories or territories open rather than signing other manufacturers, so the licensee should expect to pay a premium for this contractual bonus.

Of course, if a license is renewed at the end of its term, new categories, distribution channels, geographic regions or other rights may be added. All terms are renegotiated at the end of the original contract's duration; some partners are not able to agree to new terms and end the arrangement, while others revise the agreement and continue the relationship.

CONTRACTS BETWEEN LICENSING AGENT AND LICENSOR

The licensor and its agent also detail the particulars of their relationship in a contract. Many of the provisions parallel those found in the licensor-licensee agreement. Following is a brief synopsis of some of the elements in a licensor-agent accord.

The contract specifies the term of the agreement, which is usually two years, often with the option to renew if the agent meets certain performance goals. It outlines the agent's compensation, including its cut of royalties, advances and guarantees, as well as any other fees, such as monthly retainers or fees for responsibilities outside the scope of the basic agreement. The document also summarizes any decreases in the agent's commissions over time, to take into account that established licensing programs are easier to maintain than start-ups. It includes reporting and payment schedules and procedures, as well as auditing provisions. Most licensors retain the right to approve all agreements negotiated by the agent.

The pact explains which properties the agent will handle and states that the licensor is and will remain the owner of those properties. It should also specify if the relationship is exclusive, exclusive only for certain categories or nonexclusive; itemize the agent's duties; and set forth the division of costs and expenses. The licensor will probably bear the cost of registering trademarks, for example, while the agent assumes responsibility for the day-to-day costs of administering the effort.

Finally, the contract should stipulate what constitutes grounds for termination and what happens after the contract ends. Most agents continue to receive commissions on royalties for a certain period after termination (sometimes indefinitely), since their work led to many of these sales.

Licensors or their master agents have similar contracts with international sub-agents around the world. These contain many of the same provisions. In particular, they must outline the responsibilities of the agent, especially in cases where an agent in another country has granted rights for a product that will be sold in the sub-agent's region. In this case the agent's tasks will center on brand management duties, such as advertising and gaining distribution, rather than on selling the property. Compensation will differ in these cases and the specifics must be outlined in the contract. Agreements with sub-agents should also deal with how specialized distribution channels, such as e-commerce, will be handled in the agent's territory.

Licensees and their licensing consultants also agree to a contract outlining the consultant's duties, compensation, cost coverage and the term of the contract, among other provisions.

OTHER ISSUES

Outside of the licensing contract, there are a number of other documents, some more binding than others, that occur within the scope of an existing or potential licensing relationship.

Some licensors want prospective licensees to sign confidentiality or nondisclosure agreements before showing them a property. Companies maintain different policies toward these documents, but some will consider signing one if they and their attorneys feel the licensor has adequately protected the property in a legal sense (making the property unique). If a potential licensee does not view a property as sufficiently different from other brands, even given legitimate trademark status, it is unlikely to sign a nondisclosure document that could come back to haunt it later.

If a property is properly trademarked and copyrighted, a confidentiality agreement is theoretically unnecessary; in addition, the fact that licensing is a business of relationships prevents most licensors and licensees from stealing from one another. Major licensees typically decline to sign such an agreement; they often have projects already in the pipeline that could be construed as similar and want to prevent accusations of theft if a similar yet unrelated property or product comes to market.

Another type of agreement is the "deal memo." Many licensing partners draw up a deal-point memorandum, or deal memo, to assist them in communicating with each other. This document specifies the basic points of a deal in plain language, exclusive of legal fine points such as warranties and indemnities, and is not binding. It acts as the foundation for discussing the key terms of the future licensing agreement, such as definitions, timing and financial parameters. A signed one- to two-page deal memo containing the dozen or so key points in the agreement allows the partners to proceed with product development while their attorneys hash out the multiple-page final contract. This procedure is sometimes essential to get products to market on time.

Letters of intent sometimes serve as a prelude to licensing contracts, but most licensors do not consider them worthwhile. Deals still fall apart even with a signed letter of intent. Most prefer to move from the deal memo straight to the contract. Some public companies sign letters of intent for financial reasons; they can publicize the existence of the letter to boost their value in the markets.

There are also contracts between licensees and their sublicensees and subcontractors, subject to approval by the licensor. These manufacturing contracts contain provisions regarding the sublicensee's relationship to the license (namely, that it holds no ownership rights). They also state that the sublicensee must destroy all molds related to the license once production is complete, that it must not produce more than the licensee orders, and other requirements. Many of these are intended to prevent counterfeiting by the subcontractor, but are difficult to enforce.

Direct-to-retail and retail exclusive deals also require contracts between the licensor and retailer/licensee. Direct-to-retail agreements are similar to the licensor-licensee contract discussed in this chapter, with added provisions that relate to the specifics of the deal. A direct-to-retail or retail exclusive contract must contain the details of where the products are to be sourced, who is responsible for the royalty payments, who bears responsibility for product development, what is the mix of exclusive, nonexclusive and direct-licensed products, and who assumes the cost and responsibility for creating signage, packaging, advertising and other marketing materials, among other provisions.

Licensors also forge contracts with service and non-retail product licensees, promotional partners, licensees that acquire the property for promotional use, and all other partners. Each is similar to the licensor-licensee contract but is tailored to the specific situation, depending on the use of the property, the term of the agreement, and method of payment (royalty, flat fee, in-kind services or some combination of these).

CHAPTER 10:
COUNTERFEITING

Counterfeiting is a big problem for licensors and licensees. Infringement devalues licensors' trademarks and copyrights and causes licensees to lose sales. From fake Calvin Klein purses on the streets of New York to counterfeit Chicago Bulls caps outside the arena to unofficial Mickey Mouse figurines at flea markets in Italy to fake Pokémon merchandise in Southeast Asian stores, no property type or product category is exempt.

Observers often use the terms "infringement," "knock-off," "piracy" and "counterfeiting" interchangeably, but there are subtle differences among them. Counterfeiting and piracy both refer to the fraudulent copying of an item, while infringement denotes encroachment on a property owner's rights. Knock-offs also suggest the making of unauthorized copies; this term refers to cases where items are similar but do not offer an overt brand connection. For instance, a knock-off artist might emulate a jewelry design but not attach a specific label's name to it.

Of course, any popular property will eventually face competition from "coattails" properties as well. These are licenses that have many of the same attributes as the original property and follow on its heels trying to capitalize on its popularity. (Think of all the animé properties that came to the market in the wake of Pokémon.) These are not illegal, but contribute to market oversaturation.

HOW BIG A PROBLEM IS COUNTERFEITING?

Evaluating the amount of counterfeit goods sold each year in the U.S. or worldwide is difficult due to the fly-by-night nature of the industry and the sheer number of venues where illegal products are sold. Infringers can be legitimate businesses by day and counterfeiters after hours, or employees of authorized licensees (or friends of employees) who steal designs and set up shop. They are capable of shutting down or moving at a moment's notice and are often located in countries where regulations against such activities are either not in place or not enforced.

Published measurements of the amount of counterfeit licensed merchandise sold each year have ranged from $1 billion to more than $80 billion, suggesting how tough it is to get a handle on the numbers. No one specifically tracks the portion of the market related to licensed goods and even the estimates for all trademarked merchandise are unreliable.

Experts agree that counterfeiting is a major concern, however, especially for licensors and manufacturers associated with top-selling properties. A popular license — whether short- or long-term and regardless of its source — will be ripped off. Anecdotal evidence provided by licensors and licensees suggests the scope of the problem: Half of all Pokémon merchandise in the amusement industry in Spain in the property's peak year was counterfeit, for example, while 90% of sports merchandise on the Brazilian market, mostly related to soccer/football, is pirated.

The Licensing Letter estimates that, as a rule of thumb, the street value of counterfeit goods associated with a given property is equivalent to at least 10% to 15% of the total retail sales value of all officially licensed merchandise based on that property. The percentage is much higher for very hot properties, properties that become popular unexpectedly before a licensing effort is in place, or properties without aggressive anti-infringement activities; some observers gauge counterfeit sales at equal or more than the retail value of official merchandise in such situations. Less-popular properties, naturally, do not attract as much counterfeiting activity, since fewer consumers demand merchandise, either official or unofficial.

COSTS

Administering an anti-counterfeiting program requires identifying unlicensed merchandise and taking action against its manufacturers, as well as trying to prevent its occurrence in the first place. Licensors spend significant time, effort and money combatting the manufacture and sale of knock-offs. The National Football League, for example, reportedly has spent 30% to 50% of its licensing royalties from the Super Bowl on protecting its marks in conjunction with that event.

Costs vary depending on what actions licensors and licensees take to prevent, or at least reduce, counterfeiting. In most cases, licensors bear the bulk of the cost, but key licensees may participate as well. In some cases, the licensor and its agent split costs 50/50, while in other cases the licensor, agent and one or two key licensees share the costs.

The costs of an effective anti-counterfeiting program are almost always greater than any return from court cases. The focus of most efforts are on prevention; going after violators sends a message to other potential infringers more than it leads to any significant financial gain.

TRENDS IN COUNTERFEITING

Unfortunately, infringers are sophisticated. Their production and packaging methods are good enough that consumers and retailers sometimes find it difficult to distinguish a piece of counterfeit merchandise from the real thing. Ten to 15 years ago, licensors and others could identify illegitimate products at a glance. Counterfeit goods lacked a hangtag (an identifying label attached to a garment or other product) or sewn-in labeling, or possessed a tag vastly inferior to those on legitimate merchandise. The products themselves were of poor quality, featuring misspelled logos, poor color reproduction, cheesy designs and cheap materials.

Today, many counterfeiters manufacture high-quality merchandise with accurate color, reproduce designs and logos very similar to legitimate goods, employ materials close or identical to what licensees use and accurately replicate hangtags and packaging. Infringers invest in expensive manufacturing equipment, often of the same type purchased by authorized licensees.

Through the use of computers, they can steal actual designs and product specifications without detection, avoid leaving a paper trail and have knock-offs on the market within a few months (or less) after a legitimate licensee announces a new product line.

Some counterfeiters manage to get products to market well before the legitimate licensee does, significantly impacting sales. When no other products are available but the counterfeits, the illegal merchandise has a window of opportunity to take advantage of consumer excitement, which may fade by the time the official products arrive, especially for a short-term property such as a musical act.

The Internet has also made counterfeiters' job simpler. It is easier to hide from law enforcement and easier to dupe consumers with shoddy merchandise (as long as the photos on a website are high quality). It is also easier to distribute merchandise on a worldwide basis.

In spite of all this bad news, the fight against counterfeiting has progressed in many ways. The U.S. judicial system is aware of and concerned about the problem and law enforcement aggressive against it. The courts now hold retailers liable for selling counterfeit merchandise, even if they had nothing to do with its manufacture, as opposed to the early 1990s when licensors could prosecute only the hard-to-locate pirates. This gives flea markets, local mom-and-pop stores and all retailers an incentive to keep an eye out for counterfeit merchandise, avoid purchasing it and alert licensors to its existence. Technological advances for hangtags and other labeling make illegitimate merchandise easier to find, at least until infringers catch up.

Internationally, where much of the counterfeit manufacturing and sales occurs (especially in Asia and Latin America but almost everywhere worldwide), many governments are implementing better laws, especially those that are lobbying for entry into the World Trade Organization. Enforcement still lags in most regions, however. While the situation is getting better very slowly, counterfeiting remains a huge problem globally.

Licensees, licensors, agents and other observers have pointed out that counterfeiters' increased sophistication means that, rather than illegally copying any brand or property, they tend to focus on licenses that will be best-sellers. In other words, there is more counterfeiting than ever on the hot properties each year, while secondary properties have less than before. Meanwhile, less counterfeiting occurs on classic properties and some corporate brands than in the past, primarily because counterfeiters are aware that the property owners are actively policing the market and aggressively taking action. With short-term properties, on the other hand, the window of opportunity is short and licensors have their hands full with other issues, so criminals can get in and out of the market before anyone can catch up with them.

WHAT CAN BE DONE?

Anti-counterfeiting initiatives have three major objectives. First, licensors want to prevent infringement from taking place. Second, by closely monitoring the marketplace, they hope to quickly discover any illegal activity that does occur. Third, they want to take action against counterfeiters that harm their trademarks. The first is the most important, although many licensors tend to devote more energy to the last two.

PREVENTION

Education is the primary tool in any attempt to prevent counterfeiting. Licensors try to inform manufacturers, retailers and even consumers about the existence of counterfeiting and to explain how it hurts each of these groups. They remind manufacturers that counterfeit merchandise cuts into their sales, that they are better positioned than licensors to run across unofficial merchandise and that it benefits them to tell licensors about suspected piracy so the latter can take action.

Property owners tell retailers they can become involved in litigation if they purchase illegitimate merchandise and emphasize that counterfeiting can lead to higher prices and anger from consumers. They also stress that carrying illegal goods may harm retailers' relationships with licensees and licensors, which can be a deterrent when hot or strong classic properties are involved. Most importantly, licensors keep retailers informed on who the official licensees are, so they do not mistakenly purchase illegal merchandise.

In reality, consumers may not really care if they are buying official licensed merchandise, as long as they like the item and feel it is fairly priced. Some may feel cheated, however, if they thought they were buying authentic merchandise and it turns out to be unauthorized. Some licensors, therefore, attempt to remind consumers of the existence of counterfeit merchandise and warn them of the possibility of purchasing knock-offs.

Another consumer incentive is that the cost of licensors' expensive anti-counterfeiting efforts could, in the long run, be passed on to manufacturers in the form of increased royalties, then to retailers in the form of higher wholesale prices and ultimately to consumers in the form of higher retail prices. In other words, counterfeiting can eventually hit consumers in their pocketbooks. Licensors also appeal to consumers' sense of right and wrong.

Some licensors have encouraged consumers to contact them if they think they spot counterfeit merchandise. For example, they have run ads in consumer magazines containing a toll-free number to make reporting violations easy. Sports leagues and studios are among those that have taken this approach.

Publicity

Licensors rely on publicity and advertising to educate all of these constituencies (supplemented by personal day-to-day communication with licensees and retailers). Publicity releases sent to trade and consumer publications motivate the media to help inform the business community and the public about seizures of illegal merchandise as well as anti-counterfeiting litigation and successes. Some licensors disseminate general information on counterfeiting and why it is a problem.

All of this publicity and advertising is also directed at potential counter-feiters. Infringers read trade and consumer publications, too. When they realize that retailers, licensees and consumers are all involved in the licen-sors' anti-counterfeiting mission and that the licensor is making a big mon-etary and human resource commitment to its effort, some potential pirates may think twice before infringing on that particular trademark. Of course, if the property is popular enough, criminals will feel it is worth the risk.

Labeling

Licensors typically require all licensees to use identical hangtags and labeling. Not only does this support a consistent marketing message, but it helps prevent knock-offs by making authentic merchandise easier to iden-tify. In many cases, licensees are required to purchase the labels from a single official supplier; in others, the licensor gives them the proper artwork so they can source the tags from their own suppliers.

Hangtags can be duplicated by counterfeiters. As a result, licensors are looking for ways to make hangtags and labels more difficult and costly to copy. Property owners use holograms or other specialty printing techniques on hangtags, labels, stickers, packages and the product itself. While counter-feiters can learn to replicate holographic and other labeling and packaging, it is more expensive than traditional methods and many infringers do not bother, preferring instead to maintain their profit margins.

These technologies can be prohibitively expensive for some licensors and licensees; if they are losing a small portion of their business to counter-feiters many experts believe the costs of such labeling is unjustified.

Legal Protection

Licensors' number-one preventive measure against counterfeiting is to adequately protect their properties under trademark, copyright and other applicable laws. Full registration provides the best support when pursuing counterfeiters through legal channels and is therefore a potential disincen-tive to infringers. If a licensor's properties are not fully registered, it still has some legal rights based on its creation of the property (copyright) and its commercial use of it (trademark), but the more thorough the registration the better the chances of success in the courtroom and the lower the chances of infringement.

In addition to copyright and trademark law, the right of publicity may provide protection in some states when dealing with infringement of celeb-rity names and likenesses (see Chapter 8). The concept of "trade dress" may apply when a knock-off product or packaging is similar to a licensed item without being an exact duplicate. The U.S. judicial system considers trade dress, or the "look" of a product or its packaging, protectable even though there is no mechanism through which to register it. (Licensors can register elements that are part of the look of a product, such as names or logos, as trademarks.) Patent protection may apply to some licensed products.

Secure Image Transmittal

It is also important to use common sense by preventing authorized artwork or specifications from getting into the wrong hands. Most licensors recommend holding back on detailed specifications for logos or graphics until a company signs a contract naming it an official licensee, especially if the two parties have no track record together. Because of the length of product development in some categories, however, many licensors ship artwork once a deal memo is signed but before the contract is final, to ensure products get to market on time.

The Internet gave rise to concerns about the ease of stealing, but many licensors rely on the web as a means of distributing artwork that is more secure than shipping printouts or CD-ROMs. They use password-protected websites and encrypted e-mail to securely transmit camera-ready images. Some licensors automatically log users off their site if they have not clicked in a certain amount of time; this can be a sign of unauthorized downloading.

DETECTION

Tips from manufacturers and other informants comprise the major method of detecting counterfeiting activity, since licensees, retailers and even shoppers are in closer day-to-day touch with the market than licensors are.

Most major property owners also maintain a network of private investigators in the U.S. and abroad. They help verify the incidence of counterfeit merchandise and assist local law enforcement in taking action against infringers.

A licensor's employees also serve as its eyes and ears in the marketplace. They go out into the field to spot-check for unlicensed merchandise and keep a lookout while doing their own shopping or traveling. They are stationed at likely venues for counterfeiting, such as sports events, fan rallies or conventions, and check out street vendors and flea markets.

Most major licensors enlist the help of U.S. Customs to stop illegal merchandise from coming into the country from offshore counterfeiting centers such as Asia. Once a licensor registers a trademark, it can record it with Customs. The agency can then refuse importation of merchandise it believes to be counterfeit. Other governmental bodies can also be useful for helping to detect unlicensed merchandise. They include the U.S. Postal Service, U.S. Trade Commission, U.S. embassies, the FBI, local law enforcement bodies and the U.S. Marshall. Customs, police departments and other organizations in countries around the world can also be helpful for licensors both in and outside their borders.

Some larger licensors have assigned a dedicated staff member to police the Internet for infringements on a full-time basis.

REMEDIES

As mentioned earlier, trademark and copyright laws are the primary tools to protect against and pursue counterfeiters in the U.S. Federal trademark legislation provides the best security for most licensed properties, while individual states also offer trademark protection to various degrees. In fact, more states have legislated that counterfeiting is a felony (meaning penalties of jail time in addition to fines) and their law enforcement personnel are actively enforcing the laws. About half the U.S. states are now considered to have strong anti-counterfeiting laws.

Two types of remedies are available under both trademark and copyright law: civil (e.g., pertaining to the rights of individuals) and criminal (pertaining to crime and its punishment). Either may be appropriate depending on the situation.

Licensors have a number of options in terms of possible remedies if their marks are infringed, depending on the area of law they invoke. Which is best—trademark, copyright or another body of law— depends on the situation. This chapter does not attempt to sort out all the alternatives. Property owners, in association with their legal counsel, should weigh the effectiveness of each against its cost.

Most licensors first attempt to turn infringers into legitimate licensees, especially if, as is sometimes the case, they are using the trademark or copyrighted entity without realizing they need permission. Either they do not understand trademark law or they believe the property is in the public domain. If the counterfeiting is of this relatively innocent type, the licensor will usually try to iron out a contract with the manufacturer, allowing it to continue producing merchandise as a royalty-paying licensee. Many manufacturers are willing to agree to this.

If the counterfeiter is infringing knowingly or refuses to become a licensee, the next step is typically a cease-and-desist letter from an attorney. This action is relatively inexpensive and is effective in many cases. The letter informs the counterfeiter that the licensor is aware of the situation and will take legal action if the manufacturer does not immediately stop the production and sale of offending items.

If the counterfeiter ignores the cease-and-desist letter and/or refuses to work with the licensor, the matter moves to court, where several legal remedies are available depending on the specifics of the case. They include seizures of merchandise and equipment, restraining orders or injunctions prohibiting the company from continuing its infringement, and/or the closure of the illegal operation. Infringers find these actions costly and annoying, although in many cases they manage to set up shop again quickly and consider reacting to such situations part of the expense of doing business.

Ultimately, if a counterfeiter is convicted of a crime, it faces jail time or fines. Judges can award monetary damages to the licensor as well, with amounts calculated based on estimates of lost sales or the infringer's profits from the operation. Again, licensors should evaluate the costs before seeking any remedy. A property owner may want to receive damages, but the costs of litigating can be prohibitively high. Most licensors prefer remedies that will put and keep the counterfeiter out of business over those that bring in a monetary settlement.

It is critical that licensors keep records of all anti-infringement activities, including copies of cease-and-desist letters and records of efforts made to police the market for counterfeiting activity. This documentation will be used as evidence in any court proceeding and demonstrates that the licensor is serious about protecting its marks and has taken an active role in maintaining their value. Lack of such evidence could weigh against the licensor; infringers could argue that the mark is weak and they were not aware it was legally protected.

The procedures and bodies of law available in different countries vary, although they often parallel those in the U.S. Since counterfeiting is a global problem, licensors and licensees must educate themselves on the particulars of the legal system and enforcement procedures in individual countries. They must also weigh the benefits and costs of aggressive action in a particular region against the amount of sales being lost due to counterfeiters there.

Even when the expense of a global anti-counterfeiting effort is high, it is important to remember the necessity of policing the market on a worldwide basis in order to protect a property's trademark status.

WORKING TOGETHER

Competing licensors benefit from working together for the common good when it comes to anti-counterfeiting activities. When a flea market features counterfeit merchandise based on one property, chances are it sells unofficial products based on other properties as well. Therefore, licensors that pool their monetary and human resources against a pirate will maximize the damage done to its operation and reduce the likelihood it will infringe in the future.

While there have been a number of official efforts among licensors, agents and licensees to band together against counterfeiters, such as The Coalition to Advance the Protection of Sports Logos (C.A.P.S.), most cooperative efforts are more informal. Many permanent, official efforts tend not to generate much interest, largely because of conflicts of interest among the competitive members. On the other hand, licensors, agents and licensees are increasingly willing to work together on a case-by-case basis when an incidence of counterfeiting involves merchandise based on all of their properties. The companies' combined resources are more effective and generate more publicity than going it alone.

EXAMPLES OF ENFORCEMENT ACTIVITY

The following examples illustrate scenarios of enforcement activity typical in the licensing business, as well as the types of results a licensor might expect:

- In 2001, investigators Kessler International and the New York City Police seized more than 5,000 watches with an estimated street value of $200,000 in a raid. The watches infringed on luxury trademarks.

- During the 2000 World Series between the New York Mets and the New York Yankees, Major League Baseball served lawsuits against 492 counterfeiters in three weeks and seized 39,000 units of t-shirts, sweatshirts, caps and lanyards infringing on the trademarks of the two teams, along with MLB's World Series and Subway Series marks. Two hundred seventy-nine of the complaints and more than 18,000 seizures occurred at the celebratory parade for the winning Yankees; the remainder occurred outside the two stadiums.

- Seizures during the Sidney Olympic Games in 2000 included pins, badges, watches, beer mugs, soccer balls, caps, boys' apparel, picture frames, refrigerator magnets and rugs made in the U.S., Hong Kong, China, Indonesia, Pakistan, the Philippines, Thailand, Taiwan, Malaysia and Republic of Korea. Units seized of the listed items alone numbered more than 12,000.

- In 1997, five people were arrested for violating North Carolina laws on infringement during the first round of the NCAA Division I Men's Basketball Championship in Winston-Salem. In the same incident, police seized more than 200 t-shirts, $500 in cash and a mini-van that was home to the counterfeiting operation.

While these examples center on activity surrounding fashion and sports properties, all property types, from entertainment to music to corporate trademark to art, can witness significant illegal activity. These examples simply serve to illustrate some of the steps licensors can take as part of their anti-counterfeiting programs.

CHAPTER 11:
INTERNATIONAL LICENSING

The licensing business has become global, with most licensors, no matter what their origin, planning to sell merchandise in countries outside their home borders. TV co-productions now typically involve companies in several countries, with each retaining a stake in merchandising in their own regions and worldwide. More than 50% of U.S.-origin films' box office accrues overseas, with the proportion of licensing revenues following close behind. Most corporate trademarks and fashion labels have a global or at least multi-territory reach, often from the beginning of their lives but, if not, through gradual expansion. Musicians attain global fame quickly, while contemporary artists are aware of the potential of international markets and are targeting them in their licensing efforts.

International territories currently account for just over one-third of total worldwide retail sales of licensed merchandise (global sales were $109 billion in 2001, according to *The Licensing Letter*), while the U.S. and Canada together account for 64.5% (with Canada representing approximately 10% of that). *Figure 12 (page 184)* shows worldwide retail sales of licensed merchandise by geographic region.

Rates of per-capita spending on licensed merchandise in the U.S. and Canada *versus* other regions suggest that international territories offer more room for growth. The spending rate per person in the U.S. and Canada is more than triple that in the next highest-spending market, Japan ($223 *versus* $69 in 2001, according to *TLL*). Per-capita spending in foreign markets may never exceed U.S. levels, but it is reasonable to assume that greater increases will come from areas with lower current levels of spending. *Figure 13 (page 184)* shows per-capita spending rates on licensed merchandise worldwide.

Not only do U.S. consumers dominate the worldwide licensing market as purchasers, but U.S. companies are the primary source of licensed properties as well. EPM Communications estimates that 75%-80% of properties available worldwide originated in the U.S. in 2002. The percentage has been declining slowly as more licensors from around the world enter the business or expand their activities; in 1998 it was estimated that 85% of properties worldwide came from the U.S.

While it used to be rare for non-North American properties (especially in the entertainment sector) to succeed in the U.S. market, this has changed. Pokémon from Japan and Teletubbies and Bob the Builder from the U.K. have been among the highest-profile licensed entertainment properties in the U.S. in the late 1990s and early 2000s. Meanwhile, some U.S. properties record greater sales of licensed merchandise overseas than in the U.S.; examples include Giordano Art (Sad Sam and Honey), DIC's Inspector Gadget (a top property in France), and Warner Bros.' Tom & Jerry. The British

Figure 12
2001 WORLDWIDE RETAIL SALES OF LICENSED MERCHANDISE BY GEOGRAPHIC AREA

TERRITORY	TOTAL RETAIL SALES	SHARE OF TOTAL
U.S./Canada	$70.30 billion	64.5%
Western Europe	$25.85 billion	23.7%
E. Europe/Commonwealth of Ind. States	$110 million	0.1%
Australia/New Zealand	$1.6 billion	1.5%
Japan	$8.8 billion	8.1%
S.E. Asia/China	$12.1 billion	1.2%
Latin America	$925 million	0.8%
Other	$250 million	0.2%
TOTAL	**$109.05 billion**	**100.0%**

Numbers may not add up due to rounding. Other includes India, Middle East, South Africa.
Source: The Licensing Letter; EPM Communications

Figure 13
PER-CAPITA SPENDING ON LICENSED MERCHANDISE BY GEOGRAPHIC AREA

TERRITORY	1998	2001
U.S./Canada	$236.38	$222.82
Western Europe	$56.91	$65.61
E. Europe/Commonwealth of Ind. States	< $1.00	<$1.00
Australia/New Zealand	$68.92	$66.66
Japan	$91.74	$69.24
S.E. Asia	< $1.00	<$1.00
Latin America	$1.91	$1.90
China	N/A	<$1.00

Source: The Licensing Letter; EPM Communications

fashion label Burberry claims Japan and Spain as its largest markets. Overseas territories can account for as much as 65% to 70% of licensing revenues—or sometimes more—for selected North American properties. Others are focused more on their home territory; just 5% of Barney the Dinosaur revenues were attributable to non-North American territories at the time it was purchased by HIT Entertainment in 2001.

Some properties launch internationally simultaneously with their debut in the home region or, in some cases, even before they are introduced locally. Properties of any type can become popular anywhere in the world in today's global business environment, and licensing occurs wherever the popularity of the core brand allows. Guy Begin, a Canadian artist, rolled out his licensing effort in Japan first, along with Canada, before entering the U.S. market.

Properties can succeed on a global basis without the U.S., although the North American market obviously remains a key objective for most licensors due to its sheer size and per-capita spending levels.

LICENSING ENVIRONMENT BY GEOGRAPHIC AREA

Following are capsule descriptions of the status of the licensing business in markets outside the U.S. These brief snapshots are not comprehensive—and capture only a moment in a fast-changing environment—but serve as an introduction to the key licensing markets.

CANADA

Licensors often grant licensees rights to the Canadian market along with those to the U.S. Canada is a small country in population and larger licensees often consider it too tiny to be worthwhile as a standalone territory, given the high investment required. Economies of scale are significant when Canada is added to the U.S., yet U.S.-based licensees sometimes lack interest in servicing Canada properly and thus lose potential sales.

Some licensees, most of them Canadian, service Canada alone, while other Candian-based manufacturers, including Irwin Toy, cover the entire North American territory.

Many of the properties that do well in the U.S. sell strongly in Canada also, although licensing executives should not view the nation as identical to the U.S. Not only does this perception of Canada as the 51st state offend Canadian consumers, but it can harm sales levels, since tastes vary between the two countries. There are also differences in strategy, timing, media exposure and other factors.

Still, the market parallels the U.S. in many ways. For example, Canada has witnessed retail consolidation as the U.S. has, except to an even greater extent. (The market for licensed goods is weighted heavily toward mass-market chains in Canada, while the high-end market is small.)

Licensors and licensees should remember that Canada has two official languages — English and French — requiring bilingual packaging. Tastes in French-speaking Quebec may differ from those in the rest of Canada;

some French-language properties can succeed in Quebec but not in the rest of Canada.

Several properties have originated in Canada and then moved south. They include the preschool book/TV property Caillou; beer brands such as Molsen and LaBatt's; and designer Alfred Sung, among many others.

WESTERN EUROPE

Licensors are increasingly adopting a pan-European outlook toward the continent, as the introduction of the euro as currency in 2002 promises to simplify accounting, the lowering of borders has made preventing exports difficult and more licensees are able to service the whole market. Still, licensing executives must remember that Europe is composed of many distinct markets within the larger economic union. Each region differs and should be considered in its own right rather than simply as part of the European Community.

Parallel imports — products that come into a country from a foreign manufacturer and are similar or identical to those produced by a domestic licensee — create an unattractive competitive situation for licensors and licensees alike. In spite of the fact that licensors technically cannot prevent their licensees from exporting products to European countries not covered in their licensing agreements (as per European Union rules), licensors restrict their licensees in effect to one or a few markets by dictating language, specifications and other characteristics that limit the products' marketability in a practical sense, and by implementing financial penalties such as "superroyalties" for distribution outside the authorized region. Licensors can also effectively prevent parallel imports by making it clear they will choose a new licensee at the end of the contract period if existing manufacturers do not abide by their wishes.

Still, despite all licensors' efforts to the contrary, there is really no such thing as an exclusive deal in Europe, unless a single licensee holds rights for the whole continent. Pan-European deals minimize parallel imports, but are impractical in many cases. Few licensees are truly capable of pan-European distribution and therefore are likely to ignore some countries in favor of those territories where their strength lies.

Languages vary from country to country, which affects a licensee's packaging and product specifications. (The populations of some countries speak several languages.) Tastes are also diverse. A licensed product that sells well in Scandinavia may not work at all in Italy, while a property that is popular in France may never successfully cross the border into England, at least without significant changes. The comic book character Astérix, for example, has been among the most popular in France and other French-speaking territories for decades, but has experienced a tough time as a licensed property elsewhere, with the exception of publishing. Several countries within Europe have strong domestic properties, although properties from the U.S. are, in most cases, embraced as well.

The retail landscape is different from one country to another. Hypermarkets (full-line discount stores) distribute a large percentage of licensed merchandise in France, while department stores drive sales in the Scandinavian countries of Sweden, Norway, Denmark and Finland. Mom-and-pop stores dominate in Italy. Germany and the U.K. are much stronger mail-order markets than other European territories.

Manufacturing capabilities vary from country to country, as well. The Benelux possesses a small manufacturing infrastructure and must rely primarily on imports. The European toy industry is concentrated heavily in the U.K. and France, while Spain is a strong producer of candy. Virtually all countries are home to numerous apparel and paper goods licensees and these categories are nearly always granted to local manufacturers.

Entertainment and media exposure in Europe is fragmented. Countries such as Germany have numerous pay and free television stations, many with full children's TV schedules (including some channels exclusively for kids). This has caused the entertainment licensing sector in Germany to become crowded, with hundreds of properties vying for limited shelf space.

The Western European countries that account for the greatest sales of licensed merchandise are the U.K., Germany, France and Italy. Entertainment and fashion licensing dominate the market, but corporate, art and other types of properties are active in some territories. In fact, the continent represents one of the most diverse licensing markets in the world after North America.

EASTERN AND CENTRAL EUROPE

Eastern and Central Europe, including the Commonwealth of Independent States (the former Soviet Union), are still in their infancy as licensing markets. Capitalism is taking hold but the manufacturing infrastructure, while improving, is underdeveloped, with many potential licensees lacking capital, modern equipment and know-how. Furthermore, inadequate legal protection, monetary, economic and political strife, lack of discretionary income and illegal activity (including a large black market) all contribute to difficulties for licensors.

In the key licensing territories of Poland, Hungary and the Czech Republic, mass market retailers have expanded and are carrying licensed merchandise and starting to experiment with licensed promotions. The number of media channels has increased, allowing for more exposure to and demand for Western and Asian entertainment properties, as well as global brands that advertise on TV or in print. Many licensors from Europe and the U.S. are entering the market—including Germany's TV-Loonland, which signed a programming and merchandising representation deal with Nox Music, a Russian multimedia company— a development that is helping to educate local property owners and manufacturers on accepted licensing techniques. The base of potential licensees is growing and diversifying. Discretionary incomes are rising.

Licensors are approaching Eastern and Central Europe in a number of ways. Some have set up subsidiaries there, some enter the market through joint ventures with local companies, some look for local licensees and use the services of licensing agents specializing in the region, and some begin by exporting merchandise into the territory from Western Europe.

Overall, the market is small and will continue to grow slowly in the near term. Most observers see the region as having great long-term potential.

JAPAN

Japanese consumers demonstrate a significant appetite for character, fashion, sports, trademark and art-related merchandise. Domestic properties such as Sanrio's Hello Kitty and Japanese fashion designers have done well there, not to mention an abundance of publishing/animation (manga/animé) franchises, as have imported properties from the U.S. and Europe. Classic characters such as Peanuts and Betty Boop, corporate trademarks such as Pepsi, Budweiser and Jeep, museums, design and art-related properties such as Christian Riese Lassen and Lynn Hollyn, American celebrities such as James Dean, Audrey Hepburn and Marilyn Monroe, sports icons such as golfer Arnold Palmer and European and American fashion labels such as Burberry, Pierre Cardin and Paul Stuart have all succeeded in the Japanese licensing business. (Local corporate brands have seen very little licensing activity.)

No matter what the source of a property, most licensors recommend approaching the market with a strong brand identity that is apparent on all products and hangtags, packaging and in-store signage. In general, Japanese consumers value an emphasis on product design and quality.

Entertainment licensing in Japan is dominated by "cute" classic characters such as Hello Kitty, Doraemon and Paddington Bear, as well as animation/comic book/videogame properties such as DragonBall Z, Pokémon, Yu-Gi-Oh!, Anpanman and Sailor Moon. The latter (and some of the former) are characterized by their presence in a multitude of media, including films (which normally do not do well here as standalone licensed properties) and by their ability to generate billions of dollars worth of merchandise sales at retail in a market a fraction the size of the U.S. Most of the action-oriented animation properties originate in Japan, but many of the top classic properties come from the U.S. or the U.K. (Properties from outside Japan sometimes need to be altered to appeal to Japanese consumers.)

Other traits typical of the Japanese market include a very strong but long-to-complete system for legal protection; a focus on properties with long-term potential; a slow decision-making process within businesses; boutique-driven distribution (both freestanding and in-store); an emphasis on exclusive licensing agreements; and a "lifestyle" approach to nearly any type of property. Licensees are typically large, vertically integrated trading companies such as Mitsui and Itoken that are active in industries from apparel to automobile manufacturing. Some of the mechanics of licensing are different in Japan from elsewhere; for example, royalties routinely are based on the retail price.

While nearly all product categories benefit from licensing here, Japanese consumers are exposed to more licensed foods, high-tech products such as cell phones and web-connected (i-mode) phones, and transportation (cars, planes, trains) than those in other countries.

Most licensors who have done business in Japan agree it is essential to work with a local partner, whether a retailer, a strong master licensee or a local agent. (This is true everywhere, but especially here.) Business practices, local customs, retail distribution and tastes differ greatly from those in the West and Westerners who go in without local assistance run the risk of failure.

The Japanese licensing market has been contracting since the late 1990s, due to the overall weak economic environment in the country and the overproliferation of properties. Per-capita spending on licensed merchandise plunged by more than $20 between 1998 and 2001. Still, it is a key market and lucrative for property owners that succeed there.

ASIA (OUTSIDE JAPAN)

Other Asian territories include Greater China (People's Republic of China, Taiwan and Hong Kong), Korea, and Southeast Asia (including Singapore, Thailand, Indonesia, Malaysia, the Philippines and others). Licensors view China in particular as having massive growth potential, although it is currently a challenging market to enter. (Hong Kong and Taiwan are active, albeit small, licensing territories.) Low discretionary income, government intrusion into all industries, a difficult retail infrastructure and political problems between China and the West are among the factors that make licensing tough. Still, U.S. properties including Playboy, Looney Tunes and Sesame Street are gaining a foothold there in categories such as publishing, foods and apparel. The sheer size of the population makes this region a great opportunity.

Southeast Asia and Korea were adversely affected by the Asian financial crisis in the late 1990s. They had represented a fast-growing area for licensed merchandise, despite some significant barriers, and still comprise a significant market, although not embracing licensed properties as fast as licensors had hoped. Many diverse countries make up Southeast Asia, some of which find licensed merchandise appealing and some less so. Many have small populations, making both importation and in-country manufacturing costly. Media is fragmented and there is little mass market retailing, with mom-and-pop shops dominating. Economic and political environments vary from country to country and counterfeiting is rampant (with Thailand being one main offender). Many infringers operate in these territories, selling their pirated merchandise in local markets as well as exporting them to the U.S. and other regions. Communication can be difficult and there are relatively few licensing agents on the ground in the region.

Classic characters such as Garfield, Mickey Mouse and Hello Kitty; a few upscale trademark and fashion properties; and international sporting

Figure 14
SELECTED INDIGENOUS LICENSING PROPERTIES, BY TERRITORY OF ORIGIN

CANADA
Caillou
Canadian Football League
Hockey Night in Canada
Labatt's
Molson
Moosehead Beer
Polka Dot Shorts
Wimzie's House

GREAT BRITAIN
Beatrix Potter
Bob the Builder
Budgie the Little Helicopter
Burberry
Dr. Who
Magic Roundabout
Mr. Bean
Mr. Blobby
Mr. Men & Little Miss
Noddy
Paddington Bear
Postman Pat
Rover Group
Spice Girls
Teddy Tum Tum
Teletubbies
Thomas the Tank Engine
Thunderbirds
Wallace & Gromit

CONTINENTAL EUROPE
Armani
Astérix
Babar and Celeste
Benetton
Compagnie des Wagons Lits
Dick Bruna art
Die Maus
Gnomes
Gucci
Italian Football League
Hugo Boss
Krizia
LEGO
Lucky Luke
Marimekko
Moomin
Nighty Night, Sleep Tight (Nou Nou)
Pierre Cardin

Pingu
Porsche
Pumuckl
Smurfs
Spirou
Tabaluga
Tintin
Volkswagen

ASIA
Akira
Anpanman
Astro Boy
Doraemon
Dragonball
Godzilla
Hello Kitty
J-League
Kampung Boy
Keroppi
Kimba
Nippon Professional Baseball
Pokémon
Ponkickies
Sailor Moon
Speed Racer
Ultraman
Yu-Gi-Oh!

AUSTRALIA/NEW ZEALAND
Bananas in Pajamas
Blinky Bill
Flat Cats
Foster's Lager
Hafta, Just Hafta
Johnson & Friends
Ken Done
Love Is...
Ozzy
Viva La Wombat
The Wiggles

LATIN AMERICA
Monica's Gang
Pele
Senninho
Xuxa

Note: This list is not exhaustive.
Source: The Licensing Letter;
EPM Communications

events such as the World Cup tend to drive much of the licensing business in Southeast Asia. There are few domestic properties; Kampung Boy is a Malaysian comic/TV property that has gained a foothold.

The main product categories are affordable products such as low-cost apparel and stationery, but there are other opportunities. Warner Bros./Cartoon Network licensed Unilever for Powerpuff Girls detergent in the Philippines.

AUSTRALIA AND NEW ZEALAND

Australia and New Zealand together comprise a small territory in total population, but they make up for their size with their enthusiasm for licensed products. Culturally, they have similar customs and tastes to those in the U.S. and the U.K. Sports and entertainment properties are popular, as are art and fashion brands. American and U.K. licenses do well here—it has been one of the best markets for The Simpsons, for example—but there are numerous strong indigenous properties as well. Some of the licenses that have originated in Australia and New Zealand include Blinky Bill, Love Is..., Viva La Wombat, artist Ken Done, Bananas in Pajamas, The Wiggles and Flat Cats.

Australia is dominated by two major retail chains (one of which, Coles Myer, has been under financial stress) and they account for the lion's share of retail sales of licensed merchandise. The number of media outlets is growing, which is likely to increase fragmentation and add properties to an already saturated market.

While Australia is a huge area geographically, the majority of the population and most of the sales of licensed goods are concentrated on the East Coast, where Melbourne, Sydney and most of the large cities are located. Australia and New Zealand have a full complement of licensing agents, many of which handle Asia as well as their home territory.

LATIN AMERICA

The countries of South and Central America (including Mexico, which is more similar licensing-wise to Latin America than North America) have grown in importance as licensing markets, although they are still in a relatively early stage of development. Brazil in particular has become a key territory, followed in significance by Mexico, Argentina, Chile, Peru and Colombia.

U.S. properties tend to be the most visibly licensed in Mexico, thanks to the two countries' proximity. Brazil, on the other hand (which has the fourth largest population in the world and is by far the largest licensing territory in Latin America) has an active indigenous licensing market, including properties such as Mauricio de Sousa's Monica's Gang and various television presenters, singers and sports celebrities. U.S. properties, especially from the entertainment/character sector, can do well there.

Some of the obstacles facing the region include economic and monetary instability; high import duties; massive counterfeiting; inexperienced licensees and a relatively small number of licensing agents; communication challenges; poor infrastructure in some areas, such as mail delivery; and the difficulty of getting royalty income out of the respective countries.

OTHER TERRITORIES

By far the majority of all licensing activity occurs in the territories discussed above. The rest of the world currently accounts for .2% of the worldwide total, according to estimates by *The Licensing Letter*.

Licensors view the Middle East as having significant potential but most are currently testing the waters there; cultural barriers (Pokémon was banned in Saudi Arabia), the lack of a mass-market retail structure, violence, political strife, anti-U.S. sentiment, terrorism and war are among the challenges. Africa is another underdeveloped licensing market, but severe economic hardship and political instability in many regions means growth is probably several years away. Some licensed merchandise is available in Africa, primarily through exports from licensees based in South Africa (which is the most developed territory by far). Licensors consider India another possibly lucrative market, due mainly to its huge population, but economic and cultural factors have kept the majority of global licensors out to date. It has a large entertainment industry that is starting to spread its wings internationally (especially in animation), which may lead to more domestic licensing activity.

Figure 14 (page 190) lists a selection of properties that originate in non-U.S. territories.

STRATEGIES FOR INTERNATIONAL LICENSING

As with a domestic licensing effort, there is no single correct strategy for licensing on a global basis. Each property differs in its attributes and in its relevance and recognition in countries around the world. But there are a number of factors licensors should consider when embarking on a licensing program outside their own territory.

First, they should legally protect their properties in all countries where they plan to do business and where their marks are likely to be infringed. Copyrights registered in the U.S. apply in most major licensing territories worldwide, but licensors must file trademarks separately in each country or region. Since expenditures add up quickly for a global licensing program, property owners must weigh the costs and benefits of trademark registration in each territory to maximize protection while keeping spending in line with what potential revenues will allow. In the case of TV coproductions and other properties where ownership is split among companies in more than one country, trademark costs and registration responsibilities may be divided among the partners.

In general, licensing practices are becoming more similar from country to country, although there are still significant differences in the specifics of each market, as will be discussed in detail below. Strategies tend to be similar for a given property in multiple territories, although the product mix, distribution plan, amount of exposure and other details vary. Licensors want to tailor the program so it will succeed in each country, but at the same time maintain a consistent brand image on a global basis. Royalties, guarantees and advances are also converging at similar levels around the world, with some exceptions.

No matter what territories are involved, international licensing requires patience and flexibility.

CHOOSING PARTNERS

Most licensors recommend partnering with a local company in each territory that can provide expertise on business practices, consumer tastes, customs and retail structures. Licensors have many options for entering a new territory:

- They can work with a master licensee. Martha Stewart expanded her business in Japan in 2001 by partnering with the trading company Seiyu, which planned to publish a Japanese version of her magazine and merchandise her products (some imported, some adapted to the market and some created specifically for Japan) in 226 retail stores.

- They can retain a licensing agent. Licensors typically select a local agent in large territories; smaller territories are often overseen by agents in nearby countries. Agents do not need proximity; the Italian soccer club Juventus retained a U.K. company to represent it in Japan and the rest of Asia. (See more on international sub-agents later in this chapter.)

- They can ally with a retailer. Pink Panther has signed a worldwide direct license with Hennes & Mauritz (H&M) for junior's apparel; other licensors ally with retailers for a single country only.

- They can use a network as an agent. The BBC allowed U.S. network NBC to license its show The Weakest Link in the U.S. and arranged similar deals in other countries where the program's broadcaster had licensing expertise. It handled other nations internally.

- They can select a joint-venture or strategic-alliance partner. The New York Yankees (along with the co-owned New Jersey Devils and New Jersey Nets) and U.K.-based soccer/football club Manchester United created a strategic alliance where each would sell each other's licensed goods and market each other's brands in their home territory. Manchester United has a similar deal with the World Wrestling Federation.

- They can launch a locally staffed subsidiary. This is a big investment for a start-up program, but gives the licensor full control. The strategy is typically used only by the largest studios, networks and corporate and fashion licensors.

- They can handle the licensing program in-house. Everlast

handles its global licensing from its U.S. office, signing master and local licensees around the world and distributing its own products globally.

As the examples show, licensors often use a combination of these strategies, for example overseeing the licensing program from its home office but signing master licensees and/or local agents to handle the property in certain countries.

Another strategic question for licensors is how to source products in each country. Again, there are several options; most licensors use a combination of these techniques depending on the specifics of their property and the countries they plan to enter:

- They can sign local licensees in each country. This is the norm in categories such as stationery, where differences in culture and specifications, as well as a lack of multiterritory licensees, leave few alternatives.

- They can grant rights to pan-regional licensees. Lego signed pan-European licensees in several categories, such as footwear, eyewear, helmets and scooters, supplemented by local licensees.

- They can authorize a single licensee for worldwide distribution. This is often the case in categories such as toys, videogames, footwear and perfume; local distributors typically sell the products in individual countries where the master licensee does not have strong distribution.

- They can sell their internally produced core products worldwide or in certain countries, either directly or through a local distributor. Skechers USA, a footwear label, distributes its own products in France; it previously used a local distributor but took all tasks in-house in 2002.

Local licensees have expertise in their respective territories and relationships in place with local retailers; they will also treat the region as more important than a non-domestic licensee might. On the other hand, some licensees are capable of worldwide or pan-regional distribution and have local expertise through subsidiary offices around the world.

Licensees and licensing agents in small territories such as Italy, Israel or Scandinavia sometimes complain of a lack of interest in their regions from U.S. licensors. These territories account for a lower total volume of merchandise sales, and thus lower royalty revenues, than some of their neighbors, although the cost of entering these markets can be just as high. U.S. licensors may not take the same care in choosing local agents or licensees in these regions, perhaps tacking them on to agreements with licensees in larger, nearby countries. This action further reduces sales in the secondary nation.

LICENSEES' STRATEGIES

Licensed manufacturers are expanding their geographic boundaries, with many selling outside their own borders and some having worldwide capabilities. Many of these companies align themselves with properties that have global popularity or appeal; if they are in an industry that requires a large investment in product development or retooling, a broader geographic grant of rights helps them spread these costs over a larger market. Other licensees work with a mix of local, regional and global properties.

Many toy and videogame companies tend to have worldwide distribution and link with entertainment properties that have international recognition. Footwear and perfume companies partner with global celebrity or fashion brands. Other categories tend to comprise fewer global manufacturers, but instances exist; some apparel companies have global licensing deals with sports leagues, for example.

Few licensees, even if they are able to take on worldwide rights, truly have global or even pan-regional distribution. They have a strong presence in some countries but not in others. Therefore, master licensees typically work with local distributors, sublicensees or subcontractors in certain nations within their territory.

Licensors look for existing distribution as a key criteria in selecting a licensee for a particular territory. Yet there are times when a licensee can use a license to expand its presence into additional regions. Mag-La Worldwide used its license with Mr. Clean to strengthen its position in Europe when it was granted an extension of its agreement for cleaning tools and household gloves, adding Western Europe to its existing North American contract.

FACTORS TO CONSIDER BEFORE ENTERING A NEW REGION

In addition to ascertaining that a property is popular, or can become so, in a territory, a licensor should learn as much as possible about the specifics of a region before launching a licensing program there. Expanding into a given territory may not be worthwhile if too many factors seem to weigh against a property's success.

Following is a brief checklist of important points for licensors to investigate before making a decision to enter a new territory:

- The political situation, including wars, elections, border disputes, riots or possible coups d'état. These lead to changes in the business environment that could affect licensing. South America, the Middle East and Eastern Europe are among the regions where these considerations are especially important.
- Economic factors, such as disposable income levels, inflation rates, taxes and currency fluctuations. These have an impact on potential revenue levels as well as on the types of products that will succeed. Australia implemented a 10% goods and services tax in 2000 that increased prices of licensed products in categories such as publishing and apparel, which had not been taxed before. At the same time, the country's currency devaluated against the U.S. dollar and British pound, changing the

revenue picture for licensors outside the region and licensees that export.

- Trade considerations. Trade agreements such as NAFTA (the North American Free Trade Agreement) and pacts within the European Community, Asia or Latin America influence licensing decisions, as do import duties and tariffs. For example, high duties for a particular product category would favor signing a local licensee over importation.

- Retail structure. Distribution methods vary among territories, so finding out what types of retailers dominate within a region is critical. It would be folly to try to impose a mass market strategy on a country where department stores account for the bulk of sales. Western distribution methods are not feasible everywhere, although the expansion of Toys 'R' Us, Foot Locker and other U.S. retailers may make western practices more prevalent worldwide. The presence of a black market and its ability to syphon sales from legitimate retailers also is an important consideration in some territories.

- Tastes and culture. Regional tastes determine what types of properties and merchandise will do well in a country. Licenses popular in France do not necessarily succeed in Germany; Japanese properties can do well in Italy and Latin America but not as well in Scandinavia. Comic books are a booming industry in Japan but virtually non-existent in Israel. Publishing is very important in Europe — it accounts for more licensing revenues than all other merchandise categories combined for some licensors — but is of less importance in Latin America. The Hang Ten fashion label appeals to juniors as well as men in Japan but only to men in Mexico.

- Size. The number of inhabitants of a region affects potential sales levels, as does population density, population growth and demographic factors such as the number of children. Geographic size also influences licensing decisions; larger regions are more likely to vary culturally and linguistically within a single territory.

- Media. The status of the publishing, broadcast and cable television, Internet and film industries within a region helps determine a property's marketing plan there. Specific considerations include the total number of media outlets and their relative audience size; the amount of advertising and which medium attracts the lion's share; whether media outlets are privatized or government-owned; how many movie screens exist; and whether global media — such as some cable networks — reach the population. Media exposure varies from country to country; as of 2000, Bob the Builder was on for 10 minutes a week in the

U.K. but planned for five half-hours per week in the U.S.

- Trademark and other bodies of law. Some countries possess very good systems for legally protecting properties and some do not. Some have set up adequate procedures on paper but do not enforce them. Legal processes in some countries are time-consuming. All of these considerations play into the likelihood of counterfeiting and dictate the time frame necessary for introducing a property. Some countries require anti-infringement measures even if the licensor is not actively licensing its property there. The U.S. has laws regarding product liability insurance; many other countries do not (causing licensees outside the U.S. to balk at U.S. licensors' demands for such protection). Countries such as Denmark have strong laws regarding unfair competition, which may affect "coattails" properties.

- Infrastructure. The strength of the manufacturing base within a region, in general and/or in specific categories, affects a licensor's ability to grant rights to local licensees. If facilities and technological capabilities are outdated and companies lack manufacturing know-how, licensors may find it worthwhile to consider imports rather than domestic licensees. The condition of transportation systems affects how efficiently licensees can distribute merchandise; the status of telecommunications influences marketing and day-to-day business operations.

- Seasons. The southern hemisphere has weather patterns opposite those in the northern hemisphere; it is hot in the south when it is cold in the north. This affects marketing schedules for items such as apparel, accessories, footwear and suntan lotion. Vacation times vary, meaning peak selling periods for inflatables and toys in general do not mesh. Each region has its own holidays, which affect business schedules and peak selling seasons. In the southern hemisphere, the summer holidays and Christmas overlap, which concentrates toy sales even more during that holiday period than is the case in other regions.

INTERNATIONAL LICENSING AGENTS

As noted earlier in this chapter, retaining a licensing agent (sometimes called an international sub-agent) is one of the key methods of entering a territory and maintaining a licensing business there. Hiring an agent in an international territory brings local business expertise, contacts with licensees and retailers in the region, and knowledge of local customs and tastes.

The criteria used to select an international sub-agent are similar to those for a domestic licensing representative. They include the level of trust between licensor and agent, the agent's history with certain property types, the experiences of licensors who have worked with the agent in the past, the typical strategies the agent implements and its plan for the property, the agent's ability to cover certain geographic areas itself or via a network of colleagues, the number of properties represented, the cost structure and the services offered, as well as references from licensees and licensors that have worked with the agency.

Several licensing agents are in business in each major territory, with the most active licensing regions usually boasting the greatest number of agents. A range of agencies operate in the U.K., for example, while few South American companies specialize in licensing. In some countries, such as Japan, it is essential to hire a local agent (or a master licensee or retailer that will perform the tasks of an agent).

A U.S. licensor can work with an agent in each territory or with one master agent for each large region (e.g., Western Europe). The master agent will sometimes retain sub-agents in each country or region within the greater area (e.g., the Philippines within Asia). In many instances, a licensor's U.S. agent may act as a global master agent, in turn retaining international sub-agents around the world. Some licensors work with a total of 10 to 20 agents worldwide for a property or family of properties. The more levels of agents, the less each agent receives from the total commission, since the typical international agent fee of 35% must be split between the master agent and sub-agent in each territory.

Fee sharing also comes into play when a licensor or master or regional agent signs a worldwide or pan-regional deal for a particular category. The agreement precludes a local agency from signing a licensee in the same category in its own nation. In such a scenario, the master agent's fee is divided with the local agent (typically in a 50/50 split but situations vary). Each case is subject to negotiation; some agents charge a "consulting fee" in lieu of or in addition to their share of the commission. Local agents earn their share of the fee by assisting the master licensee in finding local distribution and supporting marketing initiatives in their territory.

As more licensing deals encompass multiple territories and as the licensing business has become more sophisticated and more difficult, the role of the international agent has changed. The bulk of its work used to consist of sales of rights to licensees in its region. Now, agency staffs spend more of their time on brand management duties such as arranging retail promotions, keeping licensees informed about property developments, ensuring strong distribution, advising on media strategies, etc. The sub-agent's relationships with all members of the trade in its country are as important as its contacts with manufacturers.

Some agents are adding services to enhance their businesses as they face more split commissions, not to mention competition from licensors with in-house licensing departments and networks who are taking on agenting duties. Many offer PR or consulting services for an additional fee, for example. Others are becoming licensors by taking financial stakes in the entertainment properties they represent. In some territories, such as Europe, there has been consolidation among agents as companies merge or are bought by networks or producers.

For more detailed information on international licensing, see *International Licensing: A Status Report*, published by EPM Communications.

CHAPTER 12
PROMOTIONAL LICENSING

Most licensors promote and advertise their properties, as noted in Chapter 5, with initiatives often partially financed by licensees' contribution to a central marketing fund. This promotional support has become an important factor in a property's successful launch and longevity and has become a critical consideration to licensees and retailers as they decide with which properties they will associate. At the same time, manufacturers must advertise and promote their licensed lines, either individually or in conjunction with one or more other licensees of the same property, regardless of the amount of licensor support.

Promotional activity surrounding a property or licensed product line can take many forms and licensors, licensees and retailers are expanding the list of possible techniques as they try to distinguish their properties from the competition. All the partners linked to a license are working together to create marketing initiatives that will increase the property's chances of success. Yet, while more promotions are multifaceted and integrated, solo efforts are also effective.

Promotional backing is important for all types of properties. A home video release gets as much support as a feature film. A corporate brand owner supports its core properties with multimillion-dollar campaigns; these help the licensed products, while the licensed products and the marketing programs supporting them reciprocate by strengthening the brand. Even small licensors, such as entrepreneurial artists, understand the value of promoting their properties to whatever extent their budgets will allow.

The term "promotional licensing" refers to licensing deals that are short in duration and do not involve changes to the product itself but, rather, an association between a property and an existing product. These alliances can comprise part of a property's overall marketing support, as noted above, or they can stand alone, as in the case of Dairy Queen's long-term partnership with King Features for Dennis the Menace, which creates visibility for the character but does not back a wide-ranging licensed merchandise effort. It is simply a lucrative promotion that benefits both companies.

Promotional tie-ins can involve both long- and short-term properties of every type, from corporate trademarks to musical acts to book characters. They can vary in scope from $60 million, multipartner efforts, such as those Disney arranges when it launches a home video of a feature film, to a simpler promotion such as the use of James Dean in an ad for McDonald's in Australia.

A single multifaceted, multipartner promotion may involve some or all of the following techniques, among others: premiums; radio advertising or giveaways; TV and print advertising; rebates; in-store boutiques and point-of-purchase displays; cross-promotions (e.g. cross-couponing); packaged goods and retail tie-ins; contests involving mail-in responses, interactive phone technology or the Internet; free or purchase-with-purchase premiums; or personal appearances. (These techniques will be discussed in more detail later in the chapter.) Licensed promotions can target consumers and/or the trade (e.g., retailers and distributors).

Promotional licensing has two major benefits for a licensor: It generates income and provides additional exposure for a property. For manufacturers, promotions add value to a licensed line by increasing consumer awareness, boosting sales, enhancing brand loyalty and encouraging new customers to sample. In addition, a licensee may be able to increase its sales substantially by providing premiums, even if it is not a primary promotional partner. Comic books, trading cards, plastic cups, prepaid phone cards, watches, squeeze bottles, plush figures, PVC figurines and small toys are among the most popular types of premiums, but the possibilities are unlimited if there is a fit between the property, the promotional partners and the product.

Licensors must be careful to ensure that premiums are either distinct from any of its licensed products available at retail, or that retail licensees provide the premiums. Any competition between retail and promotional products will not only hurt the licensees involved, but could also harm the property as a whole through real or perceived oversaturation.

Promotions occur at any time during the life cycle of the property. An anniversary, the launch of a new fashion collection, a video release or the introduction of a brand extension are all common times to promote. A good thematic match between a property and a tie-in partner can engender a promotion at any time, regardless of whether it is timed to coincide with a significant property milestone.

TIE-IN PARTNERS

In addition to licensees and licensors, several other constituencies are participants in licensed promotions. Entertainment companies such as movie theater chains, home video distributors, music labels, film studios and cable and broadcast networks tie in with all types of properties to magnify awareness and spur increased sales or viewership.

Retailers utilize licensed tie-ins, including mass market, department and all kinds of specialty stores; fast food restaurants; drug and grocery chains; and video rental outlets. Licensed tie-ins build store traffic and drive sales of licensed products based on the promoted property, as well as merchandise that has nothing to do with the tie-in. Retail partners can also raise their company's profile and reinforce their image as a fun place to shop. Licensed tie-ins with an element of exclusivity cause the retailer to become a destination for a certain property or product line, at least for a limited time.

Most retail promotions contain an element of exclusivity, whether for an entire property or one licensed product. Exclusivity could be defined as an exclusive promotional window, an exclusive period of time for selling products before they go into broader distribution, or one exclusive product tailored to the retailer.

Packaged goods companies and other manufacturers who are not retail licensees associate with licensed properties. As noted, a promotional partner's participation differs from that of a retail licensee in that the tie-in usually does not alter the product itself. In other words, Nestlé, whose Butterfinger candy bars have been involved in tie-ins with The Simpsons, used the characters in advertising and promotional materials but did not reshape the snacks into the image of Bart Simpson. In the case of Blue's Clues pasta shapes or Clifford fruit roll-ups, both licensed products, the food itself incorporated the shape or other characteristics of the property. (Promotional alliances occasionally involve licensed products as part of the tie-in; for example, Tiger Woods' endorsement deal with Nike also comprises signature merchandise.)

A packaged goods partner's involvement with a licensed promotion can include a variety of elements, such as on-pack advertising, the use of the property in packaging, cents-off coupons, cross-promotions with licensed or non-licensed products from other manufacturers, and tags within regularly scheduled advertising. These companies hope their participation will lead to increased sales, higher consumer awareness and excitement, and greater advertising exposure. Food and beverage companies, apparel, accessory and footwear marketers, and health and beauty firms are among the frequent manufacturer-participants in licensed promotions, but any type of company can be involved if there is a good fit between product and property and compatible objectives between licensor and promotional partner.

Media partners — radio stations, television stations and networks, magazines and newspapers — also become involved in tie-ins, both nationally and locally. Their inclusion offers other participants more exposure, since media partners usually provide print space or air time to support the promotion. In return, the media companies benefit from being associated with a highly visible property. On-air, in-print or online contests can increase readership, listenership, viewership or traffic.

Internet companies are frequent media partners, despite the financial problems the dot-com industry suffered in the 2000s. E-commerce companies, Internet-related hardware and software marketers and web entertainment producers and distributors are all viable partners for properties targeting demographic groups that rank high in Internet use. These include, but are not limited to, teens (both male and female), college students and young men. Some of the Internet partners are standalone companies; larger media companies often integrate their online divisions into corporate licensed promotions.

Larger tie-in partners sometimes involve several of their divisions or companies in a tie-in. Kellogg's global alliance with Disney involves several of its food divisions, including products such as Pop-Tarts and Eggo Waffles, as well as its Kellogg's cereal brands.

The participation of a greater number of companies (related or unrelated to each other) in a single promotion increases the tie-in's cost-effectiveness for the partners, since each bears a smaller slice of the total burden, while maximizing consumers' exposure to the property. Thus, licensors often seek one or more (noncompeting) partners from each of these sectors: fast food, retail, packaged goods and media.

AN OVERVIEW OF PROMOTIONAL TECHNIQUES

The main element of a licensed tie-in is the property itself. It is therefore highlighted throughout the various facets of the promotion, including in broadcast or print advertising, in newspaper inserts, on packaging and/or on hangtags. Personal appearances by celebrity endorsers or costumed characters at stores, promotional events and press functions also enhance the property's visibility. One of the licensor's main objectives is to increase consumers' personal connection with the property; it will consider any technique that can enhance shoppers' interaction with and perception of the license, be it a character, brand, sports event or artist's image.

Licensors and their partners emphasize the property in trade as well as consumer elements. Retailers and distributors may have a chance to meet key personalities associated with the property, visit behind-the-scenes venues such as a locker room or TV production set, or attend an event such as a film opening or concert. Contests encourage employees and colleagues of the promotional partners to do their best to support the tie-in, such as creating large in-store displays or otherwise highlighting it to shoppers.

Licensor Saban (now owned by Disney) created a trade promotion in support of its Power Rangers property in 1999. It wanted to increase sales and traffic at Wal-Mart stores and needed the support of Wal-Mart employees to do so. Saban created a contest to see which stores could create the best displays of Power Rangers merchandise, using video, audio or any other element that would attract attention. Winning stores, which were selected on the basis of photos of their efforts, won cash prizes. The contest was promoted in-store to extend the excitement to consumers.

While incorporating the property itself into all promotional elements is the key to any licensed promotion, other facets of the tie-in vary depending on the capabilities of the partners, the objectives of the promotion, the characteristics of the property, the target consumer and the budget.

As with any licensing partnership, there must be a fit between the property and the promotional elements. Rexall Sundown's Rugrats vitamins included an in-pack offer for Rugrats-themed calendars; the hook was that children could keep track of their vitamin-taking by recording it in the calendar. Thus there was a good match between the premium, the property and the product.

Every promotion is different; in fact, "to cut through the clutter" by creating something unique is the point of a tie-in. Still, certain promotional techniques are utilized routinely. Here is a checklist of some of the alternatives licensors and licensees use as elements of their promotional activity:

- Premiums. These are usually inexpensive items that incorporate the property's logo, a character, a design or a personality's likeness. Licensees can distribute them free, as Hormel did with Clifford books as part of a kids' meal promotion, or sell them as a purchase-with-purchase or standalone item. Licensors and licensees should design the premium so it is unlike any retail products available, both for competitive reasons and to make it desirable to consumers. Premiums, such as those found in quick-service restaurant tie-ins, are often collectible or are created so they interact with each other, causing consumers to want the whole set.

- Rebates, discounts and cross-marketing. One or more of the products involved in a promotion — licensed or not — may be tied to a money-off offer. Sometimes several partners provide rebates through a bounce-back mechanism in which the purchase of one item entitles the consumer to rebates or discounts on other items. On-pack or in-pack coupons drive consumers from one product to another as well as promoting the overall licensing program. A line of collectible figures from JoyRide Studios based on videogame characters includes codes and secret strategies that enhance game play, encouraging game owners to buy the figures and *vice versa*.

- Contests. Sweepstakes or other types of contests personally involve customers (or trade partners) in the promotion. Typical prizes include visits to sets or sports arenas, the chance to meet celebrities and/or win free merchandise.

- Publicity. Print and broadcast publicity, directed at consumers and the trade, cost-effectively increase the number of impressions a tie-in generates.

- Events, tours and personal appearances. These elements promote good feelings and personal involvement on the part of consumers and the trade alike. Allowing consumers to attend a sporting event or visit a set or go backstage at a concert creates a similar personal interaction.

- Nonprofit overlays. Many consumers (and trade partners) appreciate the fact that their participation in a promotion results in some benefit for a nonprofit organization. These overlays also drive associated licensed merchandise sales, when licensees donate a portion of proceeds to the nonprofit group. Mulberry Neckwear donated a percentage of proceeds from sales of its Nature Conservancy ties not only to the Nature Conservancy but also Zoo Atlanta, while wildlife artist Karen Bierce earmarked a portion of her licensing royalties to two environmental programs.

- Changes to packaging and hangtags. Packaged goods companies and other participants add the property's logo or a special promotional logo to their merchandise during the promotional period. The special packaging or labeling generates additional consumer impressions for the property and calls out the partner's association with it.

- In-store display materials. Point-of-purchase materials and other in-store signage in high-traffic areas create a greater impact for the promotion throughout the store. Options include tabletop cards, shelf talkers, banners, video monitors, concept-shop displays, posters and placemats (in quick-service restaurants).

- Internet components. Internet-related companies can be promotional partners or the web can be used as one element within a broader promotion. Artisan Entertainment supported its property Tangerine Bear with a trailer, games and certificates on Claus.com in 2001, while Sony promotes its films with ticketing, trailers, auctions and targeted e-mails on Yahoo! networks. In many cases, two or more partners' websites drive traffic to each other, as was the case in a tie-in between Hotwheels.com and Walmart.com in 2002.

- In-school and at-home educational marketing. Children's entertainment, literary and other properties often lend themselves to educational materials sent to parents, schools, preschools, day care centers and caregivers. The packets include games, contests and activities and serve to increase awareness and goodwill among children and their parents. Nelvana promoted its Little Bear direct-to-video feature with a mailing of a half million activity kits to families with preschool children; Timex created educational activity kits, distributed through schools to 3 million youngsters.

- Advertising/endorsements. Advertising and endorsements (by spokespeople or spokescharacters) are often part of multifaceted promotions but can be standalone efforts. They can involve radio, television, print or other media. Many entertainment licensors and agencies that represent celebrities have dedicated staff working with ad agencies on these opportunities. John Wayne appearing in televison commercials for Coors and Wonder Woman for Minute Maid orange juice are examples that have occurred in the U.S.; many advertising tie-ins occur in non-North American territories as well.

- Cross-merchandising and co-packaging. Cross-merchandising in-store creates a bigger impact on consumers and increases impulse purchases. Co-packaging provides added value and spurs more purchases for both products involved. One-gallon cans of Disney paints, marketed by Sherwin-Williams, are merchandised in Wal-Mart stores with Disney stencils and stencil

paints. In-store concept shops gathering all property-based products in a single location make a big splash at retail.

■ Product placement. Many movie-related promotions involve
product placement within the film. Television series can also
host product placement initiatives, as can Internet entertainment vehicles and other electronic media. Jeep has arranged
for placement of its products in a licensed videogame, Tony
Hawk's Pro Skater 3.

Licensors and their partners can integrate all of these components, and
others, in various combinations, depending on their objectives, the nature of
the property and the audience.

CASE STUDIES

The following examples illustrate a few of the promotional combinations possible and show the diversity of potential programs. Some include
multiple and some single partners, some involve entertainment properties
and some other types of licenses. Each features different categories of tie-in
partner and techniques specific to the needs of those partners. This is not a
comprehensive list, but gives an idea of the scope of promotional alternatives:

■ A 2000 promotion for a direct-to-home video release based on
Nelvana's Franklin included merchandise boutiques at Sears
(featuring apparel, toys, videos and home furnishings); movie
preview trailers in-store at Sears photo departments, operated
by Lifetouch Photo Studios; and a tie-in with 1,200 Applebee's
restaurants featuring placemats and drinkware depicting
Franklin and promoting the video. Radisson Hotels was another
partner.

■ In 2001, Kmart promoted its Route 66 apparel (a licensed private label) by selling an exclusive Route 66 Barbie in a limited
edition of 75,000.

■ The Southeastern Conference, a collegiate organization, tied
in with Hibbett Sporting Goods, a southeastern U.S. sporting
goods chain with 200 locations. The retailer carried an exclusive range of apparel and accessories with the SEC and member university logos. Regional marketer Golden Flake potato
chips was a presenting sponsor; coupons on 610,000 bags of
potato chips gave purchasers discounts on the apparel.

■ After the Peanuts comic strip stopped running original versions
in 2000, licensor United Media maintained awareness through
a Days Inn hotel promotion that offered a free video of a Peanuts TV special with a one-night stay. Meanwhile, Wendy's ran
a kids' meal tie-in and the Children's Museum of Manhattan
hosted an exhibit of Schultz artwork. Auto racer Jeff Gordon
drove a Peanuts car.

- Save the Children authorized Pepsi to feature images from the nonprofit organization's portfolio of artwork for holiday-themed cans for Christmas 1999.

- When the classic U.K. TV series Thunderbirds was relaunched in Japan in 2000, it was promoted in two ad campaigns, one for a mobile phone company and one for an apartment complex.

- Health store retailer GNC was the official vitamin store of NASCAR in 2001. It introduced an exclusive NASCAR children's vitamin and sponsored a car on the NASCAR circuit.

- A Cartoon Network promotion with retailer Mervyn's in 2001 allowed customers to bring their cable bill into the store and receive a 15% discount on Cartoon Network merchandise, which was displayed in boutiques in 270 stores. Cartoon Network worked with its local cable affiliates on the effort.

- Teletubbies agent (at the time) itsy bitsy Entertainment created Teletubbies Get Up and Go! exercise day to promote its video and book lines (both of which had specific tie-ins to the event) and its PBS show (which ran a tie-in special). Several national fitness organizations for children endorsed the project.

- Fashion label Op created a branded music CD with a surf theme, which it distributed in 2001 through gift-with-purchase offers and at events.

- The launch of Canadian designer Alfred Sung's fragrance Pure was backed by a $1.5 million ad campaign and nearly 2 million scent samples distributed in stores.

- Kroger grocery stores tied in with the 2001 film *Shrek* by offering customers who purchased $300 or more in one of its 2,000 stores a child's admission or adult matinee ticket to the film. The chain also sold merchandise in-store, some of it exclusive to Kroger. Selected stores' bakery departments featured Shrek-themed baked goods.

- In Australia, the preschool TV series Hi-5 tied in with Kellogg's Rice Bubbles cereal in 2000, with the centerpiece being a contest for a chance to win breakfast with the cast. On-pack promotion covered 1.2 million boxes; 1,000 merchandise packs were secondary prizes. In-store signage and television advertising supported.

- Cartoon Network teamed with Delta Airlines in 2000 for a promotion that involved premiums, in-flight programming and five jetliners painted with the Powerpuff Girls characters. Nippon Airlines painted a plane with Pokémon imagery in a similar effort.

- The 100th anniversary in 2001 of the Wright Brothers' first flight was the occasion for limited-edition merchandise and other promotional ties, as well as the use of the celebrities in advertising. Advertising historically has represented the Wright Brothers' estate's main source of income.

- Jim Henson promoted its Muppets brand upon its 25th anniversary in 2001 by creating a fan convention, MuppetFest! The event, the first of a planned annual series, included auctions, puppet workshops, contests and panel discussions.

- Coca-Cola was the sole promotional partner for the first Harry Potter film in 2001. Efforts involved messages on 850 million Coca-Cola, Minute Maid and Hi-C packages, reading tours, in-store promotions, TV ads, book giveaways and library donations, as well as a gift of $18 million to Reading is Fundamental, a nonprofit group. Other giveaways included more than 29 million free Coke products and 9 million movie certificates. Contest prizes included trips to England.

- The film How the Grinch Stole Christmas in 2000 was supported by a tie-in with the U.S. Postal Service that involved in-store merchandise and custom signage in 33,000 post offices and retail stores, as well as Whoville cancellations.

- Marvel Comics superheroes were painted on several Monster Trucks competing in the U.S. Hot Rod Association's Monster Jam circuit in 2001. Depictions of the Marvel-sponsored trucks in turn appeared on merchandise such as backbacks and toys.

- As part of its effort to transform Jurassic Park from a film franchise into a brand, Universal Studios launched the Jurassic Park Institute in 2001. The educational initiative included a website, in-school materials, museum exhibits and an online kids club, as well as merchandise such as nonfiction books about dinosaurs.

- In 2001, the book character Arthur celebrated its 25th anniversary with retail tie-ins at bookstores, many involving in-store birthday parties. Licensee Little Brown published a special anniversary book and other licensees created 25th anniversary products and promoted the celebration on-pack. The Pizza Hut Book-It program and *Parenting* magazine ran Arthur-related contests; sponsors of the latter included Border's bookstores. A museum tour and an American Library Association tie-in were also part of the festivities. The Book-It contest, which involved doing literacy-related good deeds, attracted entries from 1,300 classrooms, while the *Parenting* writing and drawing contest received upwards of 10,000 submissions.

VALUING PROMOTIONS

Unlike retail licensing, which is associated with a defined payment structure based on a royalty, guarantee and advance, there are no set rules for promotional remuneration. Deals often contain a licensing fee of some sort, but partners frequently contribute advertising, on-package exposure or other promotional elements in lieu of cash for at least part of the payment.

The more complicated the promotion, the more complex the payment structure. A simple agreement granting a licensee the rights to a property for a series of ads will probably require payment consisting of a flat fee or percentage of the media buy, although the amount of the fee is negotiable; some licensors have rate cards for such activity but that usually serves as a starting point for discussion. On the other hand, a complicated scenario incorporating many of the promotional elements discussed above might involve tradeouts, cash or some combination of the two, with each partner responsible for a unique compensation structure depending on their involvement.

Promotional partners supply added value in various ways aside from cash. One participant may provide premiums. Another could mention the tie-in at the end of its existing TV ads or devote one or more of the ads in its print schedule to the promotion. A manufacturer could incorporate the property and/or the tie-in into its packaging. A retailer or a licensee could furnish in-store signage, flyers or point-of-sale materials. Media companies could donate air time or print space, while a producer could offer access to a set as a contest prize. A single partner could be responsible for several promotional elements.

Many of these costs are incremental to the provider; the company has to create packaging or run advertising whether it is involved in the promotion or not. But the partner's contribution adds a component of value to the tie-in, exposure that other partners would have to pay to acquire.

The fee for the use of the license, which is usually one component of the total compensation package for high-profile or well-established properties, and which the partners will agree to pay if they value the association with the property, varies. For a long-term or wide-ranging exclusive promotion, a licensor might view a fee in excess of six figures as reasonable. A leading soft drink or fast food company might pay in the low- to mid-seven figures for a high-profile film, in addition to committing to in-store promotional activities, signage and/or premiums, while a short-term promotion might bring in fees in the $10,000 to $50,000 range. Some licensors ask for a 10% royalty on the cost of each premium as well. Licensors of an unproven property might waive the fee, allowing licensees to pay in in-kind services exclusively.

Negotiations proceed until all partners are satisfied that what they supply to the promotion, whether cash, added impressions or other variables, is fair in view of the benefit they will receive in increased sales, greater awareness, goodwill or whatever their goals may be. In some cases, each element of a promotion commands a separate fee, but licensees usually prefer one lump payment because it allows them more flexibility in implementation.

Licensors and their partners typically publicize the value of their promotions in terms of the amount of advertising expenditure required for an equivalent number of impressions. (Published reports and analysts' estimates use the same yardstick.) A video tie-in valued at $60 million would suggest that the added number of impressions achieved through the activities of all partners would cost $60 million to generate through advertising. The "value" does not refer to the total cost of the promotion or to the amount of money that changed hands.

Multimillion-dollar promotions are common, especially for tie-ins surrounding entertainment properties. Promotional activity for the video release of the film How the Grinch Stole Christmas was valued at $20 million; a Kellogg-Disney cereal promotion at $20 million; the Jimmy Neutron film and franchise launch at $50 million; and the Chicken Run film at $100 million. All were multifaceted campaigns including advertising, retail and packaged goods tie-ins, events and premiums, contests, online and in-school components, and/or charity elements.

While the big promotions — those valued in the tens of millions of dollars — receive the most attention, not all tie-ins must be costly. Events or publicity-driven campaigns can cost $100,000 or less, depending on the elements and number of partners involved. Each participant must weigh the cost of the promotion—or their contribution toward the total cost—against potential awareness and sales gains.

MEASURING RESULTS

It is often difficult to quantify the results of a licensed promotion. Measuring increased awareness, goodwill and "excitement" — among the major objectives of a licensed tie-in — is not a science.

Tracing which results are attributable to which part of the promotion can also be a challenge, especially for complex, multipartner efforts. Licensors even find it hard to ascertain which results, if any, are traceable to the use of the property itself — the promotion's reason for being — rather than to other elements of the tie-in.

Measurable (but not necessarily traceable) elements of promotional alliances include the number of coupon redemptions, the number of contest entries, the number of calls to an interactive phone line, the amount of traffic to an online site, and the number of premiums sold or given away. Toys 'R' Us and Kids 'R' Us tied in with Toy Story 2 in 1999; the promotion included game pieces with UPC codes in 250 circulars. Consumers had to cut out and bring the pieces into a store, where they scanned them at one of five price-check machines in each location to see if they won. This structure allowed the retailer to track traffic that came from the circular into the store.

Indirect gauges include the box-office take for the promoted film *versus* other, comparable releases; store traffic, attendance or sales levels during the promotion *versus* nonpromotional or other tie-in periods; and awareness of the property and the partners' brands, as measured by recall studies at periodic intervals before, during and after the tie-in.

The following results, from published reports, corporate press materials, interviews and presentations, illustrate some of the legitimate yardsticks by which to measure a tie-in's success:

- A Superman Racing promotion in 2000—consisting of an event where top auto racers in each racing league drove Superman cars—generated 14 million broadcast and 16 million print impressions from a press conference that cost $100,000; licensed merchandise sales pegged to the event reached $35 million.

- When Kellogg's tied in with the Grinch film on 100 million packages, it saw a 13% sales lift in stores where promotion-specific floor graphics were used. In all, total dollar sales were up $11 million, volume sales up 4.5 million units and volume share up 1.7% during the promotional period. Sixty-five percent of retailers participated, the highest ever for a Kellogg promotion to date.

- A Cartoon Network online and network promotion in 2000 to support its Toonami programming bloc required kids to watch the bloc's shows to learn the special codes needed to play an online game. This set-up drove them back and forth between the two media. The online site got 3.5 million page views in the first week, an increase of 60% in weekly page views and 75% in unique users.

- A MasterCard ad featuring Curious George increased sales of Curious George children's books by 20% in 2000.

- A 1999 tie-in between Rugrats and Mott's was credited for a 20% sales increase for the Mott's brands over the previous year.

- A sweepstakes for the summer 2000 X-Men movie in conjunction with the Internet site Fandom generated a total of 57,930 unique users, with each visitor entering the site an average of four times for a total of 226,670 impressions. It was estimated that 25% of the first weekend's moviegoers had logged onto the web for information about the film.

PROMOTIONAL AGENCIES

Both licensors and their tie-in partners sometimes retain promotional agencies to assist them in creating effective promotions. Licensors use the agencies to come up with unique strategies for their properties and to bring in appropriate partners, while licensees hire them to seek properties with which they might associate promotionally. Promotional agencies also can help creatively by producing advertising, designing and sourcing premiums and coming up with point-of-purchase materials.

Choosing a promotional agency is not unlike choosing a licensing agency or licensing consultant. Their track record, ideas regarding their clients' properties or products, references from past and present clients, current portfolio of properties or companies represented, and proposed financial package are among the factors potential clients should weigh before selecting an agency. Business journals such as *Entertainment Marketing Letter* and *PROMO* list contacts and describe current promotions involving agencies.

PROMOTIONAL SUCCESS FACTORS

The factors that support a successful licensed promotion parallel those behind a positive retail licensing relationship. All partners need to be honest about their objectives and what they are able to contribute to the promotion. This openness must start at the beginning of the alliance and continue throughout the promotional period. All partners should inform each other immediately when a film release date changes, a designer delays a collection, one of the partners cannot meet a deadline or a television cast member quits.

Honesty and realism are also crucial when it comes to predicting the results of a promotion. Excess inventory of premiums or specially marked products remaining after a tie-in wipes out profits generated during the promotional period, while too little inventory can harm sales and damage retail and consumer relationships.

Participants should be forthcoming about the lead times they need to maximize the impact of the promotion. Packaged goods companies usually require at least eight to 12 months to prepare a tie-in; retailers need six to seven months or more. On the other hand, entertainment companies sometimes have to put together a promotion just two or three months prior to the release of a film, thanks to the changeability of movie release dates or lack of available artwork.

All partners should have compatible goals and similar target markets. As with retail licensing, the property and its partners should match in terms of the image they hope to project and the creative elements they feel support their brands.

The fit between the property and the partners' products and customers is also critical. The Nickelodeon character SpongeBob SquarePants matched up well with a Got Milk? milk mustache campaign; since he is a sponge, he was unable to maintain his mustache for long before it was absorbed. Minute Maid orange juice is so healthy that it turns a regular woman into Wonder Woman. Talbot's used Jane Jetson to promote its online store; just as on TV, she can order an outfit with one click. The job-search website Monster.com tied in with the film property Monsters, Inc. in a promotion that included a movie trailer and ticketing. While these examples all come from the entertainment realm, the fit between property and partners must be there no matter what type of license is at the center of the tie-in.

As the marketplace for promotions becomes nearly as saturated as the market for licensed products, creativity and uniqueness can help a tie-in effort succeed. A Shrek/Burger King promotion in 2001 included television advertising with animation created specifically for the ad. Commercials featured characters from the film as customers in a Burger King restaurant, with dialogue relating directly to the restaurant chain. Since the creative execution was obviously unique to the situation (rather than involving film clips as usual), these ads stood out to consumers.

When promotional elements are well integrated, offering a consistent message and driving consumers back and forth among the various partners, fans and shoppers will connect with the property and the products or services involved. This personal interaction is a key factor in a successful promotion. A Rugrats tie-in with Embassy Suites involved a sweepstakes that gave the winner a five-day trip to Hollywood to meet the show's animators, who drew the winner into a Rugrats mini-movie. The promise of this type of connection makes a promotion attractive to its target audience.

Of course, all promotions should make sure to maintain, if not enhance, the integrity of the property. Nickelodeon's deal with Gateway Computers does not allow Rugrats or Blue's Clues characters to talk specifically about the brand in commercials, although clips are allowed. The network does not want it to appear as if the characters are endorsing the product. Any promotion that harms the core property's image is a failure for the licensor, no matter how many sales or how much awareness it generates.

All partners should sign off on all promotional elements (even those with which they are not directly involved). Each should be confident that the total tie-in reflects well on its business. The key is that all participants feel they are involved in a win-win situation, where each ally's cost (whether measured in cash or tradeouts) is fair and its gains equitable.

CHAPTER 13
FINAL THOUGHTS

Despite the difficult environment facing the licensing business today, new participants continue to enter the licensing business daily. They include small manufacturers hoping to boost their consumer profile by associating with a licensed property to large corporations mining their portfolio of brands for new revenue streams. As a result, competition among properties and licensees is acute. In the face of this market glut, a common-sense approach to licensing makes more sense than ever before. Me-too and ill-conceived licensing efforts will fall by the wayside as innovative and distinctive programs succeed.

Contraction in retail shelf space, increased selectivity on the part of retail buyers and the greater number of properties available all combine to make gaining shelf presence difficult. Only a small percentage of properties can get past the retail gatekeepers and have a chance to attract consumers' attention. Those that do tend to be a mix of the highest-profile event properties, evergreen brands and unique niche licenses that can truly be positioned as exclusives.

Most licensors now view the entire world as their potential market, knowing that their home territory alone may not be enough to support their property. Global licensing efforts have become the norm. Yet it is not easy to introduce a property and implement a strategy on a worldwide basis, given the differences in cultures, tastes, retailing, media and business practices from country to country. Licensors must tailor their properties and tactics to the specifics of each nation, yet maintain a consistent image around the world. To do this, they need to gain an understanding of how licensing works in each country where they plan to do business.

The fast pace of technological change gives rise to a number of new demands on licensors and licensees alike. They must cope with new and future distribution channels (e.g., e-commerce), media exposure outlets (interactive TV), business practices (using the web to streamline the licensing process), product categories (new electronic game formats or interactive toys), and asset-management methods (via electronic databases). The exact nature of many of these developments is not yet known; what is recognized is that changes will occur quickly and continuously, and licensors, licensees and their partners must be well-positioned to meet them.

Customer sophistication is another challenge. Shoppers no longer desire licensed merchandise just for its novelty, as they did a decade ago. Even intense fans of a property or loyal consumers of a brand do not necessarily translate this enthusiasm into licensed product purchases. Licensors and licensees must attract customers by targeting them personally, creating a long-term and satisfying connection between the shopper and the property, and providing products consumers cannot resist. This is not easy to do, given the saturated marketplace and the average shopper's busy life.

The best licensing strategy for a property depends on its unique characteristics, its competitive situation and its target audience. Some licenses lend themselves to a single line of products and others to a full multicategory program. Yet licensing executives agree that there are common traits behind every successful property.

Licensors and licensees should carefully consider the fit between product and property, matching each partner's target demographics and ensuring that the property makes sense in association with the product, service or promotion. At the same time, successful licensing programs are those that stand out from the competition and remain fresh throughout their lifetimes — whether of short or long duration — through promotional activity, new product introductions, new media and/or entertainment vehicles. This holds true for any type of property.

Licensing participants enhance their chances of success if they select partners whose objectives parallel theirs and nurture the relationship through honesty, open communication, fair treatment and an understanding of each other's businesses and goals. A realistic outlook also helps. An honest assessment of a property's characteristics will lead to a sound licensing strategy, while making overoptimistic promises is a prelude to failure.

Licensors and licensees who spend enough time and effort on the planning process will reap the rewards, but remaining flexible is equally important. Market conditions and consumer whims change quickly; the ability to keep abreast of emerging trends and react in a timely fashion is a key criterion for success. Licensees and licensors who have thoroughly analyzed their properties, products, markets and customers are better poised to adapt to changes quickly and appropriately.

Members of the licensing community are ahead of the game if they have thought through the objectives of their licensing program *before* setting their strategy. It is surprising how many jump into licensing simply because "I know it's a way to increase my business," yet they have not considered exactly what goals they hope to achieve through licensing nor which of these objectives takes priority. There are many valid reasons to embark upon a licensing program, but strategies vary depending on which goals are most important. Measuring success also relies upon the upfront establishment of achievable milestones.

Licensors and licensees should not ignore niche opportunities. Targeting a small segment of the population with a property that appeals directly to them can be more successful than shooting for wide success. Niche consumer bases are often easier to reach and communicate with, they respond to properties they feel are tailored just for them, and they appreciate being the first to be offered a unique property.

Even with all the market challenges, growth opportunities exist for niche and general-interest properties alike. New product categories, innovative properties, unexplored marketing techniques and underdeveloped geographic regions emerge continuously and create the potential for successful licensed products and services. A creative approach to licensing, in combination with planning and flexibility, will drive many licensing partnerships in the future. That, and a bit of good luck!

PART 4:
APPENDICES

LICENSING BUSINESS GLOSSARY

Note: Phrases in ***bold italics*** signify cross-references. Please refer to individual listings.

– A –

Access. The ability to acquire reproducible art based on a property. Mainly relates to art licensing, where a manufacturer can use a ***public-domain*** work royalty- and permission-free, unless a third party (e.g., a museum) controls access and charges a fee for permission to use the work.

Added value. A benefit that makes a product more attractive in the eyes of consumers. A premium, a discount or a license can all add value.

Advance. Part of the payment required for a license, usually due upon signing of a licensing contract. Often a portion of the ***guarantee*** rather than an additional payment.

Advertising. A method of promoting a property or licensed product line. The licensee, the licensor or both may advertise a licensed product or property.

Advertising adjustments. Variations on required royalty rates tied to advertising. A licensor may require an additional few percentage points on top of the royalty for a general advertising fund or may allow a lower royalty in return for advertising expenditures by the licensee.

Allowable deductions. Authorized deductions in the sales figures upon which royalties are applied. Usually limited to 2%-3% of the total. Licensors allow very few such deductions; common examples include freight, cash/volume discounts and ***returns***.

Ancillary merchandise. Secondary products related to a company's core product line; often licensed. A magazine publisher would consider licensed videos or tote bags based on its titles as ancillary merchandise.

Ancillary revenues. Additional revenues coming from sources outside a company's core product lines. For the owner of a corporate trademark, royalties from licensing (outside of ***brand extension***) would often be considered ancillary revenues.

Application. 1) The way in which a property can be incorporated into a product. 2) The first step in registering a trademark or copyright. 3) A form by which licensors can screen potential licensees, often representing the first step in the licensing negotiation process. See ***licensee evaluation form***.

Arbitration. A preferred means of dispute resolution in the event of a conflict between licensor and licensee.

Auditing. A means of verifying that licensees have remitted accurate royalty payments. Licensing contracts usually contain a provision allowing the licensor to audit the licensee's books.

Authors. 1) Writers. Well-known authors of licensed books can earn a royalty in addition to that paid to the trademark holder. 2) In copyright law, the creator of a work.

– B –

Back-end revenues. In entertainment, investors often recoup their costs on the back end, that is, through royalties from home video, foreign TV sales and other monetary streams. Licensing royalties are often a component of back-end revenues.

Behavioral characteristics. Traits exhibited by a group of consumers, such as where they prefer to shop or what types of entertainment they enjoy. Knowing a target market's behavioral characteristics helps licensors and licensees effectively reach them.

Benchmarks. Milestones at which royalty rates can rise. Benchmarks in a graduated royalty deal could be based on a property's overall performance or, more typically, on the sales of the product line.

Big 3 discounters. The three major national discount department store chains: Wal-Mart, Kmart and Target.

Blockbuster. A property that generates significant licensed merchandise sales, usually within a short time period.

Boilerplate. A contract containing standard provisions. Often used as a basis for negotiating an individual licensing agreement.

Bounceback mechanisms. Promotional elements that tie various partners together. For example, a purchase of one product may lead to a discount on another product or service.

Brand. 1) A property that, over time and with significant investment, has gained value among consumers and is perceived by consumers as having a consistent image or message. 2) Often used by licensors to refer to any property, especially one positioned as a current or future evergreen.

Brand equity. The value associated with a brand by consumers.

Brand extension. An additional product line under an existing brand umbrella. Brand extensions into related areas outside a manufacturer's area of expertise are often licensed.

Brand identity, Brand image. The perception, on the part of consumers, that there is a single image joining all products under one brand name. Usually enhanced by consistent packaging, labeling and point-of-purchase materials.

Breach of contract. A violation of one of the provisions in a licensing agreement; grounds for termination.

Bricks-and-mortar retailer. A traditional retailer that has a physical store or stores, as opposed to an e-commerce retailer.

Bridge. A term in the apparel industry for mid- to higher-priced apparel. A level between mass market products and designer collections.

Built-in audience. A group of fans of a property who become the primary target market for licensed merchandise associated with that property. A property such as Star Trek or Elvis Presley has a built-in audience.

Buyers. Retailer personnel responsible for purchasing products for a given department. Jurisdictions vary from retailer to retailer.

By-products. Products or ingredients that are created during a manufacturing process but not needed for the item being produced. By-products are sometimes used as ingredients for other licensed items associated with the original product. For example, by-products from the whiskey distilling process could be used in the manufacture of a licensed whiskey-flavored barbeque sauce.

– C –

© symbol. A mark used to show copyright ownership. The creator of a work of art or authorship can employ the symbol even if the work is not registered with the Copyright Office.

Cannibalization. The process by which one distribution channel or manufacturer subtracts sales from another distribution channel or manufacturer associated with similar products. Sales of a licensed product in a discount store may cannibalize sales of a similar, higher-priced product at a specialty store.

Capital. The financial assets or worth of a manufacturer or other company. Licensors select licensees that possess adequate capital.

Cartoon Q. A survey conducted by Marketing Evaluations that measures the popularity of cartoon characters.

Category killer. A type of retailer known for a wide selection of products in a certain product category, as well as low prices. They compete with specialty stores and mass merchants. Examples include Toys 'R' Us; Bed, Bath and Beyond; and Sports Authority.

Category manager. An employee of a licensor or licensing agent that is responsible for sales and brand management within a given product category or categories. Many licensors structure their departments by category rather than property responsibility.

Cease-and-desist letter. A letter from an attorney that asks a counterfeiter to immediately stop its illegal activity and threatens legal action if it does not. One of the first and most cost-effective steps in an anti-infringement program.

Central marketing fund (CMF). A licensor-controlled fund financed by licensee contributions, matched by the licensor. Licensees donate 2%-3% on top of their royalty; the money is used to finance promotional activity benefiting the property.

Certificate of registration. A document from the Patent and Trademark Office signifying the registration of a trademark.

Civil law. Laws dealing with the rights of private citizens. Civil law provides for protections against counterfeiting and remedies if it occurs.

Classic properties. Properties that have a long life marked by strong, steady sales (with cyclical ups and downs). While a true classic has multigenerational appeal, many licensing executives refer to any property with long-term potential as a "classic."

Classifications, Classes. In trademark law, categories of products. Licensors must register trademarks in the classifications within which they expect to market merchandise.

Clicks-and-mortar retailers. Retailers that have both physical stores and an e-commerce presence, particularly if their offline and online activities are interrelated.

Close-out. The sale of merchandise at a very low price (often below cost) in order to reduce inventory in a short time. After a licensing contract terminates, licensees may dispose of inventory for a finite period, which can lead them to settle for close-out prices.

Co-branding. An arrangement where two brands appear on a single product. Often achieved through licensing, with both the licensor's and licensee's brand being given equal weight on the package, rather than the licensor's taking precedence as is typical.

Co-insured. An additional party named on an insurance policy. Licensors demand to be named as the co-insured on licensees' product liability, personal injury and/or property damage policies.

Co-op money. Financial contributions by licensees or licensors to a retailer's promotional or advertising efforts.

Coattails. A product or property that tries to emulate the characteristics of a successful property or product that came before it. While not illegal (as in *counterfeiting*), these copycat products tend to underperform compared to the original.

Collateral materials. Sales materials used to help promote a licensed product line, including brochures, flyers, sales packets. Must be approved by the licensor if the licensed property is featured in conjunction with the materials.

Commitment. A licensee's support of a property, outside of monetary compensation. Can include a promise to market a large number of products or make the licensed line a major focus for a season. Licensors may agree to a greater licensee commitment in lieu of a high guarantee.

Common law. The body of law based on legal precedent rather than on written laws. The *right of publicity* is based largely on common law.

Concept shops. Retail areas devoted to merchandise, from various product categories, based on one licensed property. Accepted as one of the most effective ways to drive retail sales of licensed merchandise. Also known as *in-store boutiques* when located within another retailer and *free-standing stores* when independent.

Conceptual drawings or models, Concept stage. Early representations of what licensed products will look like. Usually must be approved by the licensor as part of the product approval process before production of the licensed line can proceed. The definition of what constitutes the concept stage varies by licensor.

Concession stands. Retail areas at theme parks, sports arenas or concert venues that sell merchandise related to the event. Concession stand merchandise is often sourced by the licensor for that purpose only, rather than being licensed.

Consolidation. The existence of fewer retailers or manufacturers or licensors within a given sector of the licensing business. Retail consolidation has hit department stores; sports apparel licensees and entertainment licensors have consolidated as larger companies have purchased smaller ones in related fields.

Consumer awareness. The level of recognition that a property has among its target market.

Consumer backlash. A negative perception by the public toward a property or product, due to a controversy, oversaturation or the fact that licensed goods are viewed as inappropriate.

Contract. The agreement between licensee and licensor, licensor and licensing agent, licensor and retailer, licensor and promotional partner, or manufacturer and licensing consultant. Outlines the rights and responsibilities of each party.

Contract negotiations. The process of agreeing upon the provisions contained in a licensing contract. Virtually every point in a deal is negotiable depending on the circumstances.

Control. The ability of the licensor to maintain the value of the brand, even when products associated with it are manufactured by licensees. The product approval and licensee selection processes are key components of maintaining control.

Conversationals. Apparel and accessories featuring designs that encourage comment. Ties and socks, often licensed, are among the major conversational categories.

Copycat. See *coattails*.

Copyright. The laws governing the protection of works of art, music or literature from *infringement*.

Core products. A company's primary product line. Can be manufactured in-house or licensed to other manufacturers.

Cost of goods sold. The unit cost of each product sold. Royalties, which accrue upon sales of each unit, are considered a component of the cost of goods sold.

Costumed characters. Actors portraying licensed characters, logos or mascots. Usually present at live promotional events supporting a property. Especially common for entertainment or publishing-based characters and corporate and team mascots.

Counterfeiting. The act of illegally copying a product. Counterfeiting is a major concern of licensors and licensees.

Coverage. In the syndicated television business, a measure of the portion of households that can receive a syndicated television show. Stated as a percentage of total U.S. television households.

Criminal law. Laws pertaining to crimes and their punishment. Provides for protection against counterfeiting and remedies if it occurs.

Cross-collateralization. The tying together of various facets of a property financially. Revenues from two properties, two retail tiers or two geographic areas could count toward the same guarantee, for example, or merchandising revenues and revenues from other sources could combine toward the recoupment of an investment in an entertainment production.

Cross-licensing. The combination of two or more properties on one licensed product.

Cross-merchandising. The joint retail display of two or more different licensed products based on the same property. Cross-merchandising tends to increase sales and is appropriate for properties of all types, including designers, characters, sports and trademarks.

Cross-packaging, Co-packaging. The act of combining two or more licensed products based on the same property in the same package for one price. Examples include videos with plush toys and action figures with comic books.

Cultural differences. Variations in tastes, product specifications, media exposure, retailing and other characteristics from country to country. Cultural differences have a significant impact on global licensing strategies.

Customs. 1) Governmental departments in each country that oversee imports and exports. Customs officials around the world are key allies in the fight against *counterfeiting*. 2) Businesses and lifestyle practices in a given country. Variations in customs affect international licensing tactics.

– D –

Deadline. The target date by which a certain action must be completed. Deadlines such as product introduction dates and first shipping dates are often included in a licensing contract, because they are crucial to the success of the licensing program.

Deal memo. A document, signed by licensor and licensee, that outlines the key points to be included in a licensing contract. While not binding, a signed deal memo allows partners to proceed with product development while the details of the final contract are being negotiated.

Dealer networks. Wholesalers or retailers that sell a manufacturer's core products; examples include automobile dealerships and soft drink distributors. Provide opportunities for sales of related licensed products.

Demand. Consumers' desire for licensed products tied to a given property.

The ability to meet demand while it exists and to anticipate its decline, so as to prevent excess inventory, are key factors in a licensing program, especially from the point of view of licensees and retailers.

Demographic group. Consumers with similar *demographic traits*. Licensors and licensees can target them in the aggregate.

Demographic traits. Characteristics including sex, age and income level. Demographic traits are major factors in determining the strategy for a licensing program.

Department stores. Stores, often upscale, that sell a wide variety of merchandise grouped into different areas. Prices tend to be higher, volumes lower and customer service greater than in *mass market* stores.

Detection. The process of seeking out and discovering counterfeit activities. Usually involves the cooperation of licensors, manufacturers, retailers and customers, as well as private investigators and governmental departments.

Developers. In the electronic game industry, people who create videogames and the game architecture that makes play possible. Developers usually receive a royalty, in addition to that earned by the trademark holder.

Differentiation. 1) The act of distinguishing a manufacturer's products or a retailer's store from its competitors'. Associating with a licensed property is one method of differentiation. 2) The act of creating a difference between upscale and mass market products to avoid *cannibalization*.

Dilution. A decrease in the value of a brand. Product overproliferation, lack of quality and entry into inappropriate distribution channels can all contribute to brand dilution.

Direct market. In the comic book industry, specialty comic book stores (as distinguished from mass market stores). The direct market accounts for most sales of comic books, except those targeted at young children, and provides an outlet for licensed merchandise based on comics, science fiction and other properties.

Direct-to-retail deal. A licensing agreement in which a retailer acts as the licensee for an exclusive product or range of products.

Disposable income. The amount of income that consumers have left over for purchases after they pay their required expenses. The average disposable income of a property's target audience will determine appropriate licensed product categories, distribution and price points. Average disposable income varies by country.

Disposal period. A period of about 30 days after contract termination, during which licensees are allowed, on a nonexclusive basis, to sell off remaining inventory produced under the terms of the agreement. Disposal usually occurs at *close-out* prices.

Distribution channels. The methods by which licensed merchandise reaches the consumer. Distribution channels include traditional retailers of various types, as well as mail order, teleshopping, the Internet and concession stands.

Distribution license. An agreement allowing a company to distribute products manufactured or created by third parties. Differs from a retail product licensing agreement, which allows the manufacture or sale of newly created items based on a property. Examples include rights to sell home videos of theatrical films or television episodes, to market a product in a foreign country or to distributed licensed goods as premiums.

Distribution tiers. Levels of retail stores. The three major distribution tiers are upstairs, including department and specialty stores; mid-tier, including less upscale department stores such as Sears and JCPenney; and downstairs, including discount stores, category killers, convenience, variety, food and drug stores.

Distributors. Companies that buy from manufacturers and sell to retailers (or other customers), outright or on consignment. Licensors must authorize any distributors employed by their licensees.

Divisional merchandise managers. Retail employees that supervise buyers of various product categories. Licensors seeking to put together *concept shops* must usually approach personnel at the DMM level or higher, since buyers are responsible for bottom lines within their departments only.

Downstairs. A distribution tier with low prices, high volume and low levels of customer service. Includes discount department stores, *category killers*, variety, convenience, food and drug stores.

– E –

E-commerce. Retail sales that occur over the Internet rather than in a physical store. The most successful ventures to date usually involve *clicks-and-mortar retailers* or divisions of larger corporations, rather than *pure-play Internet companies*.

Endorsement. The association of a property (often a live or deceased celebrity but sometimes a character) with a product, implying use. An endorsed product does not involve altering the merchandise itself, as a licensed product would. Endorsements are usually compensated with a flat fee, or a fee and a percentage of merchandise sales, if any.

Entertainment vehicles. Films, film sequels, television shows, home videos, videogames, publishing, Internet entertainment and live events that serve to add excitement to a property. All are opportunities for additional merchandise sales and for promotions supporting the property.

Estate. Rights belonging to the heirs of a deceased celebrity. Royalties that come from from licensing the name, likeness, signature, etc., of a deceased celebrity usually go to his or her estate.

Exclusivity. An agreement granting a single licensee all rights to use a property in a particular product category, territory or distribution channel. Exclusivity can be defined broadly or narrowly. See also *retail exclusives*.

Exploitation. The commercial use of a trademark. Licensors must exploit their *trademarks* in various classifications of products to prevent third parties from questioning the marks' validity in those classes.

Exposure. The amount of opportunity consumers have to see or hear about a property. Advertising, publicity, entertainment and media vehicles, and live events can all enhance a property's exposure.

Extension of contract. The expansion of a licensing agreement to include additional properties, products, territories, duration or distribution.

— F —

Fad. A product, property or pop-culture phenomenon that is embraced by a wide slice of the populace very fast; then, after a short duration, its popularity plummets. Licensed properties that become fads can sometimes transform into long-term franchises over time.

Fan shops. Specialty stores that exclusively sell licensed merchandise, particularly sports apparel or character-based merchandise.

First-look deal. An agreement where a licensee is allowed the first opportunity to consider a licensor's future properties before the licensor takes them to other potential partners. Usually one component of a long-term, multiproperty deal.

First shipping date. The date at which manufacturers must make their first shipment of a licensed product line to retailers. Usually written into the contract because of the importance of having merchandise in stores in time for key selling seasons.

Fit. The appropriateness of an association between product and property in terms of product application, target audience, licensee's and licensor's objectives and other criteria. Applies to both licensed merchandise and promotions.

Flat fee. An alternate method of payment for a license, usually in conjunction with promotional licensing. Sometimes applies to products, particularly when several licensors are involved, in which case a flat fee per unit may be charged in lieu of a royalty; this is rare and is usually intended to simplify accounting.

Flea markets. Retail environments at which counterfeit merchandise is commonly discovered.

Flexibility. The ability to adapt to changing market conditions. While thoughtful strategic planning is important to the success of a licensing program, flexibility is also key.

Flop. A licensing program that fails to drive licensed merchandise sales. Licensing efforts that are considered flops overall may still be associated with some successful product lines; some strong-selling properties are considered flops if they do not meet too-high expectations.

Franchise. A long-term property that is comprised of many elements. In entertainment, a franchise would include films, publishing, television, videogames, promotions, licensed products and other facets.

Free goods. Licensed products that are given away, such as samples. Can be royalty-free, within limits.

Free-standing stores. Independent retail outlets focusing on one property or family of properties. One type of *concept shop*.

Full-time licensor. A property owner whose associated products are all licensed rather than being manufactured in-house. Fashion labels can opt to become full-time licensors if royalty revenues for licensed lines exceed profit margins for products manufactured in-house, for example.

$-$ G $-$

Gatekeepers. Entities that stand between the property and the consumer, such as broadcast and cable networks, Internet distributors and retailers. Licensors and licensees must sell the gatekeepers before they can sell to consumers.

Generic merchandise. Nonlicensed products.

Goodwill. Value associated with a property. Owned by the licensor; contracts contain a provision stating this fact.

Graduated royalties. A payment structure in which the royalty rate rises (or, in rare cases, falls) as specific sales or performance benchmarks are attained. An increasingly common method of compensation.

Grant of rights. The major provision of a licensing contract, outlining what properties, products, territories and distribution channels are authorized under the agreement.

Gross margin. The difference between manufacturer's sales price per unit and *cost of goods sold*, divided by sales price (stated as a percentage). In industries where licensed products do not command premium prices, royalties cut into manufacturers' gross margins.

Grounds for termination. Actions on the part of either the licensee or the licensor that would cause the licensing contract to become invalid. Grounds for termination are outlined in the agreement.

Guarantee. A minimum royalty payment, usually based on expected sales. Actual royalty payments accrue against the guarantee; whatever remains of the guarantee amount after total royalties are tallied is payable at the end of the year or contract period. If royalties exceed the guarantee, no further money is owed. (In rare cases involving non-exclusive licensing agreements, the guarantee is a performance benchmark, rather than a required payment.)

$-$ H $-$

Hangtags. Hanging labels on licensed merchandise such as apparel. Hangtags and other labeling are usually consistent across all licensed products in order to enhance *brand identity* and make spotting counterfeit goods easier.

Hard goods. A retail term referring to products not made of textiles, such as toys or furniture. The opposite of *soft goods*.

Hits. 1) A measurement of Internet usage that gauges how often web browsers clicked on a website. 2) Successful (often blockbuster) licensed properties.

Holograms. An expensive-to-duplicate method of printing labels or hangtags. Can also be incorporated into the products themselves. Often used as a means to counteract infringement, since they are easy to spot and costly to copy.

Home runs. Another name for *blockbusters*.

Hot properties. The most popular properties within a given year. Usually refers to *short-term* rather than *classic properties*.

Hypermarts, Hypermarkets. Huge retailers featuring low prices and large selections. A major distribution channel in some countries, such as France; expanding worldwide. Carrefour is a hypermarket.

– I –

Impressions. The cumulative number of times consumers see or hear of a property. The use of a property on packaging, in advertising, in entertainment and in live events all contribute to the total number of impressions generated.

Impulse purchases. Products bought by consumers on the spur of the moment, without prior planning. Many licensed products, especially those based on entertainment or character properties and/or sold through distribution channels such as supermarkets or convenience stores, are impulse purchases.

In-store boutiques. Another name for *concept shops* when located inside another store.

Incremental costs. The difference between costs associated with a licensed tie-in and costs that would accrue anyway. For a promotional partner, the additional cost of placing an ad mentioning a tie-in specifically, within an existing advertising schedule, versus the costs for the ad originally planned within that schedule, would be an incremental cost.

Indemnifications. Protections against lawsuits by third parties. Licensees indemnify licensors against personal injury suits involving a licensed product, while licensors indemnify licensees against suits charging that the trademark infringes on other marks.

Infrastructure. The systems in place in a given region for manufacturing and transporting goods, and for communication. The state of a geographic territory's infrastructure is an important factor in the decision of whether a licensor should enter that territory.

Infringement. The unauthorized use of a trademark.

Injunctions. Court-ordered restrictions on a party's activities. A court can issue an injunction against an alleged counterfeiter, barring the continued manufacture and sale of the goods.

Installed base. The number of consumers and/or businesses that already own the hardware necessary to use a given technology. Applies to electronic games and multimedia; the size of the installed base for a particular platform determines the current potential market for software sales related to that platform.

Instant classic. A property that has high expectations for long-term success before its launch and meets those expectations, at least initially. Often used in the 1990s to describe Disney animated feature films such as *The Lion King*.

Interactive multimedia. A term referring to technologies that allow the user to input and manipulate information as well as receive it (interactive) and that combines sound, video, computer and other technogies (multimedia). Formats can include online and offline platforms or combinations of the two. A current question is whether there will ever be one standard for interactive multimedia.

International copyright convention. One of a number of international agreements, including the Berne Convention, dealing with copyright protection. Most countries subscribe to either Berne or to the provisions of another international copyright convention, or are parties to separate bilateral agreements covering copyrights. The existence of these copyright conventions and treaties means that a copyright registered in the U.S. is valid in most other key licensing territories as well.

International sub-agent. A *licensing agent* operating in a territory outside the licensor's home region. May be retained by the licensor or by a master or regional licensing agent working with the licensor.

Internet. A channel for distributing entertainment and other content, disseminating marketing information, posting artwork, and selling merchandise through e-commerce. While still a small channel for product sales, the Internet is important for business-to-business marketing and administrative tasks.

Interstate commerce. The marketing and selling of products across state borders. Interstate commerce is required for federal trademark laws to apply.

Inventors. Creators of games, toys or other products. Inventors usually require a royalty in addition to that owed to trademark holders.

Inventory control. The process of maintaining adequate production levels to meet demand for a licensed product while it is high and to prevent excess inventory after demand falls off. An especially important consideration for merchandise based on *short-term properties* or *fads*.

Invisible licensing. The act of creating licensed products that are perceived by consumers to be manufactured by the licensor rather than the licensee. Brand-extension licensing of fashion labels and corporate trademarks is often "invisible."

– J –

Joint ventures. 1) A type of business structure where two or more parties share ownership. 2) A common method of expanding into new geographic territories; an alternate to licensing or setting up a subsidiary. 3) A licensing agreement is not a joint venture; this fact is stated in the contract.

Jurisdiction. The state law under which a licensing agreement is valid and under which disputes will be resolved.

– K –

Key category. An important product category. Its significance may relate to the awareness, sales or advertising it generates (e.g. a master toy licensee for a children's entertainment property); to the way it enhances the core property and creates a connection between the consumer and the property (e.g. home video, videogames or publishing); or to the fact that it is the category for which a brand is known (e.g. sportswear for a fashion brand) or is naturally related to that category (fruit juice for a fruit brand).

Knock-offs. Illegal products that are confusingly similar to legitimate licensed merchandise. May or may not be exact copies.

Know-how. Expertise in manufacturing or marketing. The level of know-how in certain geographic territories where capitalism is in its infancy may be an important criteria in the decision of whether to expand there.

– L –

Labeling. Identifying marks on licensed products, including *hangtags*, sewn-in labels and packaging. Consistency in labeling enhances brand image and assists in spotting counterfeit merchandise.

Launch date. The date at which licensed products will appear at retail. Launch dates may vary from product to product, depending on the *rollout* strategy for the property.

Lead times. The amount of time required for products to arrive at retail after a licensing deal is completed. Lead times vary from licensee to licensee, between licensee and licensor and among promotional partners. Factors affecting lead times include length of contract negotiation, product development time, retooling requirements and time lags related to importing.

Legal marking. Placing notices on labels, printed matter, etc. stating trademark and copyright status. The act of legal marking prevents infringers from claiming ignorance of the existence of the mark and helps prove to the courts that the licensor is serious about its trademark and copyright ownership.

Legal protection. The act of registering appropriate *trademarks* and *copyrights* in order to have a legal means to counteract *counterfeiting* and *infringement.*

Legal remedies. Rewards a licensor can receive and/or punishments required for a counterfeiter when the licensor's marks are infringed. Remedies can include injunctions, damages, fines and jail time.

Letter of intent. A non-binding document stating that two parties are about to sign a deal. Licensors and licensees typically skip this step, focusing on the deal memo and final contract, but some public companies may desire to publicize a letter of intent to boost their stock price.

License acquisition. The process the licensee goes through to seek appropriate properties with which to associate and to negotiate acceptable terms for a licensing agreement.

Licensed promotions. Marketing alliances that focus on a licensed property and generate awareness for the promotional partners. Also known as licensed tie-ins.

Licensee. The party that acquires the rights to utilize a property, usually for a retail product but sometimes for promotional use or for a service.

Licensee estoppel. A contractual provision that prevents a licensee from questioning the validity of a licensor's trademarks during the term of the agreement.

Licensee evaluation form. A method licensors use to screen potential licensees. Licensees must provide sales, marketing and financial information regarding their company and outline their plans for the property. Also known as a licensee application or licensing application.

Licensee summit. A licensor-sponsored gathering of all licensees, key retailers and promotional partners associated with a property, intended to enhance communication and spur partners to work together.

Licensing. A lease agreement in which a *licensee* rents the rights to a legally protected property from a *licensor* for use in conjunction with a product or service.

Licensing agent. A company or individual that acts on behalf of the licensor in launching, administering and/or evaluating a licensing program. The agent takes over many of the licensor's duties, subject to approval by the licensor, in return for a commission.

Licensing consultant. 1) A company that represents the interests of a licensor in launching or administering a licensing program, usually on a short-term basis, in return for a fee. 2) A company that represents the interests of the licensee in seeking and acquiring licenses. Several licensing consultants specialize in serving manufacturers only. Usually paid through a retainer or some combination of retainer and commission (with the latter based on percentage of the licensed line's sales).

Licensing in. The act of acquiring a license. Licensees license in.

Licensing fee. 1) A flat fee (either a lump sum or a per-unit charge) required as payment for the use of a license. An alternative to a royalty, generally for promotions or advertising rather than retail products. 2) Sometimes used in reference to the guarantee.

Licensing out. The act of leasing rights to other parties. The licensor licenses out.

Licensing point person. Term describing the executive at a retail chain responsible for dealing with licensors and identifying licensed promotional opportunities. The retailer's key contact with the licensing community.

Licensor. The *property* owner.

Lifespan. The time period starting with the **launch date** of a property and ending when demand for licensed products ends. Classic properties have long, even unlimited, lifespans, while short-term properties have lifespans of three to five years or less.

Likenesses. Depictions of celebrities. Celebrities or their *estates* retain the right to approve the use of their likenesses, whether these likenesses are the central property or a component of another property (e.g., actors in a film, although less-high-profile talent rarely have likeness approval rights).

Litigation. Legal action against another party. Contract disputes and anti-counterfeiting activities may lead to litigation.

Logo. A graphic representation of a trademark or brand. Special logos are often created for special events, for sub-brands based on a property or as an umbrella to tie diverse properties together.

Long-term properties. Properties that have lifespans stretching over a decade or more. The strategy behind managing a long-term property is much different from that for a *short-term property*.

Low-end merchandise. Inexpensive products such as key chains, buttons and pencils. Sales are primarily *impulse purchases*.

– M –

Manufacturer's representative. 1) A *licensing consultant* exclusively representing the interests of manufacturers in seeking licenses, managing licensing programs and negotiating contracts. 2) In sales, a company that serves an intermediary in selling a manufacturer's products to retailers.

Markup. The difference between the retail and the wholesale price, divided by the retail price, stated as a percentage.

Mass market. Retail outlets with high volume, low prices and little customer service. Includes discounters and *category killers*.

Master licensee. The major licensee in a given category, with rights to several products within that category. May *sublicense* certain products to other manufacturers with expertise in those areas, within the context of its agreement with the licensor.

Maturing market. A market in which annual sales growth is slowing or leveling off after several years of large increases. Part of the natural business cycle. The licensing business in the U.S. and Canada, and in several other large territories, is a maturing market.

Measureability. The ability to tally the results of a promotional tie-in, or facets thereof, to gauge success. Coupon redemptions, calls to interactive phone lines and website hits are all measurable (but not necessarily traceable). See *traceability*.

Media buy. The total amount spent on print, television, radio and other forms of advertising. Payment for the use of a property in advertising may be structured as a percentage of the media buy or as a flat fee.

Media vehicles. Book and comic book publishing, television shows, films and sequels, videogames, computer software, websites and home video, all of which add to a property's exposure, keep it fresh and create promotional opportunities.

Merchandise mix. The types of products stocked by a retailer. A store's merchandise mix helps determine if it is an appropriate outlet for a licensed product line.

Merchandising. 1) The placement of goods at retail so as to maximize sales levels. 2) Promoting the sale of retail products in-store through advertising, promotion or point-of-sale materials. 3) Sometimes used as a synonym for retail product *licensing*.

Mid-tier. The level of distribution below upscale department stores and above mass market; examples of mid-tier retailers include JC Penney and Sears.

Milestones. Measurable performance benchmarks that, when achieved, can affect payment or other aspects of a licensing relationship.

Monetary damages. Financial payments received by a licensor when a third party is convicted of counterfeiting or infringement. The amount of damages may be based on lost sales by legitimate parties (licensors and licensees) or on the counterfeiter's profits.

Multi-partner promotions. Promotional tie-ins that involve several parties, such as a retailer, a packaged goods company, a licensor, a media partner, licensees, etc. A greater number of partners reduces each company's costs, but can create difficulties in terms of logistics. Each partner is exclusive within its category.

Multi-tiered distribution. A strategy in which licensed merchandise is distributed through both *upstairs* and *downstairs* retail channels. Care must be taken to differentiate merchandise in each tier, so that one does not *cannibalize* the other.

Music merchandising. The method by which products are sold at concert venues. Music merchandisers act as licensees, producing most merchandise, and *sublicense* other companies for certain categories. In addition, music merchandisers sometimes serve as licensing agents, arranging deals for products sold in traditional retail channels.

– N –

Naked licensing. Licensing without any attempt to control the quality of merchandise. Could lead to the loss of trademark rights.

Net sales. The sales amount upon which royalties are applied. Usually the manufacturer's sales price less certain *allowable deductions*.

Niche. A small, reachable target market. Niche licensing programs are narrow in scope — a few products aimed at a small but avid audience — but can be lucrative for licensees who participate.

Nielsen ratings. A measurement of television viewership. Used by licensors to demonstrate consumer awareness of a property.

Nonexclusives. Licensing agreements allowing more than one licensee to produce merchandise that is similar or identical and/or overlaps in distribution level and/or territory.

Nonprofit overlay. Adding a nonprofit organization as a promotional partner. Some of the proceeds from merchandise sales within the context of the promotion go to the nonprofit group, providing a purchase incentive and enhancing goodwill.

Nontraditional outlets. Distribution channels for licensed merchandise where such products are not usually sold. Selling licensed entertainment merchandise in video rental stores or movie theaters, plush toys in housewares departments or t-shirts in bookstores would all be examples of exploiting nontraditional outlets.

North American Free Trade Agreement (NAFTA). A treaty among the U.S., Canada and Mexico reducing restrictions on trade. It is one of many trade agreements that affect international licensing programs.

Notice of Allowance. A communication from the Patent and Trademark Office stating that no third parties oppose the use of a trademark. Part of the trademark registration process. The licensor has six months to exploit the mark in interstate commerce or file an extension once it has received its Notice of Allowance.

Novelization. A book that tells the story contained in a film or television show, following the plot closely. A common licensed product for entertainment properties, especially films. Novelizations tied to entertainment properties other than standalong movies tend not to sell as well as original novels.

– O –

Objectives. The specific goals of a licensing strategy. Identifying objectives should be the first step in a licensing program; the goals of the licensor and its licensees should be compatible.

Official Gazette. A monthly Patent and Trademark Office publication that posts trademark applications so parties who feel they will be hurt by a mark have the opportunity to oppose its registration.

Opposition. The act of alerting the Patent and Trademark Office that a proposed trademark will hurt an existing trademark.

Option to renew. A provision sometimes included in a licensing contract that allows existing licensees to renew at the end of the term, usually dependent on meeting certain performance or other benchmarks. Usually known simply as an option.

Outright sale. For artists and designers, an alternative to licensing. The outright sale of a design for a flat fee means that the artist loses control over and ownership of the design. Also associated with less financial potential than licensing in many cases.

Oversaturation. 1) The existence of so many products that supply exceeds demand. 2) The existence of so many similar properties that the market cannot support them all. A successful licensed property or product often breeds copycats, leading to oversaturation and ultimately to a *shakeout*.

– P –

Packaging. The container or wrapping surrounding a licensed product. Consistency in packaging helps enhance brand image and assists in spotting counterfeit products.

Page views. A measurement of Internet usage that gauges the number of times web users look at an individual page within a website. Generally preferred over *hits* as a measurement, but less precise than other yardsticks, such as *unique users*.

Pan-European licensing. The act of granting one license for all European territories rather than separate licenses for each territory. Few manufacturers are equipped to become pan-European licensees.

Pan-regional deal. A licensing agreement encompassing most or all of the countries within a region. Many licensees are not capable of distributing across an entire multi-nation territory, but if they are, a pan-regional deal can be beneficial to both licensee and licensor.

Paper trail. The paperwork associated with anti-counterfeiting efforts, including copies of *cease-and-desist* letters and other records of anti-infringement activities. A paper trail helps convince the court that the licensor is serious about protecting its trademarks and that the alleged infringer knew of the existence of such trademarks.

Parallel imports. The ability to import licensed products into one country from another—in spite of the fact that a local licensee has been granted rights for similar or identical products in the former—creating an unwanted competitive situation. Parallel imports are legal within the European Union, but are discouraged by licensors.

Penalties. Additional payments required for late royalty remittance, missed deadlines, overproduction, overshipping or other violations of contractual provisions.

Per-capita spending. In licensing, the amount spent per person on licensed merchandise in a given geographic territory. Regions with lower per-capita spending are often perceived as having more room for growth than markets with high current per-capita spending rates.

Performance criteria. Benchmarks written into a licensing contract or a licensor-agency contract that determine whether or not the contract can be renewed. Not meeting these benchmarks may also be grounds for termination, depending on the situation.

Permissions. The act of authorizing the use of a property, usually for editorial purposes. May require a fee.

Pilferage. The theft of merchandise from retail outlets. Fear of pilferage is one reason some independent specialty stores are reluctant to sell licensed products.

Piracy. The unauthorized copying of merchandise. Piracy encompasses items featuring unauthorized logos as well as copies of product designs (patent infringement).

Platform. A type of videogame hardware or computer operating system. Each platform is distinct, meaning that only software made for it can be used on it. In licensing, property owners sometimes authorize different licensees to produce software for each platform.

Play value. How fun it is to play with a toy, videogame or premium. A license applied to a toy does not add value or drive sales unless it enhances the play value of that toy.

Plush. Stuffed toys or figures.

Point-of-purchase materials. Display items or marketing materials used in-store to attract attention to licensed merchandise. P.O.P. materials include countertop and floor displays, prefabricated racks and *shelf talkers*, video monitors, posters and banners.

Policing. The process of detecting incidences of counterfeiting and tracing the culprits. The amount of policing done by a licensor depends on its properties' popularity and the amount of counterfeiting activity associated with them, as well as the resources it is willing to spend.

Preproduction samples. Product prototypes that indicate how the product will look when it is manufactured. Most licensors demand the right to approve preproduction samples before manufacturing can begin, as part of the product approval process.

Premium. 1) A promotional item that is sold or given away to consumers or members of the *trade*. Sometimes premium rights are licensed to advertising specialty distributors or premium specialists, who typically source primarily from retail licensees and sell only through licensor-approved channels; premiums also can be created for a specific promotion and sourced by the partner. 2) A higher price. Licensed products in some industries can command premiums over generic products, allowing licensees to pass their royalty cost on to consumers.

Price point. A pre-established retail price within a product category.

Private investigators. Independent contractors retained to help in the detection of counterfeiting activity.

Private label. A brand that is exclusive to one retailer. Private labels can be licensed, as Wal-Mart's *Better Homes & Gardens* and Target's Mossimo brands are.

Privatization. The transformation of industry or media from government to private ownership. As territories move toward privatization, they usually become more attractive to licensors, although the transition can create challenges in the short term.

Product approvals. The quality control process by which the licensor monitors the manufacture of licensed products based on its properties. Approvals are generally required for *conceptual drawings or models*, *preproduction samples* and *production samples*, and sometimes at additional points in the product development process.

Product category. A group of related products. Toys and Games is a product category comprised of dolls, *plush*, board games, activity toys, action figures, etc.

Product introduction date. 1) The date at which licensed merchandise is first introduced to retailers, either at a trade show or in face-to-face meetings. 2) The date products are made available to consumers. Product introduction dates are important milestones, since late products can damage overall sales for the property.

Product liability insurance. A type of insurance that is usually required contractually by licensors to back up licensees' *indemnifications*. The insurance covers both parties financially in case someone sues them over a licensed product line.

Product line. A range of related products manufactured by one licensee.

Production samples. Early manufactured products that must be approved by the licensor before full production can occur. One step in the product approval process.

Profit margins. The difference between revenues and expenses, divided by revenues (stated as a percentage). Licensors would consider licensing over in-house manufacturing if profit margins for an internally produced merchandise line promise to be less than royalty revenues for the same line, if licensed.

Promotional licensing. The act of licensing for advertising, premiums or other marketing purposes, rather than for a retail product.

Promotions. Marketing elements that support a licensing program by generating awareness. Can include sweepstakes or contests, discounted merchandise, live appearances, *cross-merchandising*, exclusive product lines or other components.

Property. A legally protected entity that forms the core of a licensing agreement. The property is what the licensor leases to the licensee.

Property-specific catalogs. Mail-order catalogs containing a selection of merchandise based on a single property or property family. Some of the merchandise may be licensed and some sourced by the licensor or its official cataloger. Products may be either exclusive to the catalog or similar to those found at retail, or some combination of the two.

Property-specific stores. Free-standing retail outlets that focus on one property or family of licensed properties. Merchandise may be manufactured by licensees or contracted specifically for the stores and is often exclusive, to prevent cannibalizing sales of similar licensed merchandise in traditional retail stores.

Property type. A property's origin (e.g., corporate trademark *versus* entertainment). Used as a classification for aggregate measurement.

Prototypes. Preproduction samples of merchandise, used to sell a concept to retailers before manufacturing begins. Prototypes look like the finished product, but are often handmade and flimsy. Licensors approve prototypes as one step in the product approval process.

Psychographic characteristics. A psychological profile of a group of people. Examining psychographic traits of a property's target market (such as what attributes of a property they value) can help determine the best way to reach them.

Public domain. The collection of properties that are, in effect, owned by the public and therefore available for commercial use without permission. Examples include properties whose copyrights have expired, trademarks that have lapsed due to lack of exploitation or monitoring, and nonprotectable events (e.g., the millennium). Some are unavailable, in a practical sense, due to lack of *access*.

Publicity. A method of generating awareness for a property through media coverage. Public events and press releases outlining the activities surrounding a property are typical publicity tactics.

Purchasing habits. Characteristics of a certain target market in terms of where they shop, whether their purchases are planned or *impulse* and whether they prefer mail order, television or online shopping over shopping in person. Helpful in determining how to reach that market.

Pure-play Internet company. A firm that does business (e.g. sells via e-commerce or creates or distributes content) on the World Wide Web only, without any physical or traditional presence (e.g. a store or a TV network). Internet ventures that are divisions of entertainment, retailing or other types of companies are not pure-play.

– Q –

Quality control. The process by which licensors (and licensees) ensure that licensed products meet predetermined specifications. The *product approval* and licensee selection processes are the major tools the licensor uses for quality control.

– R –

® symbol. The legal marking placed next to trademarked names, images, etc., to indicate they are registered marks.

Rebates. Promotional tools in which customers receive discounts on merchandise. The shopper purchases a product, then redeems a coupon entitling him or her to money back. Often one element in a licensed tie-in or cross-promotion.

Redemptions. The number of coupons returned within the context of a promotion. A method of measuring the effectiveness of a tie-in.

Registration. The process by which a trademark or copyright becomes fully protected under the law.

Release date. The date at which a home video, book, musical recording or videogame first appears at retail.

Repositioning. The process of changing a brand image or aiming a property at a different market. Licensed merchandise can help reinforce other marketing activities undertaken to reposition a brand.

Reproduction programs. Licensing efforts in which licensees manufacture exact replicas of objects in a licensor's collection. Generally applies to museum licensing programs, where art objects or historical artifacts are reproduced for sale at retail.

Reserve for returns. A portion of royalty payments withheld for a time to account for eventual returns. In industries where products are fully returnable (such as book publishing), a reserve for returns (e.g., 10%-15% of sales) simplifies accounting.

Restraining orders. Court orders barring a company or individual from continuing an illegal activity. One method of preventing alleged counterfeiters from further infringement.

Retail exclusives. An agreement between a licensor and retailer whereby the retailer has an exclusive window of opportunity in which it is the only promotional partner and/or the only source for licensed merchandise. Exclusives can take many forms and timeframes range from six weeks to indefinite.

Retail sales. Sales of merchandise, measured in terms of the price paid by consumers. Typical yardstick of the success of a licensed line; not to be confused with the partners' share of profits or with wholesale or *net sales*.

Retailers. Sellers of merchandise to consumers. Increasingly important players in the licensor-licensee-retailer partnership. Licensors and licensees must sell concepts and merchandise to retailers before consumers have access to their property.

Retainer. A payment for ongoing services. *Licensing consultants* are often paid by retainer, sometimes in combination with a commission; some *licensing agents* specializing in corporate licensing demand a retainer in addition to their commission.

Retooling. The process of adapting existing machinery for a new line of merchandise. In industries such as toys, retooling is a major cost and may prevent some companies from considering risky, short-term properties where they are not reasonably certain they will recoup their retooling investment.

Returns. 1) Merchandise that is sold to consumers and then brought back to the store for a refund. 2) Merchandise that is sold (sometimes on consignment) to retailers and then returned to the manufacturer if not sold to consumers. In industries where returns are common, such as book publishing, a *reserve for returns* is withheld from royalty payments.

Right of publicity. The legal notion that a celebrity or his or her estate has the sole right to exploit that celebrity's image and name for commercial use. No federal right of publicity exists, but some states recognize it. It is based for the most part on *common law* rather than *statutory law*.

Risk management policy. A financial strategy that ensures money will be available to defend against lawsuits. Takes the place of insurance in industries where insurance is prohibitively expensive.

Rollout. The systematic expansion of a licensing program into new product categories, new distribution channels or new geographic territories. A program's proposed rollout is a strategic consideration that varies depending on the property.

Royalty. The basic form of payment in a licensing agreement; usually a percentage of the *net sales* price of each unit of licensed merchandise sold.

Royalty compliance. The timely and accurate reporting and payment of royalties. Auditing provisions are included in licensing contracts to ensure compliance.

Royalty reporting. The act of providing licensors with accurate and detailed information on sales results and royalties due over a period of time (usually three months).

– S –

Samples. 1) Units of licensed merchandise used in the selling process rather than being sold to consumers. 2) Representations of licensed merchandise at various stages of the manufacturing process, given to licensors for their approval.

Secondary meaning. A legal term that applies to descriptive trademarks (e.g. a brand name that describes the product rather than being made up). While such marks cannot normally be registered as trademarks, they can be if they acquire secondary meaning; that is, consumers associate that name with that product alone. Contractually, licensees may be required to state that a descriptive mark has acquired secondary meaning, thus preventing them from later claiming that a mark is descriptive and unenforceable.

Seizures. Court-ordered confiscations of goods or machinery. A common remedy against illegal counterfeiting activity.

Sell-off period. A period of about one month after the termination of a licensing agreement during which licensees can dispose of excess licensed product inventory on a nonexclusive basis. After the sell-off period, the licensee cannot allow any more merchandise to reach the market.

Selling season. 1) The traditional time period during which manufacturers sell to retailers. 2) The traditional time period during which retailers sell to consumers. The latter is generally six to nine months after the former. The major consumer selling season for the toy business is in the fourth quarter, but manufacturers sell to retailers in February at the annual Toy Fair (or earlier). For apparel, the two major consumer seasons are Fall and Spring; respective selling seasons to retailers are about six months prior.

Separate guarantees. Individual *guarantees* tied to different product categories, distribution channels or territories within the same licensing agreement. Separate guarantees ensure that no single part of an overall agreement will be ignored.

Service licensing. Licensing agreements that authorize the licensee to market a service rather than a retail product. An important category of business for corporate, magazine and other types of properties.

Shakeout. A reduction in the number of companies doing business in a particular field or in the number of similar properties available. Usually follows a period of *oversaturation.*

Shelf talkers. Printed point-of-purchase materials that stand on a retail shelf. Other related P.O.P. includes shelf danglers, which hang from the shelf, and shelf extenders, which stick out. Certain retailers, such as supermarkets, are heavy users of shelf talkers and related signage.

Short-term properties. Licensed properties with a natural lifespan of as little as one year and as much as five years. Such properties may be very lucrative during that brief window.

Sidelines. A term in the bookselling industry for non-book products sold in bookstores. Many of these products are licensed.

Social expressions. A product group consisting of items that allow consumers to display their allegiances by using or wearing products with phrases or graphics. Greeting cards, t-shirts, mugs and desk calendars are all social expressions items.

Soft goods. A retail term meaning merchandise made of textiles, such as apparel and domestics. The opposite of *hard goods.*

Specialty stores. Retailers that focus on one or a few product categories. Stores are usually relatively small in square footage and can be independently owned or part of a chain. Prices are in the middle to high range, product selection is limited and volumes are low. Customer service and product differentiation are the major competitive advantages over other stores.

Specifications. The details of what a given product should look like and how it should be manufactured. Specifications include materials, colors and allowable depictions of a property.

Spokescharacter. A licensed character used in an advertisement, promotion or live appearance supporting a product; implies endorsement.

Spot checks. A method of detecting sales of counterfeit merchandise at retailers, flea markets or on the street. Licensing personnel conduct spot checks regularly, with particular emphasis on times when the appearance of counterfeit merchandise is likely.

Statement of Use. A part of the trademark registration procedure in which the licensor states that its marks are being exploited in interstate commerce.

Statutory law. The body of written state and federal laws.

Stock-keeping units (SKUs). Unique numbers assigned to each product to allow retailers and manufacturers to keep track of sales on a product-by-product basis and to help in the reordering process.

Stockpiling. The act of acquiring several licenses and paying required advances and minimum guarantees, but not bringing all the properties to market.

Store traffic. The number of people who shop at a store or eat at a restaurant during a given period. Assessing changes in store traffic is one method of measuring the success of a licensed promotion.

Strategy. The plan behind the implementation of a licensing program. A strategy should be based on the licensor's objectives and should allow for flexibility in the face of a changing marketplace.

Street value. The value of counterfeit merchandise, as measured by what customers pay for it.

Style guide. A book (or CD) created by licensors to illustrate to licensees the allowable uses of a property, its specifications and required legal markings.

Subagents. Licensing agents specializing in one territory or one product category (or a few territories and/or categories), which are retained by a master or regional licensing agent rather than directly by the licensor.

Sub-brands. Identities that pull together certain types of merchandise within the context of a larger brand, allowing segmentation by target consumer, retail tier or other yardsticks. Baby Looney Tunes is a sub-brand of Looney Tunes; the Princess Collection is a sub-brand of Disney. Playboy has sub-brands targeting different distribution tiers.

Subcontracting. The act of purchasing merchandise from a third party within the scope of a licensing agreement. The licensee has the right to market and sell the merchandise, but another company, approved by the licensor, actually manufactures it to the licensee's and licensor's specifications. Licensors sometimes subcontract rather than license to supply their own stores, catalogs or e-commerce operations.

Sublicensing. The act of authorizing a third party to create or market products within the scope of a licensing agreement, in turn for a royalty. The property owner licenses rights to a licensee, which in turn sublicenses certain categories or territories to a sublicensee, with approval from the licensor.

Subsidiaries. Companies owned by another company. Setting up a subsidiary in a foreign country is an alternative or complement to seeking licensees, retaining a licensing agent or creating a joint venture there, representing one method of launching and overseeing licensing activity in a new territory.

Sunk costs. Financial investments or fixed costs relating to a product line that are lost if the product does not do well. Different from variable or unit costs, which accrue as each unit of product is manufactured. For a licensee, sunk costs include advances and guarantees, retooling and product development investments.

Superroyalty. An additional several percentage points tacked on to a royalty rate for goods sold beyond the authorized production or geographic limit. Used in cases where the licensor does not want to or cannot terminate a contract but wants to penalize or disincentivize licensees from overdistributing.

Syndication. 1) A method of distributing television shows whereby individual stations purchase the rights to air a program in their market at a time of their choosing. Different from a network show, where a program is purchased by a network for broadcast on all its affiliates at the same time. 2) A method of distributing comic strips to newspapers. 3) A method of distributing web content over several Internet distribution channels.

– T –

Target market. The group of consumers likely to purchase a given licensed product.

Tariffs. Payments required when importing or exporting goods. High tariffs may cause a property owner to license a company within a territory's borders rather than bringing in products from a neighboring country.

Teleshopping. A distribution channel where consumers view merchandise on television and order by telephone. Includes home shopping networks, transactional television shows, infomercials and short advertisements.

Term. 1) The duration of a licensing agreement. Varies, but most commonly two to three years for sports, art and entertainment properties, often longer for fashion labels, corporate trademarks and long-existing relationships. 2) A provision in a licensing agreement.

Territory. A geographic region. One of the key elements in the *grant of rights*.

Third-party catalogs. Mail-order catalogs that sell licensed merchandise, but are not owned or controlled by a particular licensor or dedicated to a particular property.

Tie-ins. 1) Promotions in which one or more partners associate themselves with a licensed property. 2) In some industries, licensed products. Publishers refer to licensed books as tie-ins.

Timing. A key strategic consideration in setting up a licensing program. Timing issues include *launch dates, selling seasons, lead times* and *rollout*.

™ **symbol**. Used by property owners to signify they consider their trademark a brand not to be infringed. Does not indicate the trademark is registered.

Traceability. In a promotion, the ability to not only measure the success of a promotion, but to attribute that success to one promotional element.

Trade, the. Term used to describe retailers, wholesalers, distributors, manufacturers and licensors, as distinguished from consumers.

Trade dress. The total look of a product or packaging. Considered legally protectable in the U.S., although not specifically referred to in trademark law. Individual elements within the total look may be trademarked.

Trade shows. Industry conventions in which manufacturers and/or licensors can exhibit their products or properties to other members of *the trade*. An important selling tool.

Tradeouts. In a promotion, the barter of various promotional elements in lieu of cash payments.

Trademark. 1) A method of legal protection; the most common and effective method for most licensors to legally protect their properties. 2) A type of property. Refers to corporate trademarks and brands, as opposed to trademarks originating in fashion, entertainment, publishing or sports.

Transactional television programs. Television shows in which entertainment or talk is combined with a sales message; viewers are able to order merchandise over the phone during the show.

TRSTS. A survey of toy sales conducted by the NPD Group. Used by licensors as evidence that a particular property is popular with children.

– U –

U.S. Customs. An arm of the U.S. government that oversees imports. Trademarks registered with the Patent & Trademark Office can also be registered with Customs, so that counterfeit merchandise can be spotted and seized at the border. An important partner in anti-infringement efforts.

Unique users. A measurement of Internet usage that gauges the number of individual e-mail addresses that visit a site over a given period. Is often considered a better measurement of usage than *hits* or *page views*.

Untapped market. A product category or audience/consumer group that has not been targeted by marketers and shows potential for growth. Untapped markets provide opportunities for licensed merchandise sales.

Upscale products. High-priced, high-quality merchandise aimed at consumers with large disposable incomes. Volumes are low, but per-unit profits are high.

Upstairs. The *distribution tier* that contains high-end department and specialty stores.

– V –

Velocity. 1) The speed at which products sell-through at retail. A higher velocity indicates a strong-selling product line. 2) The speed at which retailers cycle away from properties that are not working. The cycle is getting shorter, meaning that properties have to prove themselves immediately; they are not given time to build.

Vendor. A retailer's term for a manufacturer or wholesaler from which it purchases merchandise. Licensees are vendors.

Volume. The amount of merchandise sold by a retailer or manufacturer, usually measured in units or *wholesale* revenues.

— W —

Warranties. Contractual guarantees that each party is able to deliver on its promises.

Websites. Licensor-, licensee- or retailer-sponsored sections of the Internet. Used to promote properties and merchandise, as well as to sell products.

Webisodic series. Internet content consisting of original entertainment distributed in a regular, episodic fashion. Segments of one to five minutes are uploaded once a week, after which they can be viewed at any time during that week or, later, from archives. A way to promote and freshen a licensed property among certain market segments.

Wholesale sales. Sales of merchandise, as measured by the invoice amount to retailers. The same as the manufacturer's selling price if sold directly, but different if wholesalers or distributors are involved.

Worst-case scenario. The worst thing that could happen as a result of a licensing agreement. Since the financial ramifications of a licensing agreement are difficult to predict, one criterion in a licensee's decision would be to look at the worst-case scenario (e.g. a large investment and minimal sales) and determine whether the company could withstand it.

FREQUENTLY ASKED QUESTIONS ABOUT LICENSING

This Appendix contains a list of questions often asked by individuals who are new to or unfamiliar with licensing. Each brief response includes a cross-reference that directs the reader to the chapter where the concept is explained in detail.

GENERAL QUESTIONS

What is licensing?

Licensing is the act of leasing the rights to a trademarked and/or copyrighted entity (the property) for use in conjunction with products or services. The owner of the rights is known as the licensor; the licensee rents the rights from the licensor. *See Chapter 1.*

How do you pay for a license?

The primary form of payment for a retail licensing agreement is a royalty, or a percentage of the manufacturer's net sales price on each unit sold. The licensee also pays the licensor a minimum guaranteed royalty (against actual royalties), a portion of which is due as an advance. There are many variations on this basic structure. *See Chapter 7.*

What is the average royalty, advance and guarantee?

It is somewhat misleading to discuss an average payment for licensing deals, since they vary widely depending on a number of factors. While royalties are commonly in the 5%-14% bracket, they can be as low as 1% and as high as 20%. Increasingly, licensors and licensees are agreeing to a graduated royalty scale tied to performance or sales benchmarks. The majority of guarantees fall between $10,000 and $50,000, but they can range from as low as $1,000 (or less) to tens of millions of dollars. Advances also vary. *See Chapter 7.*

What are the risks of licensing?

For the licensor, the most significant risk of a licensing program is the threat of losing control over the property. For the licensee, the major risk is financial loss, since minimum guaranteed royalties and investments in product development and tooling become sunk costs if the property fails. *See Chapter 1.*

What are the responsibilities of the licensor and the licensee?

In general, the licensor is responsible for maintaining the value of the property, by adequately protecting it through legal channels, keeping it fresh and desirable and monitoring and counteracting infringement. The licensor also provides marketing support. The licensee is responsible for manufacturing, marketing and selling the licensed product line. Licensees are often responsible for product development (subject to the licensor's approval), but some licensors actively develop products in-house. *See Chapter 1.*

What are the provisions in a licensing contract?

Contracts vary depending on the situation, but some of the major provisions include the grant of rights, payment and auditing procedures, the agreed-upon approval process, warranties and indemnifications. *See Chapter 9.*

Are concept shops effective ways to sell licensed merchandise? How are they set up?

Concept shops, or in-store boutiques, are recognized by licensors, licensees and retailers as one of the best ways to drive sales of licensed merchandise. Licensors take the initiative, with the support of their licensees, in setting up concept shops, meeting with appropriate retailer personnel and providing point-of-purchase materials. Concept shops are often part of a larger, exclusive retail promotion. *See Chapters 4 and 5.*

How do I forecast the financial impact of licensing on my business?

The financial impact of licensing is difficult to predict. For licensors, one method is to examine comparable properties and assess the relative strength of the licensor's property versus the others over time (an inexact science at best). Licensees should consider whether their company can easily withstand a worst-case scenario, analyze the license's effect on margins and examine whether other marketing methods may achieve the same volume increases at less cost. *See Chapters 5 and 6.*

Who initiates the licensing agreement?

Either the licensee or the licensor can make the first contact. Licensors usually offer a contract to the licensee (except in certain industries, such as publishing); it is virtually always negotiable. *See Chapter 9.*

How big a problem is counterfeiting?

Counterfeiting is a huge challenge, requiring significant human and financial resources to combat. The more popular a property, the more counterfeiting activity occurs. *See Chapter 10.*

What are net sales?

Net sales are usually defined as the manufacturer's selling price (as stated on the invoice), less certain allowable deductions (e.g., freight, cash/volume discounts, returns). Deductions are normally limited to 2%-3% of the invoice amount. *See Chapter 7.*

What is the difference between a copyright and a trademark?

Trademark registration is the primary tool for legally protecting a property for purposes of commercial exploitation. U.S. trademarks can be renewed indefinitely if the marks in question continue to be used commercially. For maximum protection, properties should be registered separately in each relevant product classification in each country where they will be licensed or where infringement is likely to occur. Names, graphics and other elements that serve to differentiate one product line from another can be registered as trademarks. Copyright is an automatic right that begins with the creation of a work of art, literature or music; it expires 70 years after the death of the creator. Registration in the U.S. is effective virtually worldwide and is suggested but not required for full protection. For most retail product licensing, copyrights are a secondary method of protecting logos and character designs. Full legal protection is expensive; licensors need to weigh the costs and benefits of multiple registrations in an effort to maximize protection while keeping costs within budgetary constraints. *See Chapter 8.*

Can I use a property that is in the public domain for free? What does it mean when the property is in the public domain?

A public domain work is, in effect, owned by the public and can thus be commercially exploited by anyone. Public domain properties are generally copyrighted properties that have expired or trademarked properties that have gone into the public domain through the trademark owner's lack of vigilance. Government-sponsored or public events are also in the public domain, although specific logos relating to them are trademarked. Anyone can use a public-domain property, assuming that the user can gain access to reproducible depictions of it. *See Chapter 8.*

Are all licensing agreements exclusive?

No. Some contracts provide for true exclusives that encompass a whole product category or geographic region, while others define exclusivity narrowly (e.g., one specific product for one minor distribution channel). Some deals are nonexclusive. *See Chapter 9.*

How is compensation structured for promotional licensing?

Compensation for promotions ranges from a flat fee (such as for advertising or endorsements), to a percentage of a media buy (such as for advertising usage), to a percentage of merchandise, food or ticket sales (such as for licensed restaurants, arcades, live event appearances), to no cash at all. A licensee may provide valuable promotional elements in lieu of some or all of a cash payment. The possibilities vary widely depending on the situation and the final package can be complex. *See Chapter 12.*

How is compensation structured for a service-related licensing agreement?

Compensation varies depending on what type of service is being authorized, but usually consists of a percentage of sales (for memberships, class enrollments, trip bookings, etc.) and/or merchandise sales, if applicable (e.g. for books or travel-related gear), as well as a fee for the license. Other payments also may be factored in. *See Chapter 7.*

What is a central marketing fund?

A central marketing fund (CMF) is a pool of money generated by a percentage of each licensee's sales (usually two to three percentage points on top of the royalty), with matching funds supplied by the licensor. The fund is controlled by the licensor and is used to put together and finance promotional activity that benefits the property and its licensees. *See Chapters 5 and 7.*

How long does it take to get products onto retail shelves after the contract is signed?

Lead times vary, but a rule of thumb is about a year from contract signing to products at retail. Some product categories require at least a year and a half, while others can get to retail in as little as three months, if necessary. *See Chapter 5.*

Are licensing deals negotiable?

Yes, all licensing deals—including nearly every component of the deal, from compensation to marketing support—are negotiable, although those involving large licensors and/or in-demand properties may be less so than those involving more competitive properties or licensors with less bargaining clout. *See Chapter 7.*

What's hot?

This is one of the most often-asked questions in licensing, posed by people who are trying to select licenses to tie in with or emulate. But it really is not relevant (except as part of a quest to become familiar with market trends); licensees should seek properties that fit with their businesses and business objectives, while licensors should create properties that stand out from the crowd. *See Chapters 5 and 6.*

QUESTIONS LICENSORS ASK ABOUT LICENSING

How are licensing agents compensated?

Licensors generally pay their licensing agents a commission, often 35%-40% of all licensing revenues. This commission can be higher or lower, depending on the specifics of the situation. Some agents also charge monthly retainers, especially in the corporate sector. *See Chapter 5.*

What is the step-by-step procedure for setting up a licensing program?

There is really no step-by-step procedure, since every licensing program is unique. All licensors should know their objectives for the licensing effort and the characteristics of their property and its target audience before setting up a strategy. Strategic considerations include which product categories to select, which distribution channels and geographic territories to target, how much to require as payment, when to launch the program and how fast to roll it out. *See Chapter 5.*

How much can I make from licensing?

There is no standard gauge of the financial potential of a licensing program. Success is dependent on innumerable factors, each of which is unique to the property, the specific licensed line or lines and the financial particulars of each deal. For planning purposes, licensors can seek comparables in terms of the performance of like properties, but should take into account their own situations. *See Chapters 5 and 7.*

Do I get to approve products made by my licensees?

Yes. In fact, the product approval process — along with the licensee selection process — is the most important way to maintain control over the program and the property's image. *See Chapter 5.*

How does the strategy for a "hot" property differ from the strategy for a classic property?

The objective for a licensing program based on a "hot" property is usually to maximize revenues and/or awareness in a relatively short window of opportunity. Thus, the licensing strategy may include wide distribution, many products and many licensees. On the other hand, for a classic property, maintaining the property's value over time is of the essence; more emphasis will be placed on avoiding market oversaturation and on keeping the property and associated products fresh over time. *See Chapter 5.*

How do I sell my property to licensees and retailers?

The more concrete information you can provide them, the better. Effective sales tools include marketing data (such as sales figures, viewership, attendance numbers, etc.); information about the property itself (style guide and other art reference, story boards, character synopses, information about how consumers perceive the brand, etc.); data about the target audience; and examples of the property's potential application on merchandise. *See Chapter 5.*

How do I decide which licensees to sign?

Selection criteria include the licensee's existing retail customer base, what the licensee is willing to pay, the financial strength of the company, the design and quality of the licensee's products, etc. The relative importance of these criteria depends on the licensor's objectives. *See Chapter 5.*

How do I decide if I should use a licensing agent?

Licensing agents offer expertise and licensing contacts to companies who lack in-house personnel with the same experience. Financial considerations also play a role: At what point does the agent's commission exceed what an in-house licensing department would cost? *See Chapter 5.*

How do I find a licensing agent?

Licensing agents are listed in a number of directories, including those published by EPM Communcations. Choosing an agent requires consideration of several factors, including the agency's specialty, track record, clients (and references from clients), plans for the property in question and proposed financial package. *See Chapter 5.*

How do I prevent counterfeiting?

Licensors can take a number of steps to attempt to prevent counterfeiting, including educating licensees, retailers, consumers and potential counterfeiters on what counterfeiting is and what the penalties are; creating consistent product packaging and labeling to make spotting counterfeit merchandise easier; and encouraging licensees, licensors and retailers to report incidences of counterfeiting. *See Chapter 10.*

What remedies do I have against counterfeiters if counterfeiting should occur?

Civil and criminal remedies against counterfeiting include restraining orders, seizures of merchandise and machinery, fines, monetary damages and jail time. The remedies sought should be balanced against the cost of pursuing them. In general, the rewards do not come close to recouping lost sales; most licensors focus more on preventing counterfeiting by sending a message than on seeking monetary compensation *per se. See Chapter 10.*

How do I expand internationally?

There is no one way to expand internationally. While international territories are considered to have significant growth potential, and often account for a large portion of a property's total business, individual licensors should examine various factors before launching globally. They include how well known the property is in various countries; the political, economic and cultural characteristics of each territory; and the methods of doing business in each region. *See Chapter 11.*

How do I decide if I need an international sub-agent?

Most observers recognize the need for a local partner in a foreign territory, whether it be a licensing agent, a retailer, a master licensee, a joint venture or a subsidiary staffed by local personnel. Foreign licensing agents have expertise in their regions and may be the most cost-effective option, especially initially. Aside from their sales efforts, they actively help manage the property within their territory. *See Chapter 11.*

When is it a good idea to forge an exclusive deal with a retailer?

Retail exclusives can be effective in a number of situations and are one of the key trends in licensing in the early 21st century. Exclusive promotions can help launch a property or create visibility for an ongoing license, while a long-term direct-to-retail deal can be financially lucrative. The only time a retail exclusive would not be appropriate is if it would harm the businesses of licensees already on board by limiting their sales or causing confusion in the marketplace. *See Chapters 4 and 5.*

What should be included in the style guide?

Style guides can be published in print or electronic form and contain designs available for use by licensees (and possible variations on those designs) each season, as well as specifications on the proper depictions of logos, characters and other elements of the property. It also describes required details to be used on packaging and labeling and specifies how copyright and trademark notices must be marked. *See Chapter 5.*

How do I keep a property fresh over time?

There are various methods of rejuvenating properties. They include creating new events or media vehicles, such as films, sporting activities, live events, television shows, etc.; launching promotions to take advantage of anniversaries, significant milestones or simply a good fit between property and partner; and introducing new product lines, either through expansion into new categories or through fresh designs. *See Chapter 5.*

What staffing do I need to oversee my licensing program?

Staffing varies from company to company depending on the property type, the scope of the licensing program, whether or not an agent is involved, and the number of properties licensed. Artists or other entrepreneurs often handle licensing themselves or with a business partner, corporate licensors may have departments ranging from one to 10 people dedicated to licensing and studios may have dozens (a rare few have 100 or more). Most observers recommend having at least one person dedicated to licensing full time, but even this rule may not apply in all cases. *See Chapter 5.*

QUESTIONS LICENSEES ASK ABOUT LICENSING

How do I decide which properties I should acquire?

The best property for a particular licensee will be one where the licensor's goals and target audience match the licensee's and where the fit between the property and product is appropriate. A number of properties may work for a given licensee, depending on its objectives and product line. *See Chapter 6.*

Where do I find out about properties that are available and who owns them?

Trade publications, trade shows and directories of the licensing business are all good sources of information. In addition, licensees can hire a licensing consultant(s) to be their eyes and ears in the licensing business. *See Chapter 6.*

What are the hottest licenses?

The hottest licenses vary from season to season. More important, however, is the fact that the hottest license is not always the best license for a given licensee. A smaller, less visible property may be much more lucrative than a blockbuster for a particular manufacturer, if there is a better fit with its products, distribution, target market and objectives. *See Chapter 6.*

If I am a small manufacturer with no prior experience in licensing, can I become a licensee?

Yes, although it may not be easy. Opportunities exist for licensees who have expertise in a certain niche distribution channel, who have an idea for a unique licensed product or, sometimes, who are willing to commit to an unproven license in its early stages. *See Chapter 6.*

What do I have to do to become a licensee?

Licensors usually require licensees to fill out evaluation forms. They ask for the licensee's plans for the licensed product line, historical data about the licensee's business, financial status of the licensee, and retail and credit references. In addition, they want to see samples of products similar to those the licensee proposes to sell under the license. *See Chapter 6.*

Is there anything like a licensing agent that represents the interests of manufacturers?

Yes. There are a number of licensing consultants who exclusively represent the interests of licensees in seeking appropriate properties to acquire. *See Chapter 6.*

How many properties do I need in my portfolio to succeed in licensing?

Some licensees acquire just one license, which becomes the basis for a significant portion of, or even their entire, business. Others acquire a whole range of properties to target different demographic groups or add variety to their product mix. Manufacturers do not want to acquire so many properties that the costs exceed the benefits, nor do they want to take on too much risk or cause their lines to compete with one another. *See Chapter 6.*

If I license a film or TV show, do I automatically get to use actors' likenesses or the movie soundtrack?

Not necessarily. Licensees should find out upfront if the use of an actor's likeness is allowed. Even if it is possible contractually, there may be problems if the actor is not fully behind the project; studios will not alienate the talent by siding with licensees. The licensor may not own rights to the music associated with a property either, but can direct you on who to approach. *See Chapter 8.*

TRADE PUBLICATIONS AND DIRECTORIES

LICENSING PUBLICATIONS

We're obviously partial to *The Licensing Letter*, but here's a list of all the major licensing publications currently available:

The Licensing Letter, 212-941-0099, www.epmcom.com

The Licensing Book, The Licensing Report, The Licensing Book International, 800-726-7667, www.adventurepublishing.com

Licensing Today Worldwide, Licensing Reporter, The Art Buyer, Nought2Twelve, 011-44-1384-440591, www.a4publications.com

License!, 212-951-6600, www.advanstar.com

The Licensing Journal, 212-597-0200, www.aspenpublishers.com

LICENSING DIRECTORIES

The EPM Licensing Business Sourcebook, 212-941-0099, www.epmcom.com

The Worldwide Licensing Resource Directory, 011-44-1384-440591, www.a4publications.com

Guide to the Licensing World, 011-44-1892-668444, www.licensingworld.co.uk

TRADE PUBLICATIONS

These trade publications are organized by the industries they cover; all occasionally feature licensing-related information.

TOYS

Playthings, 212-519-7200, www.playthings.com

The Toy Book, 800-726-7667, www.adventurepublishing.com

APPAREL AND FOOTWEAR

Children's Business, 212-630-4000, www.childrensbusiness.com

Women's Wear Daily, 212-630-4000, www.wwd.com

Daily News Record (men's apparel), 212-630-4000, www.dnrnews.com

Footwear News, 212-630-4000, www.footwearnews.com

SPORTING GOODS

Sporting Goods Business, 646-654-4500, www.sgbmag.com

Street & Smith's SportsBusiness Journal, 704-371-3100, www.sportsbusinessjournal.com

ENTERTAINMENT

Entertainment Marketing Letter, 212-941-0099, www.epmcom.com

Hollywood Reporter, 323-525-2000, www.hollywoodreporter.com

Variety, 323-857-6600, www.variety.com

Broadcasting & Cable, 212-337-7000, www.broadcastingcable.com

Kidscreen, 416-408-2300, www.kidscreen.com

MARKETING

Research Alert, 212-941-0099, www.epmcom.com
Youth Markets Alert, 212-941-0099, www.epmcom.com
Marketing to the Emerging Minorities, 212-941-0099, www.epmcom.com
Marketing to Women, 212-941-0099, www.epmcom.com
Brandweek, 646-654-5243, www.brandweek.com
Advertising Age, 312-649-5200, www.adage.com

PUBLISHING

Publishers Weekly, 212-645-9700, www.publishersweekly.com
Comics Retailer, 715-445-2214, www.krause.com

GIFTS

Gifts & Decorative Accessories, 212-519-7200, www.giftsanddec.com
Giftware News, 312-849-2220, www.giftwarenews.net
Giftware Business, 646-654-5967, www.giftline.com

GENERAL RETAILING

Discount Store News, 212-756-5100, www.dsnretailingtoday.com
Stores, 202-626-8101, www.stores.org
Supermarket News, 212-630-4000, www.supermarketnews.com
Drug Store News, 212-630-4000, www.drugstorenews.com

HOME FURNISHINGS

HFN - Home Furnishings News, 212-630-3720, www.hfnmag.com
Home Textiles Today, 212-519-7200, www.hometextilestoday.com

TRADE ASSOCIATION

Licensing Industry Merchandisers Association (LIMA), 212-244-1944, www.lima.org

TRADE SHOWS

For current listings with dates and locations, see www.epmcom.com; click on "Licensing and Merchandising" and go to The Licensing Letter. *Below the image of the newsletter click on "calendar."*

LICENSING CONFERENCES AND TRADE SHOWS

Dates and locations subject to change. Most events are annual.

Licensing Letter Symposium, EPM Communications, 212-941-0099, www.epmcom.com

Licensing Show International, Advanstar, 203-882-1300, www.advanstar.com

Brand Licensing London, Advanstar, 011-44-208-987-0917, www.licensinglondon.com

Licensing Europe, Advanstar, 011-44-208-987-0917, www.licensingeurope.net

Licensing in Latin America, Licensing Brands International, 212-614-3296, www.licensinglatinamerica.com

Licensing in Asia Pacific, Licensing Brands International, 212-614-3296, www.licensingasia.com

MAJOR U.S. CONSUMER PRODUCTS TRADE SHOWS

This is not a complete roster, but lists a few of the major shows of importance to the licensing community. Most are annual; dates and locations change each year.

American International Toy Fair, Toy Industry Association, 212-675-1141, www.toy-tia.org

Bologna Children's Book Fair, Bologna Fiere, 011-39-5128-2111, www.bolognafiere.it

BookExpo America, Reed Expositions, 800-840-5614, www.bookexpoamerica.com

Electronic Entertainment Expo/E3, Electronic Entertainment Expo, 800-315-1133, www.e3expo.com

EPM Entertainment Marketing Conference, EPM Communications, 212-941-0099, www.epmcom.com

Fancy Food Show, NASFT, 212-482-6440, www.fancyfoodshows.com

Frankfurt Book Fair, 011-49-69-2102-0, www.frankfurter-buchmesse.de

International Home Furnishings Market, International Home Furnishings Marketing Association, 336-888-3700, www.furnituremarket.org

International Housewares Show, National Housewares Manufacturers Association, 847-692-0103, www.housewares.org

International Juvenile Products Show, Juvenile Products Manufacturers Association, 856-231-8500, www.jpma.org

International Consumer Electronics Show, Electronic Industries Association, 703-907-7605, www.cesweb.org

MAGIC, WWD/MAGIC and **MAGICKids**, Magic International, 818-593-5000, www.magiconline.com

MIPCOM and **MIPCOM Jr.**, Reed Midem, 212-689-4220, www.mipcom.com

MIPTV, Reed Expositions, 800-840-5614, www.miptv.com

National Stationery Show, George Little Management, 800-272-7469, www.glmshows.com

New York International Gift Fair, George Little Management, 800-272-7469, www.glmshows.com

School & Home Office Products Association (SHOPA) Show, SHOPA, 937-297-2250, www.shopa.org

Super Show, Super Show, 305-893-8771, www.thesupershow.com

Surtex, George Little Management, 800-272-7469, www.glmshows.com

VSDA Convention, Video Software Dealers Association, 800-955-8732, www.vsda.org

INDEX

Boldface numbers refer to figures and tables

M

S

ABOUT THE AUTHOR

Karen Raugust was the Executive Editor of *The Licensing Letter*, the authoritative newsletter on the licensing business published by EPM Communications, from 1990 to 1996. She has also written and edited other EPM publications, including *TLL's Licensed Property Benchmarking Study* (2001), *The EPM Fad Study* (1998), *International Licensing: A Status Report* (1996, 1999) and *The Market for Children's Entertainment & Media* (1997). She served as a licensing consultant and was frequently quoted in the media.

Currently, Ms. Raugust is a freelance writer specializing in licensing, entertainment, and business, contributing to more than 30 publications including *Publishers Weekly, American Artist, Supermarket News* and *Animation Magazine*. Through her Minneapolis-based company, Raugust Communications, she provides consulting services that include creating marketing and business plans, compiling research reports, and writing and editing. She is the author of *Merchandise Licensing for the Television Industry* (Focal Press, 1995) and a contributor to *The Advertising Age Encyclopedia of Advertising* (Crain Communications, 2001), *The Only Sales Promotion Techniques You'll Ever Need* (Dartnell, 1996), *Contemporary Fashion* (Gale Publications, 2001), *American Women Writers* (St. James, 1999) and other titles.

Prior to her work with EPM, Ms. Raugust held positions at Union Square Press and *Editor & Publisher* magazine. She holds a BA from Carleton College and an MBA from Columbia University.

ABOUT EPM COMMUNICATIONS, INC.

EPM Communications is a New York City-based publishing, research and consulting firm specializing in marketing-oriented information. The privately-held company publishes the newsletters *The Licensing Letter, Entertainment Marketing Letter, Research Alert, Youth Markets Alert, Marketing to the Emerging Majorities* and *Marketing to Women*.

In addition to *The Licensing Business Handbook*, EPM publishes two annual directories, *The EPM Licensing Letter Sourcebook* and *The EPM Entertainment Marketing Sourcebook*, along with research studies including *The EPM Fad Study, International Licensing: A Status Report, The Licensing Business Databook, Marketing to Teens and Tweens*, and *Marketing to the 50+ Population*.

The company provides telephone-based short-term consulting services to its subscribers through "The 60-Minute Consultant" program, develops on-site seminars for subscriber companies and produces the annual Licensing Letter Symposium, EPM Entertainment Marketing Conference and other meetings.

EPM was founded in 1988 by Ira Mayer, a prominent entertainment industry journalist and marketing and media analyst, and his wife, Riva Bennett, who had been associated with various research and finance institutions.